. . . the captain of a mighty host

JOHN L. LEWIS

and

THE INTERNATIONAL UNION
UNITED MINE WORKERS OF AMERICA

The Story from 1917 to 1952

October, 1952

Published by Authority of the

INTERNATIONAL EXECUTIVE BOARD

of the

UNITED MINE WORKERS OF AMERICA

CONTENTS

ABOUT THIS BOOK

THIS BOOK IS A HISTORY in pictures and words of the most dramatic period in the story of American labor.

The pictures were gathered from every conceivable source. More than 3,500 negatives and prints of one of the most photographed men in the United States were examined by the editors. Approximately 250 were selected for reproduction in the book. These show John L. Lewis with mine workers, trade union leaders, politicians, statesmen, Presidents of the United States, captains of industry and business, auto workers, steel workers, textile workers, packinghouse workers, newspapermen, foreign dignitaries and the host of other persons—big and little—with whom the chief executive of the United Mine Workers of America has associated for the past thirty-five years. They show Mr. Lewis in Washington, Scranton, Pittsburgh, Coaldale, Indianapolis, New York, San Francisco, Wilkes-Barre, Mexico City, Paris and the other far-flung points where his work in behalf of America's coal miners has taken him.

The words, for the most part, are those of Mr. Lewis. They record, as only his words can, the story from 1917 to 1952 of "the mighty host" that is the United Mine Workers of America. They tell of the 1919 strike, the Jacksonville Agreement, Mingo and Logan Counties, "No Backward Step," the Guffey Coal Act, the organization of the mass production workers into the CIO, the "Little Steel" strike, Harlan County, Franklin Delano Roosevelt, World War II, the fight for and realization of the union's welfare fund.

This is a history of the union. As such, it is also the story of John L. Lewis during those years. For John L. Lewis and the UMWA are "One and Indissoluble."

This book is not a complete history. It is only a small part of a tremendous research project that has been under way for the past two years. This project was established by the International Executive Board of the UMWA. The Board directed that a complete collection of Mr. Lewis' speeches and writings be collected for the UMWA archives. This work continues. Each item is recorded, listed chronologically, cross-indexed by subject matter. Ultimately, it will be possible to refer to any and all statements of Mr. Lewis by date and by subject matter. Literally thousands of index cards already have been filed.

The book is, in effect, a report by the Board to the delegates attending the 1952 international convention of the UMWA. The book is made possible by the militant membership of the UMWA and their president, John L. Lewis. It is their history.

Special credit for actual publication of the book goes to the members of the International Executive Board, to Vice President Thomas Kennedy, to Secretary-Treasurer John Owens, to the officers of each UMWA District, and to the staff members of the International Union.

Here is your book—a book made possible by and dedicated to the United Mine Workers of America and their president.

REX LAUCK.

PREFACE

HERE IS THE STORY of thirty-five years. It is the story of the man—John Llewellyn Lewis—and of the men of a mighty labor organization—the United Mine Workers of America.

It begins on February 1, 1917. That is the date when the United Mine Workers Journal reported that UMWA President John P. White had named Mr. Lewis to his first post with the International Union, that of statistician.

It tells of the uphill fight by America's hundreds of thousands of coal miners. It starts when coal miners are among the most poorly paid in American industry, when sick and injured mine workers are dumped upon a human scrap heap to die or to live out their miserable existences in pain and suffering. It starts when hours of toil in the dark and damp are long and arduous, when civil rights are unknown in the prison-like mining camps across the breadth of the greatest coal-producing nation on earth. It begins when boys of tender years are forced into the pits by the economic circumstances surrounding them.

This story, of the shock troops of American labor and of the man who heads their ranks, is not always one of a steady march of progress. Great bitterness and many heartaches and much strife must be recounted. There are times, as the story unfolds, when the men of the UMWA and the man who has been their president since 1920, have their backs to the wall. But through the story there runs the theme of dedication to a cause, of vigor, determination, militancy and the unbeatable will of free men to fight for the privileges of free men.

In the field of labor, the United Mine Workers has occupied a position of unquestioned leadership. The union has been the spearhead in the struggle to establish collective bargaining in our industrial life. Its principles and policies, its strength and unity, and its outstanding leaders have been an inspiration to the millions of American men and women who toil for a living. It can be truly said that to a great extent the history of the American labor movement is the history of the United Mine Workers of America.

These accomplishments have not been attained without a struggle. Nor were they attained in a day, a week, or a year. They have been made possible only through the combined efforts of hundreds of thousands of coal miners cooperating over a period of many years. They are the result of a firm determination imbedded in the hearts and minds of the coal miners of America to build and maintain a strong, enduring union.

The union today is the product of the sweat and blood—even the lives—of men with vision, faith and courage. What light is to the eyes, what love is to the heart, what liberty is to the soul, the United Mine Workers has become to the coal miners of America. With the same firmness of purpose that has brought the union to its present magnificent development, America's mine workers face the future, confident in the ability of the organization successfully to withstand the attacks of those who would seek to destroy it.

Therefore, it devolves upon all coal miners to preserve the gains already made and to hand on to their successors in the coal mines of America an enlarged and strengthened union. This they can do. This they will do.

This book must end, of necessity. It is appropriate that it close at the start of the 1952 international convention of the UMWA. The story continues. John L. Lewis and the United Mine Workers of America still march forward together.

THE EARLY DAYS

It is thirty-five years ago. The United States is on the verge of entering World War I. A workingman's rights are few; the compensation for his toil meager. He has no right to organize, nor to bargain collectively.

In the same year, 1917, a young man not yet thirty-seven years old, is called by the United Mine Workers of America to take his first position of leadership with the International Union. The post is statistician. The man is John Llewellyn Lewis.

Through the next thirty-five years, there weaves a parallel between the advancement of the nation and the progress of its working people. As the United States resists tyranny, so do the United Mine Workers of America, under the leadership of their great ninth president, fight unceasingly for the right to live in freedom, to enjoy security and to share justly in the products of their labor.

John L. Lewis stepped onto the ladder of authority in the International Union on February 1, 1917. The February 15 issue of the United Mine Workers Journal announced his appointment as statistician under a small headline on page seven and included this brief review and comment on his earlier career:

"He was born in Lucas, Iowa, and started to work in the mines of that state at an early age. He has worked in the mines of most of the states

of the West and Middle West. Early in his career as a miner he evinced deep interest in the cause of organized labor and served as a local officer and as a delegate to district and international conventions for a number of years. In 1910 he was elected a member of the Illinois Miners' Legislative Committee, resigning in the latter part of that year to accept an appointment from President Gompers as general organizer of the American Federation of Labor. He served with marked ability in this position up to February 1 of this year, resigning to accept the position of statistician of our international organization.

"While acting in the capacity of general organizer for the American Federation of Labor, he organized the State Federation of Labor in New Mexico and a large number of federal labor unions in various parts of the country. He had full charge of the corps of American Federation of Labor organizers in the memorable campaign made by the federation to organize the employees of the United States Steel Corporation. He also officiated as legislative representative of the American Federation of Labor at Washington and represented the same organization as legislative representative in various state legislatures. During the past year he assisted several of our district organizations in their wage conferences and presided over the special

UMWA'S SEVENTH AND NINTH PRESIDENTS IN 1919; JOHN P. WHITE AND JOHN L. LEWIS

convention in the Pittsburgh district which settled the controversy in that field.

"He is a man of strong personality, a gifted orator, and his many friends in the labor movement will rejoice to know that he has been appointed statistician of our international organization."

Litigation has always been one of the major weapons used by coal operators in fighting the UMWA. The first legal blow the UMWA suffered after Mr. Lewis' appearance on the national scene was the decision of the United States Supreme Court in 1917 in the Hitchman Co. case, in which the court upheld the legality of "yellow-dog" contracts. The following is the contract that miners had to sign if they wanted to work for the Hitchman Coal and Coke Co.:

"I am employed by and work for the Hitchman Coal and Coke Co. with the express understanding that I am not a member of the United Mine Workers of America, and will not become so while an employee of the Hitchman Coal and Coke Co.; that the Hitchman Coal and Coke Co. is run non-union while I am in its employ. If, at any time I am employed by the Hitchman Coal and Coke Co., I want to become connected with the United Mine Workers of America or any affiliated organization, I agree to withdraw

from the employment of said company, and agree that while I am in the employ of that company I will not make any efforts amongst its employees to bring about the unionizing of that mine against the company's wish. I have either read the above or heard the same read."

At the time of the Twenty-sixth Convention in January, 1918, there was generally assumed to be a serious coal shortage. In a thorough report of his work as statistician, including detailed state-by-state figures, Mr. Lewis proved that the shortage was not of coal but of railway cars in which to transport it:

"There can be no question but what the members of the United Mine Workers could have produced 50 million additional tons of coal during 1917 had the railroads provided an adequate car supply. The miners were blamed for taking the usual holidays, and even for not working in case of explosions, by many who felt the coal shortage and who hastily placed the blame, without investigation, upon the mine workers."

Mr. Lewis reported on his participation in an AFL investigation of an alleged labor shortage:

"The cry of 'labor shortage' was heard long before the United States entered the war. Labor unions have a serious problem to meet in the labor-shortage bugaboo being talked overtime by Chambers of Commerce, Boards of Trade, et al., who are not suffering from an inability to secure workers, but who seek to hold wages down to the lowest level."

Later in the year President John P. White made the following announcement in the Journal:

"You are hereby notified that I have appointed John L. Lewis business manager of the United Mine Workers Journal, with full power to conduct the affairs of the Journal in line with the constitution.

"The appointment of Mr. Lewis becomes effective on and after July 15, 1917."

The Journal of that time had its problems. It was printed in three languages and was run on a commercial basis. Now with a new responsibility in addition to his work as statistician and in organizing, Mr. Lewis reported to the 1918 convention:

"To meet the growing need of educating the steadily increasing number of immigrants to the cause of trade unionism, the 1914 convention conferred upon the International Executive Board authority to print the Journal in three languages—English, Italian and Slovak.

"It is apparent that the intent of Postmaster General Burleson, who is an avowed opponent to trade unionism, is to clamp the lid down tight on foreign language publications. His department has adopted a most rigid censorship program. If the war continues, no one can forecast just where the censorship will stop, so the question with all publications printing foreign languages is whether continuance of foreign languages will meet the war-time demands of government censorship.

"The paper question has been one that has disturbed the peace of mind of every publisher in the land. Immediately following the inauguration of the eight-hour day in the paper mills, the manufacturers, true to form, endeavored to treble profits under the guise of benefiting labor.

"High cost of paper and printing materials, increased overhead expenses, increased mailing charges, all operate to increase to an almost prohibitive cost the continued publication of hundreds of uplift and labor publications in the United States.

"Therefore, the duty of maintaining periodicals that will carry the necessary publicity to keep the fundamental issues of trade unionism alive in the breasts of the people devolves itself upon the powerful trade unions of the nation. The United Mine Workers of America, the largest trade union of the world, must meet this duty in conserving the ideals of labor. The Journal should be made a real live publication. Its columns should be awake to the conditions of the times. It should be and can be at the forefront of the labor publications of the world."

John P. White retired as president of the UMWA on October 25, 1917. Frank J. Hayes, the new president, told the membership that John L. Lewis, "a man of marked ability," had been appointed vice president. The appointment again broadened his sphere of activity for he retained all other duties. A few months later, he also was appointed by President Woodrow Wilson to the National War Labor Conference Board. On becoming vice president, Mr. Lewis pledged:

"I shall vigorously prosecute the work of extending the organization into the non-union coal-producing fields of America, where freedom and justice are now denied the miners and where the essentials of democracy are refused expression. Especially must the order of things be changed in the unorganized districts of West Virginia, Pennsylvania and Alabama, where the bulk of the coal used by our Navy and in the manufacture of steel is produced."

He kept his word. During 1917 he assisted in organizing at least six non-union coal fields, attended interstate wage conferences and talked to government officials.

From the depth of his own experience, he told of the life of a union organizer at this time:

"Laboring in isolated communities, where they are often denied even food and shelter; handicapped and persecuted by the almost satanic ingenuity of the shameless agents of the non-

MR. LEWIS SOON AFTER HE BECAME UMWA PRESIDENT; WITH HIM IS FRANK HUGHES

union coal operators; insulted, abused, beaten and offered every personal indignity by murderous mine guards, their lot is far from being an easy one. Only the greatest loyalty to our cause and our union makes it possible for men to serve under these conditions. To our organizers, we owe a high place on the roll of honor."

On October 6, 1917, the union signed the "Washington Agreement" with the Central Competitive Field operators, producing some 200 million tons of coal a year in Illinois, Indiana, Western Pennsylvania and Ohio. Further negotiations with operators in the outlying coal districts in the Far West and South brought other UMWA members under contract. The agreements provided greatly increased, but widely varying, wage scales. The Central Competitive Agreement, covering approximately 200 thousand miners, continued the contract from April, 1918, to a minimum of two years or longer, contingent upon the end of World War I. Mr. Lewis was one of the negotiators and, presiding at the 1918 convention, led the hot fight for acceptance of the pact.

Opposition, as was then usual, was directed by Alexander Howat, president of District 14 (Kansas). Howat objected to the "automatic penalty" clause which the government had forced the UMWA to accept. Under the clause, miners could be fined, without appeal, for minor infractions of work rules and absences.

The year 1918 was one of unrest among the miners, a portent of the first big work stoppage under Mr. Lewis' leadership, which was to come in the following year. The 1919 Convention heard from Mr. Lewis of the successful negotiations with War Fuel Administrator Harry A. Garfield on pay raises for the anthracite miners:

"Your officers deemed it an opportune time to urge again our claims for an increase in wages and as in the meantime an increased spirit of unrest had developed in many sections, particularly in the Shamokin district of the anthracite region where more than 20 thousand men were on strike, we again telegraphed Dr. Garfield, urging further consideration.

"As a result of this insistence and after a long series of conferences in which representatives of the anthracite operators also participated, an agreement was reached providing for a definite increase to the anthracite mine workers.

"This increase amounted to from 90 cents for certain classes of outside day labor to $1.10 per day for other classifications employed inside and outside of the mines and 15 per cent over existent rates to contract miners."

Dr. Garfield and President Woodrow Wilson were not so cooperative about a raise for the bituminous miners. On October 21, 1918, the UMWA told Dr. Garfield in a letter:

"We are profoundly impressed with the necessity of action being taken in the bituminous fields similar to that taken in the anthracite region. We are so confident that the increase in the cost of living has so decreased the purchasing power of the daily wages of the mine workers, that we deem it our duty to press upon you their request for an increase in mining prices.

"A spirit of unrest is abroad throughout the bituminous coal fields. Delay will serve to accelerate it. A speedy determination of the matter alone will serve to stabilize the situation and allay the spirit of unrest existing."

Dr. Garfield wired a succinct reply:

"Am convinced that increase of wages in the bituminous industry is not called for as part of the plan of stabilization and, therefore, that no increase ought to be made at the present time."

The miners realized that further appeal to Garfield was useless. On October 31, UMWA officers and district representatives began a two-day conference at Indianapolis to discuss further steps. At the close of the meetings, Vice President Lewis said:

"We can sit here in this conference and analyze the proposition, but it will not have any effect upon the governmental agencies that are now in control and operating under laws as fixed as the laws of the Medes and the Persians.

"I feel that we cannot make any particular progress in continuing this debate upon this one principle of standardization of wages because it is a principle in which the government is deeply interested and has an agency at work upon. There is another agency, of which Felix Frankfurter is chairman, which is a general wage review committee. The members of that committee are sitting every day in conference while Felix Frankfurter, the hot dog of the labor administration, expounds his fallacious policy. We are not interested in appealing to his agency. Ex-President White refused to serve on that committee."

The miners decided to appeal to President Wilson. They telegraphed:

"It is not sufficient when Dr. Garfield states that the bituminous mine workers are not entitled to an increase in mining wages. In making such a statement, he denies to them the fundamental right of presenting facts and the reasons they feel they are justified in seeking an increase in wages."

President Wilson denied the miners' plea and supported Dr. Garfield. Mr. Lewis reported to the union:

"There was nothing further that could be done by the representatives of your organization except to acquiesce and continue in force and effect the Washington Wage Agreement until the logical date of its termination."

The press and several government officials tried to blame the war-time coal shortages on the mine workers and the eight-hour day. Mr. Lewis reported at the June, 1918, convention of the AFL at St. Paul, Minn.:

"The country is facing in the coming winter a coal famine the likes of which has never existed before in America. We say to the world that if the United States Railway Administration can furnish the mine workers with cars sufficient to transport the product we will produce, they will provide the country with enough coal.

"In spite of the fact that 35 thousand men have left the industry in the anthracite fields, the tonnage has in no way decreased, but the 140 thousand men have produced the same tonnage formerly produced by 175 thousand men. There is nothing but fallacy in the claim of the employers that the eight-hour day limits production; on the contrary it increases production. The men in the anthracite fields have increased their production nearly one-fourth of a ton per man per day."

WASHINGTON'S FIRST LABOR-MANAGEMENT CONFERENCE MEETS ON MARCH 14, 1918

Left to Right—B. L. Worden, W. H. Van Dervoort, Loyall Z. Osborne, L. F. Loree, representing employers; UMWA President Frank J. Hayes, T. A. Rickert of the Garment Workers, William L. Hutcheson of the Carpenters, Labor Policy Board Chairman William Howard Taft, First Secretary of Labor William B. Wilson, former secretary-treasurer of the UMWA; C. Edwin Michael, representing employers, Frank P. Walsh, public member, and Victor Olander of the Illinois State Federation of Labor.

The UMWA had its first serious brush with the communists in 1919. At that time, communists were calling themselves the "One Big Union." They led a strike in District 18 (British Columbia) in which they short-sightedly called out the maintenance men as well as the miners. The mines were flooded and the men were unemployed for several months as a result. The district charter was revoked. In his report to the 1919 convention, Mr. Lewis said:

"The district officials, under the provisions of the International constitution, forfeited their claims to affiliation with the UMWA.

"The 'One Big Union', like its contemporaries, the IWW, the Provincial Workingmen's Association and the Working Class Union, is founded upon the day dreams of visionaries and lacks a proper conception of the trades union movement."

John P. White, former UMWA president and later a trouble shooter, was sent to straighten out District 18 affairs and on June 14, 1920, after a special convention, the district got a new charter. It has been running its own affairs ever since.

The AFL made a major attempt to organize the steel workers in 1919 and John L. Lewis lent active aid to the campaign. At the 1919 UMWA convention he described the efforts made by the miners on behalf of the steel workers:

"I may say that the UMWA is one of the twenty-four associated international unions which have been cooperating for the past number of months in an endeavor to organize the steel workers. We have contributed our prorata in a financial way and we have contributed the services of numerous field workers.

"In conformity with our duty as one of the international organizations represented on the Committee to Organize Iron and Steel Workers, I have today appointed sixteen field workers to report to the secretary of the committee."

The drive failed because the AFL's techniques were not adequate to organize a mass production industry. It was not until 1937, when the CIO entered the picture, that a steel company signed a contract with a labor union.

An event that saddened mine workers through-

out the coal fields in 1919 was the death, on September 9, during that year's UMWA convention, of their former president, John Mitchell, beloved leader of the early struggles in the anthracite region at the turn of the century. Mitchell, fifth president of the union, served from 1898 to 1907. Funeral services were held in Scranton on September 12. In tribute to Mitchell, delegates to the Cleveland convention attended memorial services in Cleveland Cathedral after marching in a procession from the convention hall. The procession was led by Mr. Lewis, William Green and former UMWA President White. In 1924, the union dedicated a beautiful monument to Mitchell at Court House Square, Scranton. Each year on Mitchell Day, October 29, union officials lay a wreath at the monument.

Whenever a coal strike impends, a process of conditioning the uninformed to hostility toward the miners is launched by publishers and politicians. The formula, a simple one, never varies. It was used in the coal stoppage which began in the winter of 1919.

Scare headlines appeared in newspapers. Public officials, including the President of the United States, deplored and viewed with alarm. Widows and orphans "shivered" for the benefit of the newspaper-reading public. Injunctions were issued. The miners were vilified. John L. Lewis was called a traitor.

In that period, Mr. Lewis had begun a new term as vice president of the UMWA. The Journal of February 15, 1919, reported his election over Thomas Kennedy, 131,798 votes to 66,458.

Later that year, on July 15, the Journal printed an official circular, ordered by the Executive Board and signed by Secretary-Treasurer William Green stating that President Frank J. Hayes was ill and had been granted a four months' leave. Vice President Lewis is authorized to act as president, the circular stated.

Excerpts from the bare, matter-of-fact reports by Mr. Lewis to the miners' convention give a clearer perspective to the strike and its issues than the inflammatory articles written by the newspapermen of that day. He said:

"On September 23, 1919, your scale committee presented the following demands to the Convention. They were approved:

"1. 60 per cent increase in wages.

"2. Six-hour-day, five-day week.

"3. Time and one-half for overtime. Double-time on Sundays and holidays.

"4. Weekly pay day.

"5. Double shift eliminated except for maintenance and developing new mines.

"6. No automatic penalty clause.

"7. All bituminous contracts declared expired; no sectional agreements allowed; new contracts to run concurrently for two years.

"8. Internal differences referred to respective districts.

"9. Agreement for outlying districts retroactive and effective same date as that of Central Competitive Field.

"10. No contract ratified until reconvened convention passes on it. Convention to be held in Indianapolis and called by the International officers.

"11. If no agreement by November 1, International officials authorized and instructed to call general strike of all bituminous mine workers throughout the United States.

"12. Convention approve ratification of wage demands of anthracite mine workers made at the Wilkes-Barre Tri-District Convention.

"The officers of your organization met with the coal operators' representatives at Buffalo, N. Y., on September 26, but without avail.

"When the joint conference re-assembled at Philadelphia on October 9, it was clearly evident from the hostile attitude of the coal operators' representatives that they would not accept the scale proposed by the mine workers. After three days of fruitless argument, the joint conference adjourned, without any perceptible progress having been made.

"On October 21, representatives of the operators and miners responded to an invitation extended by Secretary of Labor William B. Wilson to meet with him at Washington, D. C. This meeting extended until October 24. The operators refused to accede to the request of the Secretary of Labor to meet the mine workers in joint conference until after the strike order, issued by your International Officers on October 15, was withdrawn. This meeting, therefore, resulted in a complete failure.

REVERED FIFTH PRESIDENT OF UMWA, JOHN MITCHELL, IS HONORED EACH OCTOBER 29

"On October 25, the President of the United States issued a statement declaring that our projected strike was unlawful, unjustifiable, and illegal, and on October 31 Judge A. B. Anderson of the Federal Court in Indianapolis issued a temporary restraining order to prevent your officers from promoting or carrying into effect the strike set for November 1.

"Many people, both in public and private life, expressed the opinion that the mine workers were not in favor of a strike but that they were driven to favor such action by their officers. The unanimous way in which the mine workers in the bituminous coal fields of the United States ceased work on November 1 was a complete refutation of that belief and demonstrated fully that it was a strike of the men who mined the coal.

"As a result of their unanimity, on November 8 Judge Anderson issued a temporary mandatory injunction in which he ordered the officers of the UMWA to withdraw the strike order issued on October 15. Upon receipt of this order, your International Officers called a meeting of all district representatives, the International Executive Board and the scale committee of the Central Competitive District for the purpose of considering a further course of action. After taking into consideration all the facts and having in mind as a paramount consideration the welfare of the men, women and children involved in the strike, the overwhelming opinion of the conference was in favor of complying, under protest, with the order of the court."

In a speech to the 1920 convention, Mr. Lewis said:

"I told the representatives of the government on Armistice Day that the mine workers of America were Americans. We *are* Americans. I shall never lead any organization but an American organization. If the day ever comes in the history of the UMWA when it is dominated by men who are false to the traditions of the American people and the American nation, then that day I shall cease to be an officer of the United Mine Workers of America.

"I regret that my government saw fit to inject itself into this industrial controversy between the miners of America and the coal operators. I believe that it was a mistaken judgment, a false and mistaken policy. But I say that the American nation itself, the American people, cannot altogether be held responsible for the acts of certain individuals who may be in control of the government at this time."

Mr. Lewis' report to the convention continued:

"On November 14 a joint conference of miners and operators of the Central Competitive Field was convened by Secretary of Labor Wilson. It continued until November 28. It was during this conference that Dr. Garfield advised that the mine workers were entitled to an increase in wages amounting to 14 per cent. Secretary of Labor Wilson proposed as a basis of settlement that mining prices be advanced 31.6 per cent. The operators refused to accept the proposal. The mine workers rejected the proposed basis of settlement offered by former Fuel Administrator Garfield.

"On December 6, your officers were brought into conference with A. Mitchell Palmer, Attorney General of the United States, and Mr. Joseph F. Tumulty, President Wilson's secretary. At this conference it was made plain that on

account of the widespread suffering existing among the people in different sections of the country and the approaching industrial disaster caused by lack of fuel, the government was determined that the strike must terminate. It was pointed out that the strike had passed from a mere controversy between miners and operators over a question of wages to an issue between the supremacy of the law and the ability of the government to enforce its mandates and decrees.

"Your representatives were assured that the President of the United States would guarantee the just and fair consideration of the demands and grievances of the mine workers through a commission appointed by him if the workers would accept an immediate increase of 14 per cent in wages pending final decision of the commission.

"While protesting in their hearts at the unjust attitude of the government, your International Officers decided to accept the plan of settlement of the strike proposed by the President, subject to approval by a conference of the International Executive Board, all district representatives and members of the scale committee of the Central Competitive Field.

"A memorandum of the agreement with the President reads as follows: 'In accordance with the request of the President, the miners will immediately return to work with the 14 per cent increase in wages which is already in effect. Immediately upon a general resumption of operations, the President will appoint a commission of three persons, one of whom shall be a practical miner and one of whom shall be a mine owner or operator in active business, which commission will consider the further questions of wages and working conditions, as well as profits of operators and proper prices for coal, readjusting both wages and prices, including differentials and internal conditions within and between districts. Its report will be made in sixty days, if possible, and will be accepted as the basis of a new wage agreement, the effective date and duration of which shall also be determined by the commission.'

"On December 8 a conference of district representatives, the scale committee of the Central Competitive districts, members of the International Executive Board and the International Officers decided to accept the plan and order an immediate resumption of mining operations."

President Woodrow Wilson appointed John P. White, Rembrandt Peale and Henry M. Robinson as members of the Bituminous Coal Commission to consider the dispute.

A convention was held at Columbus, Ohio, on January 5, 1920, to consider the action taken by the officers in accepting Wilson's proposal. Despite opposition to the plan, led as usual by Alexander Howat and Frank Farrington, the convention voted overwhelming approval, 1,639 votes to 221.

The front cover of the Mine Workers Journal for January 15, 1920, carried the following state-

branded as un-American and as brutal men seeking to freeze women and children. The public mind was inflamed by such false charges and the coal miners were discredited by public sentiment. But I believe that the American public now understands the coal miner better than it did a few weeks ago. It has learned that he is not the brute that he was pictured but that he is a good American citizen—a better American citizen, in fact, than those who would traduce him. All we ask is a square deal and a chance to live as American working men should live. I believe the American public is willing that we should have a square deal. It shall be our pur-

UMWA, OPERATOR NEGOTIATORS DISCUSS 1919 PACT; MINERS RECEIVE A BIG WAGE BOOST

Among those pictured are Thomas R. Brewster (front row, second from left), chief spokesman for the Central Competitive Field operators; Labor Secretary William B. Wilson, Acting UMWA President Lewis, William Green, UMWA secretary-treasurer.

---

ment by Mr. Lewis entitled "Coal Miners Are Americans":

"The action of the Columbus convention means that the UMWA is an American institution that believes in and upholds American ideals. While the strike was on, we were

pose to lay before the President's commission the facts upon which we base our demand for better conditions, and we have a right to demand that the pledge of the President that full justice will be done the coal miner be carried out. We could not and do not ask for more than justice."

He continues the story in his report to the 1921 UMWA convention:

"The U. S. Bituminous Coal Commission began its hearings in the assembly room of the American Red Cross Building, Washington, D. C., on January 12, 1920. The hearings continued over a period of several weeks, during which time the officers of each of the bituminous districts were privileged to present testimony in support of our contentions in the respective fields.

"On March 10, the majority and minority reports of the Bituminous Coal Commission were forwarded to President Wilson. The chairman of the commission, Mr. Henry M. Robinson, and Associate Commissioner Rembrandt Peale joined in the filing of a majority report. Mr. John P. White dissented.

"The International Officers made every effort to have President Wilson endorse the minority report. They recognized that a grave injustice had been done to the men employed by the day who had been given an increase in wages disproportionate to the advance accorded the men working by the ton.

"President Wilson refused and forwarded the majority report, ordering the mine workers and the operators to negotiate a contract on that basis. The operators were solidly determined to make no further concessions, so the joint agreement was accordingly signed in New York on March 31, 1920, to continue in effect until March 21, 1922.

"Briefly, this agreement provided an increase of 24 cents per ton on both pick and machine mining, $1.00 per day to day and monthly men, 53 cents per day to trappers and 20 per cent increase on yardage, dead work and room turning, upon the rates in effect October 31, 1919. The eight-hour day and all the rules and conditions of the 1916 Interstate Contract, together with supplemental agreements, were ordered to become a part of the new contract by the Bituminous Coal Commission."

The 1919 strike had ended. Despite accusations by dissident elements that Mr. Lewis had "surrendered," the miners had won pay increases averaging from 27 to 31 per cent, a raise that John P. White in 1927 called "the largest wage increase in the history of mining conditions."

In later comments on the 1919 strike, Mr. Lewis said:

"The 1919 strike demonstrated once and for all that American public opinion, no matter how sympathetic with the ideals of labor, with the woe and misery of the oppressed worker, will not tolerate open economic warfare in the form of prolonged strikes, nation-wide in scope, which affect such a vital necessity as a continued fuel supply and which would so seriously cripple our transportation and utilities, stop manufacture and force the populace-at-large to submit to the rigors of bitter winter weather, when the government itself declares to be unlawful the exercise of such economic force.

"The outcome of this strike endeavor is a complete answer to the theories promulgated by the One Big Union, the Communists and all other self-styled emancipators of American coal miners, who theorize that it would be possible by sheer force through the exercise of the strike, to compel American industry, the American people and the American Government to accede to any program, the attainment of which must be secured through the medium of a prolonged paralysis of nationwide commerce."

And despite misrepresentations, down through the years, by editorialists and political reactionaries, facts are that UMWA strikes never have paralyzed the nation—except in headlines.

Soft-coal miners who were paid a daily wage instead of tonnage rates were not satisfied with the award of the President's Bituminous Coal Commission of March 31, 1920. Stoppages occurred and new negotiations with the operators opened. Mr. Lewis reported to the membership:

"On August 19, 1920, the miners and the operators of Indiana agreed upon an increase of $1.50 per day to day labor and additional settlements on the same basis were quickly made in Illinois, Western Pennsylvania and Ohio and the outlying bituminous districts within the organization. These settlements brought the day labor rates to $7.50 per day.

There was trouble in the anthracite, too. Negotiations began the day before the President's Commission handed down its report in the bituminous case. President Lewis also reported to the convention on this situation:

"The International officers and the officers of Districts 1, 7, and 9 arranged with the anthracite operators for a joint conference for the presentation of demands made by the Tri-District Convention. The negotiations dragged on for several weeks and were unsuccessful.

"When it seemed that the breaking point had been reached and that no agreement was possible, the United States Government through its Secretary of Labor, William B. Wilson, intervened and requested miners and operators to assemble in Washington for a series of conferences. Propositions for settlement, however, proved unacceptable and the conferences adjourned May 12.

"In consequence of this failure to agree, the President of the United States on May 21, 1920, addressed a letter to the operators and miners insisting that the anthracite dispute be referred to a commission of three members whom he would appoint.

"A convention of Districts 1, 7, and 9, comprising the anthracite fields, was assembled in Wilkes-Barre, Pa., on May 24, 1920, and voted

to accept the commission as proposed by President Wilson.

"On June 3, 1920, the President created the commission, naming as members, Dr. William O. Thompson, President of Ohio State University, representing the public interest; Neal J. Ferry, UMWA Board member from District 7, representing the miners; and William L. Connell of Scranton, representing the operators.

"On August 23, 1920, Messrs. Thompson and Connell combined in the rendition of a majority report and Mr. Ferry filed an exhaustive minority report. The majority report became the basis of the present anthracite agreement, which was signed in Scranton on September 2. It is effective for two years beginning April 1, 1920, and increases the wages of contract miners 20 per cent, miners' laborers and monthly men 17 per cent, outside men $54 a month plus $60 per month for outside employees."

A PRINTER, A COAL MINER, A CIGAR MAKER CONFER DURING A 1922 WHITE HOUSE VISIT

AFL Secretary Frank Morrison (left) of the Printers, Mr. Lewis, AFL President Sam Gompers of the Cigarmakers.

So the anthracite miners also had a greatly improved contract to expire April 1, 1922.

During the course of his testimony before the Bituminous Coal Commission in 1920, Mr. Lewis spoke of the need for a shorter work day in the mines. His feeling for the hard life of the miner is an ever-recurring theme in his talks and writings. And it is his understanding of the miners which has helped him to fight so hard for his people.

"It is commonly believed that the miners enjoy an eight-hour day. They do not. In theory, yes. In fact and practice, no.

"Our contracts carry with them provisions that there shall be eight hours' work performed by the men at the working places. Where are these working places? They are far down in the interior of the earth—oftentimes miles away underground—and it requires a considerable time for a man to be lowered into the mine and from the bottom of the shaft traverse the workings to his working place. In addition to that, during the period of lunch time, the average miner who is producing coal by the ton does not have the advantage of that half-hour or hour and is not free from working in that period. The conditions underground are such that it would be practically impossible to sit down and remain idle for the lunch period and while the men who work by the day are privileged to absorb the lunch hour, the man who works at the vein of the coal continues to labor and eats his lunch at his working place like the busy executive who has a sandwich brought to his desk. Taking these conditions into consideration, the miner is underground from nine and a half to ten hours per day.

"We hold that that period of time underground is a wrong condition. We hold that it is too long a time for a man to be shut off from the sunlight and the air, and working in the fetid atmosphere of the underground workings."

That sounds like a good argument for portal-to-portal pay. It is. Except in those days, Mr. Lewis called it the six-hour day.

Mechanization in the mines has been advocated by the UMWA under the leadership of John L. Lewis consistently from the beginning. Their views on the introduction of machinery

THE TYPICALLY DETERMINED EXPRESSION IS SEEN AFTER A VISIT TO PRESIDENT HARDING

are well known now. But they were presenting the same arguments thirty-two years ago, when they told the coal commission:

"The theory of the trade unions is that the manufacturer must either equip his factory with modern labor-saving devices or else suffer by competition, but that he may not pay lower wages because of his unwillingness to secure the best machinery. Where trade unions do not exist, employers with the worst and oldest machinery and the most antiquated methods manage to eke out a precarious existence by underpaying and starving their workmen, but where trade unionism is able to enforce a definite minimum wage, these less skillful and less adequately equipped manufacturers must either introduce modern appliances or go to the wall. As a consequence, the countries, the industries, and even the individual establishments where trade unionism is strongest are those in which machinery is applied earliest and to the largest extent."

On February 7, 1920, Acting President Lewis became President Lewis. He and UMWA Secretary-Treasurer William Green informed the membership in an official notice which said:

"The undersigned desire to advise you of the

20

retirement of Brother Frank J. Hayes as president of the United Mine Workers of America. His resignation was presented to the International Executive Board at a meeting held in Washington, D. C., on February 6. This action on the part of Brother Hayes was necessitated because of ill health from which he has been suffering for an extended period. It had been hoped that his health would improve so as to enable him to resume the duties of his office, but in his letter of resignation, Brother Hayes points out that such hope is impossible.

"In conformity with the laws of the International organization, the vice president has succeeded to the office of president and Mr. Philip Murray, president of District No. 5, UMWA, has been selected to fill the unexpired term of the vice president. His selection was confirmed by a vote of the International Executive Board. Brother Murray is eminently qualified to discharge the responsibilities of this office and will immediately assume his duties as vice president of the International Union."

In the December, 1920, UMWA elections, President Lewis was opposed by Robert H. Harlin, president of District 10 and former international statistician, for the UMWA presidency. Philip Murray was opposed for the vice presidency by Alexander Howat, president of District 14.

Mr. Lewis defeated Harlin 173,064 votes to 106,132. Mr. Murray, in a closer race, kept Howat in Kansas by beating him 143,452 to 132,416.

Tired of what he felt was a "do-nothing" policy of the AFL, Mr. Lewis allowed his name to be placed in nomination six months later for the federation's presidency in opposition to seventy-one-year-old Samuel Gompers. Although he did not campaign actively, he received one-third of the votes cast. In a speech to the 1921 AFL convention after the election, Mr. Lewis said:

"I am content with the decision of the convention and the vote that was cast for me. I am more content with the action of this convention in speaking so definitely upon certain matters of progressive policy adopted by a majority vote."

It was at this AFL convention, on June 20, 1921, that Mr. Lewis successfully sponsored a resolution calling on labor organizations to assist in the vocational education of incapacitated people and to aid them in finding jobs when their re-education had been completed. This was a quarter of a century before the United Mine Workers Welfare and Retirement Fund came into being. Mr. Lewis' interest in the rehabilitation of persons crippled in industrial accidents was not an inspiration which suddenly occurred to him during the 1945 coal negotiations. He has fought for the physically handicapped all of his life.

On March 11, 1920, forty-three mine workers and eighty-two coal operators were indicted in the court of Judge A. B. Anderson on charges of conspiring to fix prices and limit distribution of coal in violation of the war-time Lever Act. Charles Evans Hughes was retained to represent the UMWA men who had been indicted.

On Mr. Hughes' argument, Judge Anderson declared a part of the Lever Act unconstitutional. He set trial, however, for the indicted miners and operators on five counts based on parts of the law he ruled were constitutional. The case dragged along until, on February 28, 1921, the U. S. Supreme Court killed the sections of the Lever Act on which Judge Anderson's injunction was based.

But the mine workers and operators were enjoined again on the identical evidence and charged with the violation of a different law, this time the Sherman Anti-Trust Act. By now Hughes had become Secretary of State under President Warren G. Harding and the UMWA had passed its legal headaches on to the able William A. Glasgow, Jr.

Trouble broke out in the mining camps of Alabama where the miners were compelled to work for low wages and under inhuman working conditions because the operators refused to accept the decision of the coal commission or negotiate with the miners. Much of the trouble was caused by the racial attitudes of some of the people of Alabama who were horrified at the UMWA's policy of organizing local unions on a non-segregated basis. This is how Mr. Lewis described the Alabama situation in his report to the 1921 convention:

"On September 1, 1920, authority was given the officers of District 20 to call a general strike of the miners of that district. Between 11 thousand and 12 thousand mine workers responded to the strike call which was made effective on the 7th day of September. Van Bittner was sent to represent the International Union during the strike."

The operators quickly launched their attack. Their tactics included all of the classical weapons used by reactionary coal barons in fighting their battles—evictions, gunmen, scabs, inflammation of racial hatred, assaults against the miners, false charges and arrests, use of the press to create hysteria in the public mind against the strikers, threats against union representatives, the National Guard ordered into mining districts, and public meetings prohibited.

Yet, Mr. Lewis reported:

"The miners stood firm and waged the unequal struggle until the month of February, when, through the instrumentality of a committee of public-spirited citizens, an arrangement was entered into providing for arbitration of all points in dispute by the governor of Alabama.

"It was believed by our members in Alabama that the case of the mine workers was so manifestly just that even Governor Kilby could not, as a public official, avoid deciding in favor of the mine workers. So the strike was terminated on February 22, 1921.

"However, on March 12, 1921, the governor rendered his award which in effect denied every contention made by the UMW in Alabama. This astounding decision may well be reckoned as the most flagrant abuse of executive and judicial authority in the annals of American public life. The Alabama miners were overwhelmed with disappointment, but true to their word, they decided to accept the decision."

The litigation and strife of this period were only "the baby figure of the giant mass of things to come." The Mingo County wars had started. The Mingo coal operators had filed a suit which became known as the "Borderland Case" and required the full attention of many lawyers for several years. The operators were beginning their long, bitter fight to break the union.

COMMERCE SECRETARY HOOVER, MR. LEWIS AND AIDES AT THE WHITE HOUSE IN 1921

NO BACKWARD STEP

HISTORIANS STATE that the great depression started with the stock market crash of October, 1929. That is merely the time, however, when Wall Street and the big-city newspaper publishers awoke to the stark reality that the nation was on the economic rocks. In the rural backroads of America and in thousands of coal mining communities, farmers and coal miners had felt the tightening grip of unemployment and insecurity from the end of World War I.

The coal miners felt it first. With the sudden cessation of war, their industry found itself with a huge stockpile of virtually unsaleable coal. Coal operators reacted with a conspicuous lack of foresight and intelligence. They slashed prices in a campaign of cut-throat competition. Then they turned to smash the United Mine Workers of America. And reverting to the tested formula and egged on by the financial interests that controlled them, the operators used every violent method in the books in their union-busting drive.

They failed. And the story of how they were beaten by the UMWA is one of the most dramatic tales in the annals of the workingman's long struggle to improve his lot.

The keynote of the period was sounded by John L. Lewis at the District 11 convention in Terre Haute, Ind., on July 14, 1921, where he said:

"I am not unaware of the conditions which prevail in the country today—social, economic, industrial, and political. Recent government statistics show that in the mines of the United States there are 242 thousand men completely unemployed. In addition, we have several million idle men in industries throughout the country. I think recent estimates run the total up to approximately four and one-half million men, and upon the basis of three dependents to each worker, it would run the total number of citizens of our country who are directly affected by this non-employment condition to some 18 or 20 million people, or practically one-fifth of our total population—a most astounding condition, a most dangerous and hazardous condition, dangerous to the welfare of our people as individuals and dangerous to the social fabric of the nation itself.

"It occurs to me that our statesmen will be required in the near future to legislate in some definite, specific manner that will operate to relieve the present condition. It cannot continue as it is. The bringing about of further reductions in wages in the various trades and occupations will not improve matters.

"I am aware that there is a tremendous influence being exerted to depress the wages of the workers of America. The coal operators of the country are doing everything possible to crys-

"NO BACKWARD STEP!" SAID MR. LEWIS IN 1921; SEEN WITH HIM IS PHILIP MURRAY

tallize sentiment in favor of wage reductions."

Soon afterward, Mr. Lewis made his famous "No Backward Step" speech. In the words that became the symbol of the UMWA's battle for survival in the 1920's, he told the anthracite Tri-District Wage Scale Convention at Shamokin, Pa., on January 17, 1922:

"One thing must be sure, not only in the bituminous coal fields of America, but in the anthracite coal fields as well—in this day there must be no backward step by the mine workers of this country.

"It makes no difference to the organized mine workers of this country that wage reductions have taken place in other industries, and it makes no difference to the organized mine workers of this country that the men employed in the non-union sections of this country in the coal industry have accepted wage reductions. We do not propose to have our standards of living gauged by the standards of living which obtain among these benighted, unfortunate people who are compelled to work for the unorganized min-

24

ing employers. We do not expect to follow the non-union mine worker down the ladder of wage reductions to the morass of poverty and degradation which prevails below, and we do not propose to have the non-union yardstick applied to our standards of living.

"The mine workers of this country do not desire any cessation of employment in the mining industry after April 1. We abhor the thought of a strike.

"And yet we do not propose to avoid the responsibilities of such a conflict by doing anything contrary to the interests of our people or by doing anything which in honor we should not be bound to do.

"When I say that we will take no backward step, I say it with an appreciation of what that policy means, and if it requires an industrial conflict to avoid taking a backward step, then the industrial conflict may come."

And the industrial conflict came.

When, on April 1, 1922, both anthracite and bituminous coal mines closed down, the conflict was on. The shutdown was, in effect, a lockout to sustain the high price of coal because the operators, flouting their contract obligation, refused to negotiate a new agreement. Mr. Lewis had warned in advance:

"There will be no strike if the bituminous coal operators deal fairly with the miners. The operators want a strike while the miners do not. The operators want a strike in order to destroy the union and in order to be able to sell their coal on hand at high prices."

The mine workers' scale committee said that they would accept no reduction in wages, demanded a six-hour day, improvement in working conditions, a weekly pay day and abolition of the automatic penalty clause. But the bituminous operators would not agree to meet with the miners' representatives.

The anthracite operators would not bargain either. The hard-coal miners were asking for $1 a day for day wage men, a 20 per cent increase in wages for contract (tonnage rate) miners and for a check-off for union dues and assessments. And they, too, issued a strike call for April 1 in case negotiations were unsuccessful.

Mr. Lewis gave the following brief account of these struggles in the bituminous and anthracite

OPERATOR MICHAEL GALLAGHER DISCUSSES 1923 COAL PACT WITH PRESIDENT LEWIS

fields in his report to the 1924 Convention:

"It was apparent early in 1922 that we were on the eve of a great struggle to maintain the principle of collective bargaining in the coal industry and to retain the wages and living standards then existing. Every industrial and financial weather vane had long pointed in that direction and the war drums of the coal operators, in both bituminous and anthracite, were beating

out their unceasing challenge to the conflict."

It came the same year and the UMWA, as Mr. Lewis reported in the Journal, was forced to fight to maintain wage levels. He said:

"Coal operators practically locked the miners out, refusing to meet in joint wage conference even to discuss a new wage agreement. The gallant five and one-half months' fight, during which all anthracite and all union bituminous coal mines were closed down, will go down in trade union history as the greatest single victory ever won by a union engaged in strike or lockout up to that period. The mines reopened with wages and working conditions intact."

There had been "No Backward Step."

Mr. Lewis realized that all labor organizations needed to draw closer to each other in a defensive alignment against management's union-busting policy.

Representatives of the sixteen railroad brotherhoods, the International Longshoremen's Asso-

THE 1923 ANTHRACITE COMMISSION MEETS IN NEW YORK; PAY HIKES, SHORTER HOURS WON

Front, Left to Right—Thomas Kennedy, president of UMWA District 7; President Lewis, John Hayes Hammond, mining engineer and consultant; Former Vice President of the U. S. Thomas R. Marshall and George Otis Smith, government conciliator. *Rear, Left to Right*—E. E. Hunt, commission secretary; C. J. Golden, president of District 9; Rinaldo Cappelini, president of District 1, and Dr. Charles P. Neil, umpire of the Anthracite Board of Conciliation.

ciation and the UMWA met in the latter part of February, 1922, and pledged mutual support in the battle against management's attempts.

Rising unemployment, spreading beyond the coal mines into other industries, moved President Warren G. Harding to create an Unemployment Conference to which he named the UMWA's president and to which he outlined an emergency relief plan in October, 1921. In a private talk with Mr. Lewis, President Harding said the miners would have to accept a wage reduction. A public statement from Mr. Lewis rebutted this as a solution to the problems of the unemployed:

"In the comfort of the conference room it is easy to forget that the unemployed are not merely a problem to be solved by debate and discussion but are a living army of human beings who a few months or weeks ago had jobs and are now jobless and, for the most part, penniless.

"Under our industrial system, the average working man can never get far from a hand-to-mouth existence. If he is frugal and farsighted, he may save a little in times of prosperity. But the opportunities are very limited, for under the best of circumstances few workers receive sufficient wages to permit of much of a margin for savings. Add to this the recurring periods of unemployment which affect almost every trade, and it is evident how difficult it is to lay anything by for the proverbial rainy day. In the coal-mining industry, the number of days of enforced idleness, according to the findings of the Bituminous Coal Commission of 1920, has never averaged less than seventy-eight days per year, even in the best of years. Thus, even in good years, the mine worker must be able to finance himself for a quarter of each year out of the earnings of the other three quarters. Extend, by weeks and months, this usual period of enforced idleness, and all his resources will be exhausted."

Mr. Lewis felt confident that the problem could be solved and submitted a detailed plan of action to meet, without delay, the most pressing needs of the unemployed. In broad outline,

A UMWA TEAM VISITS PENNSYLVANIA GOV. PINCHOT ON 1925 ANTHRACITE PROPOSAL

Left to Right—O. L. Garrison, secretary to President Lewis; Philip Murray, international vice president; Mr. Lewis, Thomas Kennedy, newly named international secretary-treasurer; Andrew Mattey, District 7 president; C. J. Golden, District 9 president.

Mr. Lewis' plan included: extension of credit, as an emergency measure, by the federal government to the unemployed workman to help him over his period of unemployment; formulation of a blueprint to cope with unemployment conditions in the future; an impartial investigation of labor costs and profits.

Mr. Lewis spelled out the effects of the depression on the miner in a 1928 statement to Congress on a bill to regulate the coal industry:

"The most important and most fundamental of the many ailments that afflict the bituminous industry is over-development. Nature has been extremely bounteous in giving us what is practically an inexhaustible supply of bituminous coal.

"Under existing law, there is no way of preventing the owner of any of this coal land from exploiting his property, mining his coal and disposing of it for whatever price he may be able to secure.

"The result of the unregulated opening of new mines, and the unrestrained development of existing mines, is that while the country normally consumes about 500 million tons a year, the present capacity of the bituminous mines is between 700 and 800 million tons a year."

In January, 1923, three months before expiration of the bituminous wage agreement, the miners and the operators of the Central Competitive Field signed a contract which kept the existing wage scale and eliminated the automatic penalty clause. But the anthracite mine workers had to strike to bring their wage scale up to the level paid in the soft-coal fields. Mr. Lewis reported to the 1924 convention on the 1923 anthracite negotiations as follows:

"The wage demands and policies of the UMWA were presented to the anthracite operators in a joint meeting, which convened in Atlantic City, N. J., on July 6, 1923.

"The anthracite operators, following their usual practice of refusing to concede anything of substantial nature in their negotiations, arbitrarily refused to give any consideration to the matter of wages. As a result, the joint conference dissolved and the anthracite mine workers, in the absence of a contract, ceased work on September 1, 1923.

"This strike seriously affected public interest

A FIRM-JAWED UNION LEADER LISTENS TO AN AIDE; MR. LEWIS AND C. J. GOLDEN IN 1923

in New England and the Atlantic Seaboard states, and resulted in public intervention by Governor Gifford Pinchot of Pennsylvania. As a result of the many conferences which followed at Harrisburg, Pa., an agreement was secured, carrying with it a 10 per cent increase in wages, a universal eight-hour day to all employees in the anthracite industry and many other improvements. This agreement was ratified at a special Tri-District Convention held in Scranton, Pa., on September 17, and the men returned to work on September 18. The agreement is effective until August 21, 1925, and is recognized by our people as a most distinct achievement.

"This substantial increase in wages gives to our anthracite members the same percentage of increases which has been received by the men in the bituminous fields since 1920."

During these negotiations, the chronic check-off issue provoked Mr. Lewis to observe on the operators' persistent inconsistency:

"The anti-union members of the National Coal Association are not so bitterly opposed to the check-off system in deducting from the wages of their employees money for payment of store bills from their swindling company stores, doc-

27

tors' fees, blacksmithing, house rent, house coal, tools, fuse, mining supplies, taxes and funds for the maintenance of baseball clubs and so forth and so forth. They prevaricate when they state that the UMWA forcibly compels them to contribute to the organization."

Like exclamation points to the economic hardships of the times and the fierceness of the operators' unrelenting campaign to cut wages and break the union were recurring outbreaks of violence in the coal fields. Some were major, like the so-called Mingo County Wars and the fight at Herrin, Williamson County, Ill., which was a bitter by-product of the nation-wide work stoppage of 1922. Others came and went quickly, leaving sudden shock, dead men and grief.

The tragedy at Herrin, Ill., occurred on June 21, 1922. Events leading to this bloodshed were reported as follows by the Journal:

"According to reports from Herrin, district officials gave the company permission to employ union men to strip the dirt from the top of the coal and to dig coal during the strike, provided the company would not ship any of the coal.

When the company had thus produced approximately 75 thousand tons of coal, it decided to ship the coal, discharged the union men and imported strikebreakers from Chicago, along with about thirty armed guards. These new men started to work and the guards were stationed around the property. They set up a machine gun at the mine."

The Journal added that a number of men, reported to be striking miners, went to the mine that morning to ask the strikebreakers to quit work. The report states that company guards opened fire and killed two men.

"This act incensed the people of the vicinity," the Journal added, "so that they stormed the mine, and killed more than a score of the strikebreakers and armed guards."

After the tragedy, Mr. Lewis issued the following statement:

"The United Mine Workers of America is not to any degree responsible for the unfortunate occurrence at Herrin, Ill. The organization has

AN EXCELLENT STUDY OF JOHN L. LEWIS IN 1923 AS HE LED FIGHT TO SAVE THE UNION

28

THE ANTHRACITE TRI-DISTRICT CONVENTION GETS DETAILS OF 1923 PACT FROM MR. LEWIS

never encouraged and does not condone lawlessness of any character. The officers of the organization are shocked and greatly deplore this tragedy. We are not, however, unmindful of the fact that sinister influences have for some time been at work among our membership to incite and inflame the spirit of violence. The ranks of the strikers are infested with thousands of detectives and secret service operatives whose employment by coal companies depends upon their ability to provoke violence and disturb public tranquillity. We have frequently called attention to this fact before investigating committees of Congress and have cited innumerable instances where outrages and murders have been committed by these irresponsible and lawless agents of the coal operators."

The story of Mingo County is typical because it contains all the elements of all of the stories of violence elsewhere. From Mr. Lewis, the 1921 Convention heard the background of the violence:

"In April and May, 1920, the unorganized miners in Mingo County, W. Va., became rest-

less because of the refusal of the operators of that section to apply the increases allowed by the 1922 Bituminous Coal Commission. A large number of UMWA local unions were formed and representatives of the UMWA were sent into the field at the request of the mine workers of Mingo County. The coal operators of that district became alarmed and, acting upon the advice of the non-union operators of the contiguous counties of Logan, McDowell and Mercer, inaugurated a lockout."

On May 19, 1920, twelve men were killed at Matewan, W. Va., in a gun battle in which the police and the people of that town faced a horde of hoodlums hired from the infamous Baldwin-Felts Detective Agency by the Mingo County operators to evict union coal miners from their homes.

In the West Virginia battle, Albert Felts, wearing a badge as a "deputy sheriff" of Harlan County, Ky., fired the first shot and was killed by Sid Hatfield, Matewan Chief of Police and one of the famous Hatfield clan. Felts had been one of the chief gunmen used by the coal operators in the Ludlow, Colo., massacre in 1913, when nineteen persons were killed, of whom twelve were miners' wives and children.

29

Hatfield, a hero of the West Virginia miners, was killed at Welch, W. Va., on August 1, 1921, by C. E. Lively, a Baldwin-Felts gunman. The Mine Workers Journal said the murder of Hatfield was probably a frame-up. He was arrested on July 28 on an allegation that he shot up the town of Mohawk more than a year before and was taken from his home in Matewan to McDowell County, "the Siberia of America." As he entered the courthouse with Ed Chambers, who had been called as witness, both were shot down by Lively and two other men.

Governor Ephraim F. Morgan of West Virginia declared martial law, but his own state courts said that the order was ridiculous without troops to enforce it. Governor Morgan swore in 130 private detectives as state militia and his "army" was supported by tonnage royalties paid by the operators, the same operators who, in later years, told Mr. Lewis tonnage royalties on coal for the Welfare Fund were illegal and would unduly raise the price of coal.

The next move was the arrest of twelve UMWA members at union headquarters while strike relief payments were being made. The Journal reported:

"Although West Virginia state police had committed innumerable other outrages in their efforts to aid the operators, this was the first time they had invaded the office of the union. Previously they had cut and slashed the tents of the colony, destroyed food supplies, poured coal oil in milk that was to have fed the children, and marched a number of men off to jail. Only a few days before they had ordered Alex Breedlove, a union miner, to throw up his hands and then had shot him dead."

Later on, seventeen miners were tried for treason against the state of West Virginia. William Blizzard, later president of District 17, was the first to go on trial because the state thought it had its best case against him. But the strained legal reasoning would not stand up, and he was acquitted. Other miners, however, had been thrown in jail on other trumped up charges and it was not until 1927 that the last one was released from jail.

The Mingo wars died down. The union had been forced to retreat. But it was not beaten. It took twelve years, but Mingo County was organized in 1933. And then it took only thirty days.

The union stood virtually alone, its back to the wall, during the dark years of the 1920's. A weak American Federation of Labor saw its ranks dwindle and wither away under the terrible pressures of unemployment and hunger.

ANTHRACITE TRI-DISTRICT STRIKE LEADERS MEET IN HARRISBURG, NOVEMBER 30, 1925

PENNSYLVANIA'S GOV. PINCHOT CONFERS WITH MR. LEWIS ON THE HARD-COAL STRIKE OF 1925

Samuel Gompers, who had been president of the AFL every year but one since its founding in 1886, died on December 13, 1924. Although there was a move to name Mr. Lewis to succeed him, the UMWA president was not interested in the post or in any other post that would mean his giving up the presidency of the UMWA. Earlier in 1924, the AFL withdrew, at Mr. Lewis' request, a resolution advocating his appointment as Secretary of Labor in President Coolidge's cabinet, a post that was open to him. The miners' leader felt he could fight labor's battles best as head of the UMWA. Four days before Mr. Gompers' death, he had been re-elected UMWA president over George Voyzey, 136,209 to 63,843. However, Mr. Lewis did feel that a mine worker should be president of the Federation. He told the AFL Executive Council his views and it reported to the 1925 convention:

"Acting President Morrison called a meeting of the Executive Council for New York on December 19, 1924. The Executive Council selected William Green, then third vice president of the AFL, as president of the Federation. He resigned as secretary-treasurer of the United Mine Workers of America and immediately assumed the work of the president of the AFL."

So Bill Green, ex-coal miner, Sunday school teacher, and Ohio state legislator, an efficient UMWA secretary-treasurer, became Mr. William Green, third president of the American Federation of Labor.

Mr. Lewis reported to the 1927 convention:

"Following this action, Mr. Thomas Kennedy, of Hazleton, Pa., for many years president of District 7, UMWA, was selected as secretary-treasurer of the International Union. Mr. Kennedy's appointment was confirmed by the unanimous vote of the International Executive Board and has met with the general approval of the membership of our organization. Mr. Kennedy is in every way eminently qualified and has long been recognized as one of the outstanding leaders in the ranks of organized labor in America."

Mr. Kennedy's subsequent career has fully justified those words. It includes twenty-two years as UMWA secretary-treasurer, four years as lieutenant governor of Pennsylvania and five years as vice president of the International Union.

31

UMWA NEGOTIATORS IN NEW YORK, DECEMBER, 1925, RENEW ANTHRACITE BARGAINING

Left to Right—Ellis Searles, editor of the United Mine Workers Journal; C. J. Golden, District 9 president; Andrew Mattey, District 7 president; Secretary-Treasurer Kennedy, Mr. Lewis, Vice President Murray.

The UMWA convention in January, 1924, authorized President Lewis to obtain the best contract he could continuing the $7.50 daily wage. The miners were asking for a four-year agreement. On February 19, 1924, Mr. Lewis signed the "Jacksonville (Fla.) Agreement," which extended the Central Competitive Field Contract for three years. He issued this statement:

"The success of the UMWA in securing from the operators at the Jacksonville joint conference a three-year extension of their present wage contract in the bituminous industry is an achievement of paramount importance to labor in general, for it establishes beyond all doubt the fact that present wage rates are none too high.

"Critics of the miners' union have charged that the present wage scale is a war schedule which ought to be deflated in peace time. But it is no longer a war-time scale. The extension of the agreement for three more years makes it a peace-time scale.

"Under this agreement, the organized mine workers of the country now have the best working conditions and the highest wage rates they have ever enjoyed."

The Jacksonville Agreement marked the beginning of the "fight to save the union." The operators of the Central Competitive Field tried to repudiate the agreement. Operators in the outlying districts refused to sign. In his report to the 1932 Convention, Mr. Lewis gave the following graphic description of the UMWA's fight during the years 1924-1928:

"Without considering curtailed production in any form; without trying to solve any of the multiplicity of problems involved in the over-development of the industry through mergers or the creation of selling agencies; blind to the adoption of any constructive program whatsoever to stabilize the industry of its own accord, the bituminous coal operators, as a result of the poor earnings in 1924, set out to ask modification of the wage scale, which had two and a half years to run.

"From December, 1924, to December, 1928, the International Union and the district organizations in the Central Competitive Field, as well as the Northern and Southern West Virginia districts, fought wage reductions with all the forces at their command. More than $8 million were spent in court costs and attorney fees involving injunctions, evictions and practically every kind of lawsuit that could be conceived and instituted by the operators or their allies."

He described typical sacrifices made by Kentucky miners and their families at this time:

"These valiant souls in District 23 enjoyed a complete organization for a quarter of a century until 1924, when the operators of Western Kentucky elected not to sign the agreement negotiated at Jacksonville that year. They locked out our people and fought for a wage reduction, and for seven months those loyal men of District 23 conducted a struggle, helped by the International Union to the extent of our ability. They endured every privation, eviction, court injunctions, mine guards, deputy sheriffs, the usual paraphernalia of industrial war.

"In that district that year, after the strike had been in progress for some time, I saw children running around the mining camps of Kentucky dressed in nothing but flour sacks, with a hole cut in the bottom of the sack so that they might poke their head and arms through and the bot-

tom sewed up around their little legs, with the print of the milling firm appearing on one side of the flour sack—a most pitiful, tragic sight.

"But that is what the fathers of these children were giving to this union. They were giving not only their own service and their own loyalty, but they were mortgaging the well-being of their children and the future of their families. They were making that fight for you and me. They were making it to protect the $7.50 day wage in District 11, in District 12, and in other parts of our jurisdiction. They were placed in the border state. They were a buffer between the union and the non-union districts and the encroachment of the operators."

In a 200-page book, "The Miners Fight for American Standards," published in 1925, Mr.

HAPPY BIRTHDAY FOR MR. LEWIS; FEBRUARY 12, 1926, AND THE HARD-COAL STRIKE IS WON

Seated, Left to Right—R. F. Grant, spokesman for the operators; Mr. Lewis, Alvan Markle, operator and conference chairman; W. W. Inglis, operator; J. A. Gorman, secretary of the Anthracite Board of Conciliation. *Standing, Left to Right*—Andrew Mattey, District 7 president; Vice President Murray, Thomas Thomas, operator; A. M. Fine, operator; Rinaldo Cappellini, District 1 president; George B. Hadesty, operator; E. H. Suender, operator; Secretary-Treasurer Kennedy, C. J. Golden, District 9 president.

Lewis answered the propaganda campaign waged by the coal operators in their attempt to belittle the wage demands made by the mine workers. This was his main theme:

"The wage structure of the United States is the base rock of the country's prosperity. The purchasing power of the American masses is the pivot upon which our whole economic system turns. A reduction in that purchasing power is instantly registered, not only in the distress of the masses, but also in the shrinkage of profits and the destruction of capital values."

He then stated another of his basic beliefs, one which has been borne out by the constantly increasing efficiency of the American coal industry under the UMWA pressure for higher wages:

"In insisting on the maintenance of an American wage standard in the coal fields, the UMW

is doing its part to force a reorganization of the the basic industry of the country upon scientific and efficient lines. The maintenance of these rates will accelerate the operation of natural economic laws, which will in time eliminate uneconomic mines, obsolete equipment and incompetent management. Any concession of wage reductions will serve to delay this process of reorganization by enabling the unfit to hold out a little longer."

The bituminous miners had contracts in 1925, but they were being repudiated by the operators. The anthracite mine workers had to strike for more than five months to win a new agreement without wage reductions. Mr. Lewis told the 1927 convention:

"The scale committee of the Tri-District Convention and the officers of the organization met with the anthracite operators at Atlantic City on July 9, 1925. From the first day of the negotiations, it was evident that the anthracite operators were determined not to make an agreement with our organization unless it contained provisions that would bring about a lessened produc-

THE LITTLE CIGAR MAKER DIES; UMWA LEADERS AT GOMPERS' FUNERAL IN WASHINGTON

Among the union leaders attending the funeral of the founding president of the AFL were *(front row, left to right)* UMWA Secretary-Treasurer Kennedy, Vice President Murray and Mr. Lewis.

tion cost through the medium of a wage reduction or, in lieu thereof, the machinery of arbitration, which would permit periodic revisions downward. Your representatives resisted such demands on the part of the anthracite operators, with the result that the joint wage conference dissolved on August 4, without agreement.

"There accordingly came into being on September 1, 1925, what was, in many respects, the greatest and most severely fought struggle which our anthracite membership have been compelled to endure. Anthracite operators, allied with the powerful anthracite coal carrying railroads and the largest financial interests of Philadelphia and New York, resorted to every conceivable method to impair the morale of our membership and destroy their confidence in the union.

"This strike continued for 170 days, through the coldest months of the winter of 1925 and 1926. It is estimated that the anthracite operators spent a sum approximating $35 million, aside from their lost profits, in their efforts to crush the United Mine Workers of America in the anthracite region.

"During this period, the Hon. Gifford Pinchot, governor of Pennsylvania, intervened with the hope of securing an adjustment of the controversy and offered a plan of settlement. This plan was accepted by the anthracite mine workers, but was spurned by the anthracite operating interests. Eventually, after the anthracite operators had fought to the point of almost utter exhaustion, they consented to meet in conference and executed an agreement for a period of five years, based substantially upon the previous offer of settlement made by Governor Pinchot.

"The strike was finally ended and the men returned to the mines February 18, 1926."

The new agreement held the line of the 1923 wage scale until August 31, 1930.

Throughout his life, Mr. Lewis has cried out against the destruction and the maiming of human life in the mines. In a radio speech from Atlantic City on August 7, 1925, he told his listeners:

"No one more fully realizes the tremendous importance of coal to the well-being of the nation than does the coal miner himself. That is the reason why the coal miner applies himself so diligently to the task of producing this necessary fuel. Because he owes a duty to the public, the coal miner goes into the dark and dangerous recesses and caverns of the earth, amid all of the terrors and hazards of these underground places, risking his life day after day.

"But let me remind you that while the coal miner owes a duty to the public in these matters, the public must not forget that it, likewise, owes a duty to the coal miner who assumes these risks and hazards and performs this great service to humanity.

"There is another very striking reason why the anthracite mine worker is entitled to fair consideration on the question of compensation, and that is the extremely hazardous character of this occupation. The anthracite industry exacts a terrible toll of human life from those brave men who produce the coal. More than five hundred anthracite mine workers are killed each year by accidents in and around the mines, and more than 25 thousand are seriously injured. Analyze in your own minds, if you can, the meaning of these appalling figures. Picture to yourselves the size of the army of these industrial soldiers who lay down their lives for the comfort and well-being of their fellowmen. Marshall these five hundred victims of the anthracite industry and let them parade, in your mind, down Main Street, five hundred strong. At the head of this parade, let there be a band playing a funeral dirge, because these five hundred able-bodied men are marching to certain death. And behind these men place the more than two thousand wives, children and dependents who are to be left helpless through the death of the breadwinners.

"And this is not all. In this same parade there will be 25 thousand maimed and crippled men, crippled and disfigured in varying degree, and 100 thousand of their dependents, sufferers from accidents in the anthracite industry. As you look upon that parade, with all of its misery and woe, we ask you to decide for yourselves whether the industry, the coal operator and the public should do all that can be done to save and protect the miner and his family."

During these back-to-the-wall years, internal disunity tested the strength of the United Mine Workers of America, sometimes almost as bitterly as the union's struggles with management.

Some of the dissension stemmed from ambitious men eager only for office, some of it from sincere disagreement over policy, some of it from embitterment over the ills that plagued the industry.

Open revolt flared in Kansas under the leadership of Alexander Howat after Howat lost the 1920 UMWA election for vice president to Philip Murray. Howat engineered an illegal strike to embarrass the union's International officers, who had promised that the men would return to work. He was ousted as District 14 president in actions outlined by Mr. Lewis to the 1922 Convention:

"The District 14 charter was revoked on the 12th day of October, 1921, by the International president. The International Executive Board did not act on that matter until the 8th day of December, 1921, and for more than ten days after the Board convened in the latter days of November, no action was taken on the Kansas matter, pending an appeal. No appeal was filed.

"There are in this convention, 125 men from the state of Kansas who have come here under an organized arrangement, not only to disturb this convention and cause confusion in its ranks, but also to do anything that may be possible to prevent the carrying out in a proper way the laws of the organization.

"They say they want a trial, that all they ask is justice, when, as a matter of fact, for nearly ten months back the International has been doing nothing in the Kansas situation but holding continual trials. In the first place, an investigating commission was sent to Kansas to hold a trial on the ground and make an investigation of the facts in the Dean mine controversy. The committee found that the mine was idle in violation of the contract. Following the committee's report, the officers of District 14 ignored and flaunted the recommendations of the committee.

"Later on, the International Executive Board summoned all parties to the controversy to appear for a hearing in Indianapolis, where each side was privileged to present the facts. After a four-day hearing, with thirty men sitting on the Board, by unanimous vote, they held that the mines were idle in violation of the contract. The decision of the Board was not complied with by the officers of District 14. That made the second trial that has been had upon that subject matter.

"A third trial was had before the last International convention and the convention upheld the action of the International officers. That made no difference to the Kansas officers. They said that they would not regard the International organization's ruling as being binding upon them.

". . . Do you know how long it would take this convention to give a comprehensive consideration to all the details of the Kansas embroglio? If you do know, you possess greater wisdom than I.

"Chaos developed in District 14. The entire district was in a turmoil and it became necessary in defense of the interest of the UMWA for the International organization to revoke the district charter."

The convention upheld Mr. Lewis and ruled that Alex Howat and his insurgents were no longer officers of District 14.

Howat was re-admitted to the UMWA in 1927 and was again elected president of District 14. He joined the Illinois insurgents and in 1930 was elected their president at a rump convention held in Springfield, Ill.

That convention was linked with the machinations of Frank Farrington of Illinois and his attempts to grab the UMWA presidency. Of all the union's difficulties, the most serious was in District 12, of which Farrington was president until he was removed from office in 1926 on proof that he was in the pay of a coal company at the same time he held office. Officers who succeeded Farrington were no better. Their "solution" to the constant turmoil caused by a dual, communist union—the National Miners Union—was to incite the miners to revolt against the International officers, to obtain an injunction preventing representatives of the International Union from functioning in Illinois, and to embezzle union funds. When proof of the dishonesty of some of the district officials was submitted to Mr. Lewis, he revoked the district charter and named Frank Hefferly and John T. Jones as provisional officers. The dissidents then called the Springfield rump convention, which met the same time as the UMWA convention in Indianapolis. Besides naming Howat president, the "Illinois insurgents" elected John H. Walker secretary-treasurer and Adolph Germer vice president.

But early in 1932 the Illinois courts threw out the injunction and Howat, Walker, Germer, Powers Hapgood, Walter Nesbit, and their followers passed out of the picture save for some frenzied hours of "disorderly conduct" at the regular UMWA 1932 convention.

Rinaldo Cappellini, District 1 president, led a brief dual union movement in the anthracite which, also, failed.

An insurgent group backed John Brophy against Mr. Lewis' leadership in 1926 over a sincere split on UMWA policies. Brophy failed of re-election as president of District 2 and was out of office until President Lewis named him director of organization of the Committee for Industrial Organization.

The Journal reported that the UMWA members had overwhelmingly re-elected Mr. Lewis to the union presidency on December 14, 1926. He defeated John Brophy 173,323 votes to 60,661.

The 1927 Miami Conference between UMWA negotiators and operators of the Central Competitive Field revealed a determination by the employers to be disunited. Some refused even to participate. They wanted to put their mines back on a non-union basis in order to scale pay down to the level of the unorganized workers in

TRADE UNION LEADERS VISIT PRESIDENT HOOVER IN 1929, THE YEAR OF THE CRASH

Left to Right—Mr. Lewis, A. F. Whitney, Trainmen; T. A. Rickert, Garment Workers; Frank Morrison, AFL secretary-treasurer; John P. Frey, AFL Metal Trades Dept.; Secretary of Labor James J. Davis, AFL President Green, William L. Hutcheson, Carpenters; Matthew Woll, Photo Engravers; William J. McSorley of the AFL Building Trades Dept.; Alvanley Johnston, Engineers; E. P. Curtis, Conductors.

West Virginia, Kentucky, and Alabama. This, according to the operators' scheme, would make it impossible for any Central Competitive Field owners to meet the union's demands. President Lewis reported to the 1930 Convention:

"The Miami Conference was not fully representative of the operating interests of the Central Competitive Field, inasmuch as the Pittsburgh Coal Company and certain other companies in the Western Pennsylvania coal fields had, previous to the expiration of the agreement, repudiated the obligation of the wage agreement and were undertaking to operate their mines through the employment of strikebreakers. The operators' delegation from Western Pennsylvania was made up of certain independent coal operators, who represented their own companies rather than any association of operators.

"It became evident in the Miami meeting that there was a steadfast intent upon the part of the operating interests represented there to refuse to make any agreement with the United Mine Workers of America that did not carry with it provisions for substantial reductions of wage schedules. The operators endorsed and supported a proposal, introduced in the conference by the Ohio operators, calling for an agreement providing for a sliding scale of wages continuously competitive with the non-union wage rates of West Virginia and Kentucky. Such an agreement would, of course, have been an economic absurdity; it would have meant that the govern-

at International headquarters. This meeting developed that the operators of all the outlying districts had agreed, under the Miami policy, to continue at work under temporary agreement, with the exception of Iowa and the Southwestern districts, and the latter were to resume joint conference following a recess to permit the mine workers' representatives to attend the Policy Committee meeting.

"April 1, 1927, brought a suspension of major production in the Central Competitive Field and in certain of the outlying districts. The shutdown continued until the early days of October, 1927, when a temporary agreement was nego-

THE PROBLEM OF JOBLESS MINERS WAS REVIEWED IN A '28 VISIT TO MR. COOLIDGE

Left to Right—Mr. Lewis, AFL President Green and Frank Morrison, AFL secretary-treasurer.

ing factor of wages in the coal industry would have been determined by the economic needs and necessities of the most unfortunate and helpless of the mine workers employed in the mountain districts of Kentucky and West Virginia.

"The mine workers' representatives at the Miami meeting voiced their opposition to such an arrangement and sought in every honorable way to negotiate a wage scale predicated upon the conditions of the industry and the necessity of our people in those areas where agreements were previously in effect.

"The representatives of the organization then returned to their several districts, and on March 28, 1927, the Policy Committee was reconvened

tiated on the basis of no wage reduction, lasting until April 1, 1928; the Illinois operators being the first to enter into this arrangement, which was followed by the operators and miners of several additional districts.

"With the termination of these temporary agreements on April 1, 1928, there came another period of strikes, the operators still maintaining insistent demands for lower wage rates. The officers of your organization were firm in their resistance of these demands and were very largely supported by the overwhelming membership of our organization.

"The demand for coal in the industry was, of course, at a low ebb, but it was currently believed that with the coming of the fall demand, the bituminous operators would have renewed their agreements. However, in the month of June, 1928, the Executive Board of District 12, in association with the executive officers of its several sub-districts and the Scale Committee of District 12, convened a meeting in St. Louis and adopted a resolution requesting the executive officers of the International Union to convene a

consideration to the changed situation. In Illinois and in Indiana, the district scale committees were able to secure a basic day wage of $6.10. In the Southwestern district, $5.00 was the best day rate obtainable. In our Northwestern districts, the basic day rates are comparatively higher, as for instance in District 22, comprising the State of Wyoming, where the basic rate for drivers is $6.72.

"A discussion in this report of the variable factors which brought about a modification of the wage policy of the United Mine Workers of America in the bituminous fields after seven years of continuous resistance would not, at this

ANTHRACITE MINERS HOLD THE LINE AGAINST WAGE CUTS IN '30 AND WIN DUES CHECKOFF

Mr. Lewis and Richard F. Grant *(to his left),* chief spokesman for the anthracite operators at Scranton, Pa.

meeting of the International Policy Committee to modify the wage policy of the International Union, in order that District 12 might negotiate and accept a contract based upon the best terms obtainable.

"The publication of this action of the St. Louis meeting created a crisis in the affairs of our organization and within a period of three weeks it was necessary to convene the Policy Committee of the International Union to give

time, be of constructive value. The membership of our organization endured the blow with remarkable fortitude and in the main rendered every assistance to their organization in the necessary revision of its wage contracts. It is the hope of all that the economic circumstances of the industry will so change as to enable our organization to regain its former wage standards."

On March 7, 1928, in an appearance before a Senate committee investigating the coal industry in Pennsylvania, West Virginia and Ohio, Mr. Lewis outlined the UMWA's program for stabilizing the coal industry:

"The tales of outrage and tyranny that come

BLACK STRING TIE, FRECKLES, RED HAIR AND SHARP BLUE EYES ACCENT THIS 1925 STUDY

from the non-union fields have weakened respect for government everywhere.

"In some respects, our industrial system is like a chain—no stronger than the weakest link—and the same metaphor also applies to the menace to our entire political structure contained in these little outlaw fiefs.

"If the American people are to be assured of a constant flow of coal, prices to secure a fair return for the men who own the mines and the men who man them;

"If American industry is to enjoy that continuity of operation so essential to the successful discharge of its social duties and to the profits consistent with sound business;

"If stability and dependability are to be established in the nation's basic industry;

"If American standards of work and wages are to be maintained in American coal mines;

"Then the uneconomic mines must be closed and closed for good;

"Unscientific freight rates must be wiped off the tariff books;

"The perpetual strife and conflict within the industry must give way to labor relations on a par with those which have achieved comparative peace in other trades.

"Above all, the American Constitution must mean what it says in every coal field of America.

"American law must run to the remotest corner of America.

"American political rights must have as equal value everywhere as the American dollar."

At a session of the same committee later in the year, Mr. Lewis regretfully said:

"Six months have passed since Congress recessed and during all this period not one single coal association, not one single leader in the industry has come forward with any proposal to correct the disorderly conduct of 'King Coal.'

"Since the adjournment of Congress, the United Mine Workers of America have accepted wage reductions ranging from 17 to 33 per cent in the unionized coal fields, not because the economic conditions and possibilities warranted such decreases but due solely to the fact that the lack of leadership within the industry resulted in no effort being made to stop ruinous competition, external or internal."

One bright spot in the skies darkened by the union-busting attitude of the coal operators in 1928 was the announcement by the Rocky Mountain Fuel Company that it favored the UMWA's organizing drive in Colorado. Miss Josephine Roche was vice president in operating charge of the company, which was the only Colorado coal firm under union contract at the time.

The bituminous mine workers were still working under the best contracts that could be obtained, but in 1930 the anthracite miners negotiated another five-year contract which still held the line on the wage scale and gave the union a modified check-off of union dues.

The joint officers' report to the 1932 Convention said:

"The Anthracite Scale Committee succeeded in July, 1930, in securing a new agreement, which carried with it the existing wage rates, the establishment of the first check-off system and laid the basis for numerous improvements in working conditions.

"The agreement was lauded in the anthracite regions by the general populace, not only for the reason that it provided for the continuation of

40

"INCOMPETENT, STUPID" WERE USED BY MR. LEWIS TO DESCRIBE EMPLOYERS IN 1928

Seated, Left to Right—Sen. Frank R. Gooding of Idaho, Financier Charles M. Schwab, Sen. James E. Watson of Indiana, John D. Rockefeller, Jr., Mr. Lewis. *Second row, Left to Right*—Sen. W. B. Pine of Oklahoma, Sen. Burton K. Wheeler of Montana, Sen. J. M. Sackett of Kentucky and Sen. J. H. Metcalf of Rhode Island.

---

the existing wage rates, but also on the ground that its duration of five years was a guarantee of industrial peace for a long period and gave further promise of promoting permanent stabilization of the industry. In truth, the successful negotiation of the anthracite agreement represents the most outstanding achievement by organized labor since the stock market crash of 1929."

Despite assurances to the contrary, soft coal operators continued to cut wages and prices. Their assurances had been made in 1929 during Senatorial investigations and in a conference with union leaders and President Hoover.

The depressed status of the coal industry was more desperate than industrial conditions in general. The UMWA was so concerned over the situation that Mr. Lewis asked President Hoover to call a conference of mine workers and operators to plan government-sponsored stabilization of the coal industry. In his wire, he said:

"Many representative coal operators have given their assurance that they would gladly attend such a conference, if the government would issue such a call. We feel that the crisis is one of such vital importance, the degradation in the coal industry so far reaching, that the conference, when called, should not be delegated to a departmental matter, but should be sponsored and aided to the fullest extent possible by your office."

In spite of Mr. Lewis' request, the idea for a conference wandered through a bureaucratic maze. President Hoover referred the request to Secretary of Labor William N. Doak, who referred it to many groups of coal operators, who referred it to a referendum. The operators then referred it back to Secretary Doak, who announced finally that a conference had no chance of success because the non-union operators' groups were against it. It never was held.

The courts always have been a standard weapon in the operators' arsenal. Never has the UMWA been wholly free from litigation and it was enmeshed especially in this strenuous period when the International Union was dug in to hold the line against wage cutbacks. Where other measures failed to prevent union activity, there was a willing judge to issue an injunction. Some of these legal battles have proved milestones in the union's progress. The Red Jacket case, for instance, was part of the operators' last ditch stand to strangle the union through "yellow dog contracts." Mr. Lewis informed the 1930 Convention:

"Prior to our last convention, the federal court at Charleston, W. Va., had made permanent its injunction against the organization in the celebrated Red Jacket case, and this decision had been affirmed by the United States Circuit Court of Appeals for the Fourth Circuit. This injunction was issued on behalf of 316 coal companies and its effect was practically to insulate some 60 thousand miners against any peaceable efforts to persuade them to become members of our union.

"Since the last convention, our counsel have sought to have this decree reviewed by the United States Supreme Court, but this application was denied in October, 1927. The Red Jacket injunction decree not only remains in effect in West Virginia, but has been accepted as an authoritative precedent for similar proceedings in other federal courts.

"In September, 1927, the federal court for the Southern District of Ohio, at the suit of a number of coal companies, issued an injunction against the organization, based upon the 'yellow dog' contract. This injunction has recently been made premanent. In September, 1927, the Pittsburgh Terminal Coal Company secured an injunction against the officers of the organization from the federal court for the Western District of Pennsylvania. A number of injunctions have been issued by state courts, including the notorious Langhan injunction granted on November 8, 1927, by the court of Common Pleas of Indiana County, Pa. A no less drastic injunction was issued by Judge Linn D. Hay of the Marion Superior Court at Indianapolis, on the application of the receiver of the Consolidated Coal Company operating at Bicknell, Ind. West

MR. LEWIS ASKS CREATION OF NATIONAL ECONOMIC COUNCIL AT 1931 SENATE HEARING

Virginia and Kentucky are fairly plastered with injunctions against the miners' union.

"The injunctions based upon the 'yellow dog' contract are designed to prevent you and your representatives from peaceably persuading the men employed under such contract to associate themselves with their union organization. The federal injunctions are enforced by United States marshals and have all the potential backing of the federal government. The state injunctions are enforced by the peace officers of the state.

"As an example of how your organization has been harassed by injunctions, your legal department has defended the organization and its members in approximately 650 injunction suits and 6 thousand eviction suits since the last convention.

"During the last ten years there have been damage suits filed against the organization with potential liabilities of $40 million. We are happy to report to you that all major cases for damages have been disposed of and that there are no judgments against the organization.

"Since our last convention, the action of the Coronado Coal Company against our organization for damages under the Sherman Act has been disposed of, the case being dismissed by the plaintiff in the federal court at Fort Smith, Ark., in October, 1927.

"The suit of the Pittsburgh Terminal Coal Corporation against the United Mine Workers for heavy damages was dismissed.

"The similar suit by the Pennsylvania Coal Co. against our organization was, by order of the same court, dismissed in May, 1929.

"The Majors case against the United Mine Workers of America for $300 thousand damages, pending in the court at St. Clairsville, Ohio, was disposed of favorably to our organization in June, 1927."

In testimony before a Senate investigating committee in 1928, Mr. Lewis had outlined the UMWA's objections to the use of injunctions in labor-management affairs:

"Enact a law that will forbid the issuance of injunctions for the protection of 'yellow dog' contracts and the hateful implications of the peonage they create. When the employer asks for this form of injunctive protection, he is asking the court not to protect his legal or property rights, but to intervene in the economic struggle between the union organization and his unorganized labor force; and, if the courts do intervene in this purely economic struggle, then it should be under conditions that will recognize the right of the trade union to organize that labor and fairly protect it in its opportunity to do so."

It was four years later that organized labor got its anti-injunction law—four years of appearances before Congressional committees, four years of pressure on Congress and the President, four years of suits and injunctions, four years of hard work by labor organizations and by some Congressmen. But the effort was worth it. The Norris-LaGuardia Act, signed by President Herbert Hoover on March 23, 1932, was a good

ILLINOIS INSURGENTS' POWER GRAB FAILS IN 1930; GREEN BACKS LEWIS ADMINISTRATION

Shown at the Thirty-First Constitutional Convention in Indianapolis are Mr. Lewis, Mr. Green and Mr. Kennedy.

THE LINES OF WORRY SHOW IN MR. LEWIS' FACE AT THE DEPRESSION PEAK OF 1932

law and it plainly limited federal court interference in labor-management affairs.

Mr. Lewis won a political victory when the United States Senate refused to confirm President Hoover's appointment of Judge John J. Parker to the U. S. Supreme Court. Judge Parker, sitting on the U. S. Court of Appeals, had written the opinion upholding the "Red Jacket" injunction in West Virginia which legalized the "yellow dog" contract in that state.

With large segments of the country still refusing to face the facts of the depression in a "prosperity-is-just-around-the-corner" haze, Mr. Lewis in a radio statement said:

"There is only one way to bring about a return of prosperity, and that is to buy it back."

In the broadcast on September 11, 1932, Mr. Lewis went on:

"The program of the United States Chamber of Commerce is to remove all governmental regulation—state and national—of industry, which shall include repeal of the Sherman Anti-Trust Law. In other words, business asks outright freedom to continue certain acts which public policy declarations have outlawed.

"Labor insists that wages and working condi-

tions must be built up to human values and public welfare standards and not held down to world-wide levels of profitless competition.

"Organized labor seeks definitely to eliminate the manufacturer whose sole ability to remain in business is geared to pauperized wage rates and cut-throat prices. This type of employer is a menace to the social and industrial well being of the nation and makes for a direct assault upon the declared economic purposes of the American people as enacted into tariff and immigration laws. The many thousands of large and small establishments, which operate on low wage scales and sell solely on the basis of depressed prices, must be forced to observe a generally recognized industrial code which shall prescribe minimum standards of employment below which employers are prohibited to descend.

"Organized labor proposes that nation-wide action be taken by and through the federal government's creation of a National Economic Council, authorized to assume the lead in economic planning.

"At the outset, we must recognize the undisputed fact that mechanization has done its work; that there is no hope for the re-employment of millions of our unemployed under the present day industrial relationship; that robots do not consume goods; that American workmen, by their efficient utilization of machines, have so multiplied their productivity that they have earned the right to enjoy the six-hour day and five-day week; furthermore, that the rates of minimum wages paid for such employment shall constitute a family standard commensurate with an American mode of living.

"Organized labor further insists that if industry is to persist in discarding men at the age of forty-five, our accepted scheme of industrial relations must be based upon such a tenure of employment, or society accept in lieu thereof the responsibility of caring for those thus thrown into the scrap heap of human want and despair."

Thus spoke the man who, in 1921, had thrown down the "No Backward Step" gauntlet to the employers. The UMWA had gone through the dark years "bloody, but unbowed." The miners' leader now was issuing the call for the many great social and political reforms that soon were to follow.

JOIN THE UNION

The "first hundred days" of the New Deal were hectic, fruitful days for America. Actions were taken and laws passed which rerouted a nation speeding down a dangerous road to economic ruin. In the history of these times, the words that "brought a new birth of freedom" to working men were the chaste, legal words in a section of a New Deal law:

NATIONAL INDUSTRIAL RECOVERY ACT

Title I—Industrial Recovery

Section 7. (a) Every code of fair competition, agreement, and license approved, prescribed, or issued under this title shall contain the following conditions: (1) That employees shall have the right to organize and bargain collectively through representatives of their own choosing, and shall be free from the interference, restraint, or coercion of employers of labor, or their agents, in the designation of such representatives or in self-organization or in other concerted activities for the purpose of collective bargaining or other mutual aid or protection; (2) that no employee and no one seeking employment shall be required as a condition of employment to join any company union or to refrain from joining, organizing, or assisting a labor organization of his own choosing; and (3) that employers shall comply with the maximum hours of labor, minimum rates of pay, and other conditions of employment, approved or prescribed by the President.

Section 7a was the child of the UMWA. It was devised by Mr. Lewis, Henry Warrum, UMWA legal adviser, and W. Jett Lauck, UMWA economist. After what Mr. Lewis has described as "forty revisions or emasculations," labor's Magna Charta was written into the NIRA. It had been lifted from coal industry stabilization bills which the UMWA had unsuccessfully tried to push through the 1928 and 1930 sessions of Congress. In a speech in 1934, Mr. Lewis said:

"Early in 1933, when the Senate Committee on Finance conducted hearings to develop specific plans as a basis for legislation designed to promote industrial recovery, the United Mine Workers of America took the position that all industry should be stabilized according to the principles laid down in the pending Davis-Kelly Coal Stabilization Bill. The now famous Section 7a of the recovery act was taken directly from the labor provisions of that bill."

Many people think of the early days of the New Deal as an era when President Franklin D. Roosevelt told Congress what laws he wanted passed, whereupon Congress obediently "rubber stamped" them in the exact form requested by the administration. But even in those "hundred days" there were men who opposed progressive legislation. Mr. Lewis spent long, weary hours and much energy convincing President Roose-

45

velt, Congressmen and industrial leaders that Section 7a was an ingredient essential to the New Deal. He told the Senate Finance Committee in June, 1933:

"Organized labor in America wants the right to organize if it wants to organize. Every employer has the right to join these trade associations, and the enactment of this bill will make it almost mandatory upon every substantial employer of labor and producer of commodities transported in interstate commerce to join an organization for his protection, and through this legislative enactment there will be a closed shop to employers and industrialists in this country in every trade and industry, and yet distinguished gentlemen have the effrontery to come before this committee and propose that, after securing these privileges for themselves, they will deny to the workmen engaged in those industries the same rights and privileges which they arrogate to themselves.

"Labor in America is tired of such hypocrisy. It is tired of being dealt with in such a manner by men who proclaim the present relationship, as was done this morning by a representative of the steel industry, as a happy state of affairs. Mr. Lamont stated that the Iron and Steel Institute, which represents 90 to 95 per cent of the producing units of the steel industry, stands for the open shop. That carries the implication that the open shop is an institution or a policy whereby the employees of the steel industry can at will belong to a union or not belong to a union, as they choose, and that the employers

are protecting the principle of the open shop and the right of the employees either to belong to a union or not to belong to a union.

"There is no open shop in the steel industry as represented by Mr. Lamont. There is no right to belong to a union in the steel industry. It is a misnomer. If any shop exists in the steel industry, it is the closed shop, closed to the man who wants to belong to a union.

"Labor will protest any emasculation of Section 7a and it says furthermore that industry has nothing to fear in a modern rationalized labor relationship such as can be set up and administered under the provisions of this act."

The National Industrial Recovery Act was signed by President Roosevelt on June 16, 1933. The law gave two important psychological openings to the UMWA and Mr. Lewis moved immediately to take advantage of them. The officers' report to the 1934 UMWA convention said:

"Coincident with the signing of the act by the President, the United Mine Workers of

America conducted a vigorous organizing campaign in all the mining districts of the United States. Systematic plans were laid out, meetings were addressed by able field representatives and the enrollment of new members took place upon an unprecedented scale. It was easily demonstrated that the mine workers employed in the non-union areas of the mining industry would enthusiastically join the UMWA if they were privileged to do so. Local unions were established, local officers selected and installed, supplies furnished the local unions, and in less than thirty days from the signing of the act by the President the complete organization of the bituminous industry was effectuated. The accomplishment was so rapid and so spectacular that many people, including some officials of the government, refused to concede it as an actuality."

The complete success of the organizing drives

30-HOUR WORK WEEK PROPOSED BY UNION LEADERS IN 1933 TO EASE UNEMPLOYMENT

Left to Right—Mr. Lewis, AFL President Green, Sen. Matthew M. Neely, W. Va.; AFL Secretary Morrison.

is recounted by Mr. Lewis in his exuberant greeting to the delegates at the 1934 UMWA convention:

"This convention will have delegates from every coal field in the North American continent north of the mines of Mexico; they are here from every section of this great land.

"Truly a great accomplishment! Truly marvelous progress! Greater progress, may I say with pardonable pride, than has been made by any other trade union organization in America. A maximum degree of accomplishment under the conditions which prevailed since we last met in biennial convention.

"We have not achieved the millennium in the mining industry. We are still facing problems in our union. The accomplishments we have performed, the progress we have made merely demonstrate the possibilities of collective action in this great industry of ours. And with this great ability of ours to serve this industry in all of the states of the Union and Canada, methinks it is a living demonstration of the fact that there is no other union like the United Mine Workers of America.

"The fact that the United Mine Workers of America have made more progress under the policies of the Industrial Recovery Act than has perhaps been the case with other basic industries is merely indicative of the fact that, having promoted the legislation, we perhaps understood its potentialities and its possibilities to a greater degree than others, we perhaps worked longer days and longer nights in carrying the message to our people and encouraging them to join in the great undertaking.

"Be that as it may, the United Mine Workers of America have substantially accomplished the task to which it has been dedicated through the years and attained the goal which it has persistently sought through the forty-four years of its history. It has at last succeeded in bringing into the fold of our union and under the banner of our organization practically all the mine workers in our great North American continent."

The second opening given the UMWA by passage of the NIRA was the opportunity to negotiate with the bituminous coal operators on a more realistic basis. The old Central Competitive Field was no longer the largest coal producing area in the country. The Appalachian operators, whose production had grown by leaps and bounds during the non-union era, formed a group with which the UMWA negotiated the first Appalachian Agreement, covering about 70 per cent of the national tonnage. The agreement provided for a $5.00 daily wage for mines north of the Ohio River and $4.60 a day in the South. The officers' report to the 1934 convention tells the story:

"Succeeding the effective date of the act, the representatives of the UMWA joined the coal operators in presenting to the National Recovery Administration the General Code of Fair Competition. Under the auspices of General Hugh S. Johnson, administrator of the NRA, wage negotiations between the representatives of the UMWA and the Appalachian group of operators (Ohio, Central and Western Pennsylvania, West Virginia, Eastern Kentucky, Tennessee and Virginia) ensued. These negotiations culminated in the negotiation of a wage agreement which was signed in Washington on September 21, 1933. This agreement covered

approximately 314 thousand men and became the basis for a code of fair competition for the bituminous industry as agreed between the operators and the NRA.

"Following the signing of the basic agreement on September 21, supplemental district agreements were negotiated locally in the various districts of the Appalachian area.

"Under this agreement and under the Code of Fair Competition, the maximum hours of labor shall not exceed forty hours per week or eight hours per day.

"We secured a code provision for the accurate weighing or measuring of coal mined on a tonnage basis, with the right guaranteed to the miners to select their own checkweighmen to inspect the weighing of their coal.

"The code further outlaws company scrip or token money and provides that wages shall be paid semi-monthly in lawful money or check without discount.

"It is also provided that the mine workers cannot be compelled, as a condition of employment, to live in company houses or to trade at company stores.

"No person under sixteen years of age can be employed about a mine and no one under seventeen can be employed to work in a mine or in any hazardous occupation in connection with a mine.

"A schedule of minimum wages for skilled inside labor and for common outside labor was determined by the code, with the provision that other classifications should maintain their customary differentials above or below these basic rates, and that piece-work and tonnage rates of pay should maintain their customary relationship to the basic minimum rates provided in the code for day labor. These wages represent an increase in various districts of from 20 to 300 per cent in the wages of mine workers and will add annually many millions of dollars to the purchasing power of the families of our membership.

"The wage structure of the bituminous coal industry, with its employee classification and especially with district and local differentials, made it necessary for the code to fix certain basic minimum rates and refer to the various districts the working out of a completed agreement.

"All of our contracts provide the machinery for settling disputes over labor relations. Where no agreements are in effect with operating companies, the Bituminous Coal Code provides for divisional labor boards to which disputes can be referred. The labor boards are each composed of a representative of the employers, nominated by the operators; a representative of the employees, named by the UMWA; and a disinterested and impartial member appointed by the President of the United States."

The officers' report to the 1934 convention continued:

"In the negotiations preliminary to the approval of the Code of Fair Competition for the

---

THE UMWA HELD THE LINE IN 1933 AGAINST EFFORTS TO CUT HARD-COAL MINERS' PAY

Seated, Left to Right—E. H. Suender, operator; R. F. Grant, operator; J. B. Warriner, operator; M. J. Hartneady, District 7 president; Secretary-Treasurer Kennedy; Mr. Lewis. *Standing, Left to Right*—Michael Gallagher, operator; A. J. Maloney, operator; C. J. Golden, secretary, Anthracite Board of Conciliation; W. W. Inglis, operator; Vice President Murray; Mart F. Brennan, District 9 president; John Boylan, District 1 president.

bituminous industry, the various steel companies operating coal mines refrained from associating themselves with the commercial operators of the industry. Apparently, these captive coal corporations hoped to continue immune from the provisions of the coal code, and, at the same time, be free from the provisions of the code promulgated for the iron and steel industry. It was later decided by the Recovery Administration that the so-called captive mining operations were clearly affected by the provisions of the Recovery Act to the same degree as the commercial operations. Certain of the steel company subsidiaries operating mines opposed the organization of their employees into the United Mine Workers of America and in a number of instances company unions were formed and promoted by the captive coal companies. The United Mine Workers of America, through many months of conference and negotiation with governmental agencies, has insisted that the captive mining operations be brought under the same agreement with the United Mine Workers of America as was the case with the commercial operators in the districts where the mines are located."

But the solid front of the steel companies was

broken in February, 1934, when the H. C. Frick Coal and Coke Company, a subsidiary of the U. S. Steel Corporation, signed a wage and working agreement with the officials of the UMWA. The contract was signed by Thomas Moses for the company.

John L. Lewis and the other leaders of the UMWA not only pressed for passage of the recovery act, but also were active in its administration. Miners served on local and regional NRA boards and the International officers were on the committee named to devise codes for the coal industry. The officers' report to the 1934 convention tells of Mr. Lewis' appoint-

president of the United Mine Workers of America was included among those appointed by Secretary Perkins and, with his associates on the Labor Advisory Board, has sought since the creation of the NRA to safeguard the interests of labor under the Recovery Act and from time to time to make constructive suggestions with relation to the codes of the various industries.

"Shortly following the organization of the National Recovery Administration, President Roosevelt saw fit to create, by executive order, a National Labor Board, the function of which would be to adjudicate strikes and industrial conflicts through mediation, conciliation and arbitration. The Board was composed of eleven

ment to two of the national boards created under the NRA:

"General Hugh S. Johnson, following his appointment as Administrator of the Industrial Recovery Act by President Roosevelt, requested the appointment of an Industrial Advisory Board, a Labor Advisory Board and a Consumers' Advisory Board, all of which were to have official status in the NRA.

"A distinguished list of industrial leaders was appointed as members of the Industrial Advisory Board by Secretary of Commerce Roper. A similar list of representatives of organized labor and nationally known economists was appointed as members of the Labor Advisory Board by Secretary of Labor Perkins. The

A BLOW AT THE HEART OF SOFT COAL'S ILLS MADE BY FRAMERS OF NRA COAL CODE IN '33

Left to Right—Secretary-Treasurer Kennedy, George Harrington, operator representative; T. G. Essington, operator attorney; Mr. Lewis, Vice President Murray.

members, appointed by the President, consisting of representative industrialists, eminent economists, and representatives of organized labor. The president of the United Mine Workers of America was named as a member of this board, and, with his associate members on the board, has rendered such service as has been possible in the midst of other duties and obligations. United States Senator Robert F. Wagner was named as chairman of the board and has functioned with distinction in that capacity. The National Labor Board has a substantial record of accomplishments and its members have labored assiduously to make a contribution to the industrial stability of the nation."

Although the main energies of the UMWA in 1933 were directed toward organizing miners and negotiating with the bituminous operators, and in NRA activities, Mr. Lewis and his co-workers, somehow found time to proceed with other work.

One of Mr. Lewis' extra-curricular posts was that of unpaid president of a labor bank in Indianapolis. So, the March, 1933, bank holiday found him burdened not only with the problem of every American citizen—shortage of personal cash—but also with the problem of paying off bank depositors. How the bank survived is told in this Journal story written by Van Bittner:

"During the industrial and financial depression through which our country has passed, thousands of banks have closed their doors and left their depositors, who have lost their money, to cool themselves in the breezes of the frozen assets of these defunct financial institutions.

"Through it all there is at least one bright spot—that is the closing of the United Labor Bank & Trust Co., of Indianapolis, of which John L. Lewis, president of the United Mine Workers of America, was president. When this bank closed its doors, every depositor was paid every penny owed him. Not a single cent was lost to the depositors."

The Illinois insurgents had maintained a "paper" district organization with John H. Walker as president until the UMWA officers reported to the 1934 convention:

"On February 27, 1933, Mr. John H. Walker, then president of District 12 by virtue of a court injunction, surrendered the charter of District 12. The affairs of the district were in a frightful condition. Under the protection of the court order, the officers had clung to the offices as long as a dollar remained in the treasury or could be secured through loans or the assumption of financial indebtedness. The assets of the district were intangible and in most instances mythical. The indebtedness of the

district organization, consisting of money owed to banks, printing establishments, undertakers, officers and field workers, delegates to conventions and dependents of deceased members reached the staggering total of $300 thousand."

Many of the insurgents had joined a dual union, the Progressive Mine Workers of America. Their violent attempts to overthrow UMWA contracts with Illinois operators led Donald R. Richberg, chief counsel for the NRA, to investigate the situation. His report said that the Progressive leaders had no control over their followers and that they were promoting violence to accomplish their aims. After the Richberg report, Mr. Lewis commented:

"Mr. Richberg found on his recent visit to Illinois that the violence in the mining areas had been caused by the unlawful attempts of the Progressives to interfere with the wage agreement between the United Mine Workers of America and the Illinois Coal Operators' Association. Criminal attacks upon men going to and from their work, night riding, bombing and shooting from ambush have all been incidental to the purpose of the so-called Progressive Miners' Union to take by force and intimidation the wage contracts to which they were not a party and in which they had no legal right of participation.

"The official statement of the Recovery Administration makes clear that the machinery of the government will not be used to impair the wage agreements of the UMWA and, in effect, calls upon the governor of the State of Illinois to enforce the law and to give protection to citizens in their inalienable right peacefully to follow their employment under wage contracts negotiated through the medium of collective bargaining.

"This statement of the Recovery Administration should open the eyes of many miners in Illinois to the fact that they have been deceived and deluded by false promises on the part of a few designing leaders and petty politicians."

The well-organized anthracite mine workers, in the spring of 1933, had to fight off attempts of the anthracite operators to reduce wages 35 per cent. The operators had made their request in 1932 and the dispute had been referred to a

51

two-man board of arbitration, George Rublee for the operators and Frank Morrison, secretary-treasurer of the AFL, for the miners. Dissenting opinions were filed, after which, according to the 1934 officers' report to the convention:

"The anthracite operators expressed dissatisfaction at their failure to agree and requested further joint meetings with representatives of the UMWA. These meetings convened in Philadelphia on April 19 and continued until April 26, 1933. During these conferences, the anthracite operators recounted again the conditions in the anthracite industry which, in their judgment, made necessary a wage reduction and insisted that the representatives of our organization acquiesce in this viewpoint. It was the contention of the mine workers' representatives in these meetings that it would be exceedingly unwise for the anthracite mine workers to agree to a wage reduction under conditions existing at that time and in view of the potential economic changes which seemed about to ensue. It finally occurred on April 26, 1933, when the conference was about to disrupt, that Secretary of Labor Frances Perkins telegraphed both the delegations of the operators and mine workers suggesting an adjournment of the conferences as follows:

" 'Due to pending legislation concerning reduced hours of operation and due to possibility of improved financial conditions to bring about a rise in prices, it is my suggestion that you delay conference on any change in present wage scale for thirty days. It is also my suggestion that you provide for reopening conference as may be desired at expiration of thirty days so as not to conflict with your agreement not to discuss wage changes oftener than once a year.'

"The conference acceded to the wish of Secretary Perkins and later developments in the bituminous coal industry and the economic situation of the nation seemed to remove the necessity of further conferences on this subject."

By 1934, the miners were able to evaluate the work NRA had done but there still remained much to do.

In a paper prepared for a meeting of the American Academy of Political and Social Science in Philadelphia on January 6, 1934, Mr. Lewis reviewed what he thought the NRA had accomplished and how he thought it should proceed:

"Organized labor is a single unit in its approval of the objectives of the National Industrial Recovery Act. Labor may differ with the National Recovery Administration in its interpretations and policies, but as to the act itself, the support of organized labor, in a fundamental sense, is without reservation. From the standpoint of human welfare and economic freedom, we are convinced that there has been no legal instrument comparable with it since President Lincoln's Emancipation Proclamation of seventy years ago.

"On the other hand, the practical application of the law up to the present time has, in the opinion of organized labor, been too restricted and too lacking in uniformity and comprehensiveness. Hours of labor have not been sufficiently reduced; employees exempted from the provisions of industry codes have been numerically excessive; price and production controls have been, as far as possible, ignored; the full cooperation of labor, as contemplated by the act, has been prevented by placing labor on the defensive in the formulation of codes, and also by forcing labor to use its economic strength, or the strike, in order to secure the mandatory guarantees of Section 7a of the act.

"Many of these points of criticism of the NRA have undoubtedly arisen from the scope and seemingly insurmountable difficulties of the test it has faced. As a whole, its accomplishments have been most heartening and laudatory. The preliminary stages, however, are now over and, in the opinion of organized labor, the time has now been reached for the application of a more fundamental and more clearly defined program.

"The representatives of organized labor realize fully that Section 7a of the Recovery Act does not impose any direct obligation on the part of the government to organize industrial workers. While we recognize the difficulties of this situation from the standpoint of the NRA, we do believe that the present procedure, which permits trade associations to submit the labor provisions of a code, places labor not in a cooperative but defensive position in connection with the consideration of these labor provisions. The labor provisions under these conditions become

MR. LEWIS IN A DIFFERENT ROLE AS HE CELEBRATES JULY 4, 1934, IN PARIS, FRANCE

---

a matter of controversy and trading through the medium of a deputy administrator.

"This being the fundamental situation, it seems to me that the NRA should put aside temporizing measures, and fearlessly apply a constructive plan for permanent economic recovery. I say this because I sincerely believe that the NRA is the only agency of the New Deal which can save us at this time. All necessary powers are lodged in the act. All that is required for the deliverance from the existing economic tragedy and the attainment of real economic recovery is for the NRA to use boldly the powers which it possesses.

"The ultimate objectives as to policy and procedure of the NRA should be immediately announced and stated to be the standards which must be included by industries in their codes. To my mind, these standards should be:

"1. Hours of work per week to be reduced, as far as possible, to a general level of thirty hours a week, of five six-hour days.

"2. Minimum wage rates of 50 cents per hour.

"3. General wage rates of 1926 raised sufficiently to produce the same weekly wage for shorter hours as earned per week before reduction in weekly schedule of hours.

"4. Production schedule as of 1926.

"The above program for the Industrial Recovery Administration would be clear cut, definite and immediately practicable, if generally applied.

"In conclusion, I repeat, that it is my firm conviction that in the adoption of a comprehensive program, as outlined by the National Industrial Recovery Act, rests our real hope for complete economic recovery. Definiteness and boldness are all that are required for its success. In its broad lines, such a program must be ultimately adopted and it cannot be put into effect too soon. Its fruits would consist not only of the employment of those now unemployed, and the realization of economic recovery, but it would also carry with it a high measure of human welfare and economic democracy, together with all the other elements of a better social and political life."

The year 1934, like 1933, was another of exceptional activity. Delegates to the January, 1934, convention passed resolutions condemning sales taxes, asking the death penalty for lynching, endorsing the soldiers' bonus and inheritance taxes. They heard speeches by Secretary of Labor Frances Perkins, C. B. Huntress, president of the National Coal Association, and William Green. And when a delegate remarked that the Communist Party was like any other political party, Mr. Lewis angrily replied:

"May the chair point out that the Communist Party, not content with political activity, has been undertaking to control the trade unions of America. The Communist Party has undertaken to destroy the UMWA.

"The Communist Party organized a dual miners' union. They financed it. They furnished it with officers. They furnished it field workers, literature and ads—a dual miners' union designed to destroy and supersede the UMWA. The name of that union organized by the Communist Party is the National Miners' Union.

"For that reason, the UMWA barred membership, not only in the National Miners' Union, but in the Communist Party, because it has, as a matter of record, directed its activities towards jurisdiction of American trade unionism. It is self-preservation of the UMWA and is simply to repel an intruder in its home that seeks to destroy the very union itself."

Later in the year, former UMWA President Frank J. Hayes, W. H. Raney and William Mitch, representatives of the International Union, negotiated a contract covering 85 per cent of the miners in Alabama. Thomas Kennedy, UMWA secretary-treasurer, won the Democratic nomination for lieutenant-governor of Pennsylvania. On March 31, 1934, a new Appalachian Agreement was signed, calling for a $5.00 daily wage in the North and $4.60 a day in the South. The miners in the states north of the Ohio River had their working day reduced from eight to seven hours a day. And, late in April, 1934, Mr. Lewis appeared before the Senate Committee on Education and Labor to support a bill introduced by Senator Robert F. Wagner of New York to strengthen the labor protections in the NRA. Although

this bill never became law, its strengthened labor provisions were written into the Wagner Labor Relations Act, which was passed in 1935 after the Supreme Court had declared the NRA unconstitutional. Mr. Lewis told the labor committee:

"The basic principles of Senator Wagner's bill have been recognized by Congress in at least two statutory enactments, namely, the Norris-LaGuardia Act and the National Recovery Act.

"This bill undertakes to put in precise form certain of these rights and privileges in a manner that will protect the purpose of the bill and prevent workers from being denied in their application the privileges accorded by the enactment of the measure.

"The right of organization and of collective bargaining is now understood by all industrial workers, but the continual denial of that right and its evasions by company unions is creating unrest and will breed revolt among the workers in industry, apart from any question of wages. This is especially true in view of the fact that the government through legislation is encouraging organization of industry. Employers were formerly not able to form these associations because of the provisions of the anti-trust laws with which they would have come into conflict prior to the passage of the Recovery Act.

"If the government is to encourage organization upon the part of employers who primarily are more able to protect themselves than are the workers, then it does seem to be entirely logical for the government at least to give the workers the necessary degree of protection in the formation of their own voluntary forms of trade unions.

"The bill introduced by Senator Wagner does not presume to make the government a party to the formation of unions of the workers; but it does undertake to protect the workers in the formation of such unions if they elect to take that action.

"In the policy of forming company unions, the employers undertake to deprive labor of the right to be represented in any broad or any national way by representatives they may elect to employ. It is a Dr. Jekyll and Mr. Hyde policy.

"I think it is unfair to the American people

for industrialists and the captains of industry in this country to be guilty of deceptions and hypocrisies in their labor relations. I think it is destructive of confidence on the part of the workers. I think it is provocative of unrest. I think it helps to crystallize discontent."

Mr. Lewis also found time in the spring of 1934 to testify in behalf of another Wagner Bill, this one calling for a federal program of low-cost housing construction. Mr. Lewis said:

"The United Mine Workers of America wish to record their approval and support of the pending bill (S. 2392) as introduced by Senator Wagner. A study of its provisions has convinced us that the fundamental principles and objects of the measure should have the earnest support of the organized labor movement.

"Our organization urges adoption of the bill

AFL LEADERS DISCUSS RECOVERY PROBLEMS AT AN NRA MEETING IN WASHINGTON IN '34

Seated, Left to Right—Edward J. Gainor, Letter Carriers; Matthew Woll, Photo Engravers; Frank Morrison, AFL secretary-treasurer; William Green, AFL president; Frank Duffy, Carpenters; T. A. Rickert, Garment Workers; Daniel Tobin, Teamsters. *Standing, Left to Right*—Mr. Lewis, Harry C. Bates, Bricklayers; David Dubinsky, Ladies' Garment Workers; John Coefield, Plumbers; Arthur O. Wharton, Machinists; G. M. Bugniazet, Electrical Workers; George Berry, Pressmen; George Harrison, Railway Clerks, and William L. Hutcheson, Carpenters.

because of two general advantages to the labor movement.

"It is obvious that it will aid the movement for economic recovery by affording additional opportunities for employment, especially in the construction industry.

"Our second reason is far more fundamental and important. It is a social and economic one of far-reaching significance; namely, that the bill makes provision for decent housing facilities, and better standards of living for industrial workers in the lowest wage or income groups.

"The members of these unfortunate groups have never before had an opportunity to secure proper housing conditions for themselves or their families. They have been forced to accept the discarded and obsolete housing of those more favored groups in the economic struggle, or have had to adapt themselves as best they could to the inadequate facilities which speculative banking, industrial, or real estate organizations have conceived for their exploitation.

"Under conditions existing around any bituminous coal mining operations, the mine worker is forced to become a tenant of the company by which he is employed, for the reason that so-called company houses are the only facilities available; and, as the operating company owns all the available land within living distance of the mines, the mine workers could not purchase

UMWA LEADERS, COAL OPERATORS MEET WITH NRA COUNSEL, MARCH 28, 1935

Seated, Left to Right—Charles O'Neill, operator; Mr. Lewis; Donald Richberg, NRA counsel; Duncan Kennedy, operator, and Percy Tetlow, UMWA representative.

land for the construction of homes, even were they financially able to do so.

"Under the pending bill, it would appear possible to rectify these conditions. In other words, not only the housing standards of the mine worker may be improved, but also his independent economic status assured."

In May, 1934, NRA Administrator Johnson had approved a temporary code for the bituminous industry with an average daily wage of $4.60. The Alabama operators, in spite of the fact that they had signed a contract with the UMWA, refused to live up to the new code. An NRA hearing was held in Washington and the Alabama operators, represented by Forney Johnston, said they "could not afford" to pay the wage scale called for by the amended code. Mr. Lewis replied:

"The chief dissenter to this order is representative of a group in the state of Alabama. In a mood of non-cooperation and studied defiance they object to the permanency of the order for every conceivable reason, logical and illogical, that they can enumerate. They seek to make a virtue of the fact that they were able, in the pre-code days, to impose upon the workers in the coal industry in Alabama more de-

grading working conditions and a greater degree of medieval barbarism in industry than was the case in any other group of the coal industry of the country. By reason of the fact that economic and social conditions in the coal industry in Alabama had sunk to a lower level than in any other section of the United States, they seek to make a virtue of that fact, and they emphasize their resistance to changing the old order and advancing in line and in tune with the rest of the industry.

"There is no logical reason why the operators of Alabama cannot pay the same wage scale and maintain the same working conditions and hours in the coal mines of that state as is done in the coal mines of the other states south of the Ohio River, with their 40 cents a day differential and equivalent differentials on tonnage rates.

"Mr. Johnston's opinion of this hearing is that it is largely stage play for publicity purposes. I assume Mr. Johnston, when he said that, was somewhat inebriated by the exuberance of his own verbosity.

"The Alabama contract was negotiated in all good faith by the representatives of the UMWA. And be it said to their dishonor, the Alabama operators are reneging on that agreement, which is not an honorable thing to do.

"They have locked out their men and they boast of the fact that 15 thousand are idle in the Alabama industry because they, the commercial operators, through Mr. Johnston, chose to repudiate a formal engagement, duly ratified, and locked out employees in violation of an order of the President of the United States, who in turn is authorized by Congress.

"I will say that every observation that has been made, every objection to the code that has been entered by the representative from Alabama operators to the amendment proposed, approved by General Johnson temporarily, has been answered by the coal operators who represent the competitors of that state in the coal industry. The men who work in the industry approve this amendment. Countless numbers of men and women who have been living in social and economic degradation in the industry have a chance under this arrangement, to go forward and obtain some of the things they so eagerly desire, to improve their social standards and their living standards.

"The coal industry is on the way back, if you please, to becoming a taxpayer, to assuming some degree of its proper responsibility in the conduct of our national affairs, and in support of our federal government. It has not been a taxpayer for a long period of time. It has not been able to support its own people. Under this program, it is going to be possible for it to support its own people.

"Mr. Administrator, I know how bored one must get sitting here day after day listening to this agony of controversy in the coal industry, but wrapped up in this proposition are the dreams of countless thousands of men who for years past have been suffering in misery because of the inability of the industry to regulate its own problems and stabilize its own affairs. And here is a chance for an industry, with the support of a benevolent government, to rise above those small quibblings in the industry,

whether they be the quibblings of a Lewis or a Johnston.

"I am going to urge, in behalf of all the men employed in this industry, that the government of the United States, acting through your offices, approve this amendment as it is now written and approved unanimously by the men who work in the mines of this country."

In May, 1934, the labor movement lost a friend with the death of William B. Wilson, a founder of the UMWA, named the first Secretary of Labor by Woodrow Wilson.

The new Secretary of Labor, Frances Perkins, had, about the same time, appointed Mr. Lewis as a United States Government delegate to the International Labor Conference at Geneva. Mr. Lewis sailed on May 30. On his return to this country, he reported:

"At this conference were present representatives of industry, of labor, and of the governments of practically all countries in the world. This gathering was significant in many ways, but most significant to me was the fact that for so many countries the delegates present were no longer representatives of industry and labor in the old sense, but were from fascist or dictator-ruled states in which labor, at least, was merely a pawn in the hands of a completely centralized governing group. This was a vivid reminder of the great changes which have taken place in the world during the past few years. In all of these countries, democracy, as we know it and love it, is dead and, still more, the number of countries of this character is steadily growing. In all the world today, there are barely a handful of states in which the old democratic principles are kept alive, and still fewer in which these principles are not threatened by hostile forces. All of us are fully aware that this threat hangs over our own country."

On July 1, 1934, UMWA International headquarters moved from Indianapolis to Washington to be near the fast-moving events in the Capital. Mr. Lewis returned from Europe and on September 1 his traditional Labor Day statement appeared on page three of the United Mine Workers Journal. He reiterated the UMWA's stand on the six-hour day, insisted that Section 7a be enforced, and that industry should take care of the unemployed. But in his last paragraph he sounded a new call—one on his mind for a long time, ever since his days as one of Mr. Gompers' young organizers and his unstinting effort in behalf of the striking steel workers in 1919—a call that he now felt had to be made:

"One more word about the organized labor movement. The time has come when the employees in mass industries must be permitted and encouraged to organize themselves in industrial unions. This is the only form of organization that will meet their requirements. The American Federation of Labor must authorize such a policy."

In the autumn of 1934, the miners cheered the Democratic sweep in the Pennsylvania elections. George Earle was elected governor; UMWA's Thomas Kennedy, lieutenant governor; and Joseph E. Guffey defeated the reactionary David Reed in the Senate race.

But elation was sobered by the depressed conditions in coal mining areas. The mine workers and Mr. Lewis knew that the NRA was not enough to save the industry. They decided that two courses of action must be taken, one to stabilize the coal industry and the other to bring all workers in mass production industries into labor unions. The first step was an appeal to the government for legislation to promote stability. The officers' report to the 1936 convention states:

"After some fourteen months' operation of the Recovery Code, sensing the reluctance of officials to enforce it and yielding to the pressure of large consumers, price chiselers began to appear and multiply in the nation's markets, and the need for more effective legislation became clear.

"In the summer of 1934, a joint legislative committee of representative operators and officials of your organization was formed to promote such legislation. After numerous sessions, it became manifest that the committee as such could not agree owing to the divergent views of many of the operators. The discussions, however, continued, and the offices of the United Mine Workers were made an open forum for operators, mine workers, wholesalers, retailers and representatives of consumers. The

results were submitted to certain members of Congress and in January, 1935, Senator Guffey in the Senate and Congressman Snyder in the House introduced the bill, since then known as the Guffey-Snyder Bill.

"Hearings were had before a subcommittee of the Interstate Commerce Committee of the Senate and a subcommittee of the Ways and Means Committee of the House. These hearings were exhaustive, particularly before the House committee, since its consideration was subsequent to the decision of the Supreme Court holding the Recovery Act unconstitutional."

Mr. Lewis has always believed that an ailing coal industry cannot pay decent wages nor provide adequate protection against injuries and deaths in the mines. He stressed this point in testimony supporting the Guffey Coal Act before the House Labor Committee:

"I speak not for the dollars invested; I speak not for the inanimate tons of coal; I speak for the human beings who go down into these coal mines and serve the public interest by getting the coal.

"This industry is a hazardous industry, the most hazardous of any industry of record. The Department of Labor reports—1896 to 1933 inclusive—accidental deaths to all coal miners of the country numbered 79,270, a yearly average of 2,085. In thirty-seven years this industry killed 79,270 of my people. The number of injuries during that same period may be conservatively computed by using the factor of fourteen and multiplying the fatal accidents by fourteen. It amounts to 1,109,780 men that were injured during that period.

"There are variations in the extent of those injuries. Some of them merely had their hands injured, their fingers mashed, or lost fingers, and others had their eyes shot out. Others had all the flesh burned from their skulls, and forever afterwards had to carry around grotesque masks to face other men. Others had their backs broken. Some lost legs, some lost arms, some were paralyzed, some sustained minor injuries of a minor nature. They had to take their chances as to what the character of their injuries might be.

"The men I represent, during this thirty-seven-year period, have carried out of these mines, on stretchers, 79 thousand dead men. Some of them were mashed into a pulp, others had their flesh so cooked by explosions that the flesh cleaved from the bone when they were picked up, and they were carried up the cinder paths of these mining communities on stretchers and into the homes of the lamenting widows and weeping children.

"Were the Congressmen ever in a mining community where all the men in the community were killed in a mine explosion? I do not know of any greater scene of human agony than to be in a community where such a thing as that occurs. Just a couple of Christmases ago, on Christmas Eve, I went to the scene of an explosion in Illinois that killed all the men in the mine. It was not a large mine, but an ancient, old, high-cost, obsolete, uneconomical mine to the operator, and the men were trying vainly to continue in operation against competition that they could not meet. They had no timber in

---

IN THE FOREFRONT, AS USUAL, THE UMWA LEADS THE FIGHT FOR 30-HOUR WEEK IN '35

Left to Right—Edward F. McGrady, assistant secretary of labor; Mr. Lewis, Earl Houck of UMWA's legal division.

it, they had no air in it, they had gas in it, and the inevitable happened—and it blew up. And for a Christmas Eve gift, the families of that community gathered around that pit head, waiting for their dead to be brought out of the mine.

"The mine workers want this industry operated upon a modern basis that at least comprehends some degree of humanity.

"I wonder who killed these people of mine for thirty-seven years? Who manages these mines? Talk about the rights of management, the inherent right to do as they please. Why, yes, with their own dollars; yes, with their own tongues. But I protest to the Congress of the United States against their right to do this with the lives of my people.

"Who was it that did not ventilate the mine? Who was it that could not buy the fan? Who was it that could not replace broken-down and worn-out equipment? Who was it that could not take safety measures? It must be those who own the mines and who manage the mines, and who prate about their pride in their management before the Congress of the United States.

"It was not the mine workers. It was not the Congress. It was not the public, although

the public bought that coal at a price during all those years that made it necessary for the coal operator to sprinkle it with human blood and pieces of human flesh. That record is appalling and it is a thing that faces these men who work in these mines every day, and it is a thing that bears heavily on the minds of every woman in the mining camp every morning when she sends her man to work."

Mr. Lewis told the House committee that railroads and other large consumers were leading the fight against the Guffey Bill because they wanted to keep prices low in spite of the fact that below-cost prices virtually had ruined the coal business in the depression years. He said:

"Those men who come here from the coal industry, favoring this bill, be they few or many, upon the operating side, are courageous men who are taking their fortunes in their hands in coming before this Congress now and urging enactment of this bill, because they are defying the crystallized, combined purchasing power of the railroads, the public utilities, the steel industries and the large manufacturers of this country, and they are daily being coerced and threatened in a commercial sense because of their courage and because of their present action.

"Why, the chairman of this committee read yesterday morning, as I understood it, a list of a number of coal companies who withdrew their support, and who had previously been supporting the Guffey Bill. It is easy to understand—commercial coercion.

"The opponents of the Guffey Bill believe in that kind of coercion, but they do not believe in a government coercing men to maintain fair practices in an industry that is stricken. They do not maintain it is unconstitutional to threaten a commercial producer on a railroad nor to have a bank squeeze him on his note, or threaten a non-extension of his note. They are for that kind of coercion. I am talking very plain, gentlemen of the committee, on these things because the mine workers are the residual sufferers of this appalling and diabolical situation. And it is diabolical in the sense that the mine work-

FIGHTING TO SAVE LABOR'S RIGHT TO ORGANIZE AT SENATORIAL HEARINGS IN 1935

ers of this country and the population of the mining communities of this country are to stand the bitter after-effects, devastating and paralyzing as they are, affecting human welfare and human property, affecting our standard of living, and affecting our very social culture through the demoralization and the confusion and bitterness and the despair in this bituminous mining industry."

During the fight for the Guffey Act, the UMWA was not only opposed by short-sighted coal operators, but also by some of the craft unions in the AFL. Mr. Lewis told the 1936 UMWA convention:

"When we were fighting against favorable odds to secure favorable action by Congress for our coal stabilization legislation, the representatives of the Machinists' Union came down before the Committee on Ways and Means and stabbed us in the back by offering an amendment to that bill which provided that any craft organization having two or more members at any coal mine could come under the collective bargaining section of the Guffey Act and that the coal operator would be under obligation to deal with the craft organization. The adoption of that amendment would have destroyed the United Mine Workers of America had it become a law and had the craft organizations availed themselves of the privileges under it."

The Guffey-Snyder Act passed both houses of Congress and became the law of the land. The officers' report to the 1936 convention said:

"As reported by the House Committee, the bill passed the House and with a few minor changes was passed by the Senate. It became a law with the signature of the President.

"Your officials feel that this report should express the grateful thanks of all mine workers to the sympathetic, liberal statesmen of both houses who supported this measure. We can here only name a few: Congressmen Snyder, Lewis, Hill, Vinson, and Boland, the Democratic whip, and Senators Neely and Guffey. Senator Guffey's name is fittingly associated with this act for its passage is largely due to his untiring advocacy."

The Guffey-Snyder Act established a fair-trade code for the bituminous coal industry and attempted to end the cut-throat competition in the industry by establishing marketing procedures and fixing coal prices on a regional basis. The bill also included a section, patterned after Section 7a, protecting labor's right to organize

61

and to bargain with management. The act was to be administered by a three-man National Bituminous Coal Commission.

And in his opening speech to the 1936 convention, Mr. Lewis said:

"The enactment of the Guffey Law by the Congress was the achievement of a dream on the part of the men in the mines and the enactment of this great measure was the first constructive act in history enacted by a government in the interests of its people for the alleviation of depression, the economic distress and the hopeless, tragic condition of the miners in this benighted coal industry."

The officers' report to the 1936 convention told of the passage of another important piece of labor legislation:

"The Wagner-Connery Labor Relations Act has had the active support of the officers of your organization. It became a law largely through the patient, persistent advocacy of the great Senator from New York. This act provides opportunity for labor in industries engaged in interstate commerce to organize free of employer domination, outlaws company unions, and guarantees the right of honest collective bargaining. A National Labor Relations Board is established for the enforcement of these fundamental rights."

The Wagner Act strengthened the provisions of Section 7a. And its enactment, together with that of the Guffey Act, provided adequate insurance against the rulings of the Supreme Court, which on May 27, 1935, declared the National Industrial Recovery Act unconstitutional.

The other part of the two-fold program was the job of protecting the United Mine Workers of America by helping other workers organize. Mr. Lewis' report to 1936 convention comments:

"While our organization has acquired greater numerical strength than ever before, and while it is also true that we have gained more prestige and become more powerful than at any time in our history, yet the work of complete organization of the bituminous industry will not be attained until the captive operations of the United States Steel Corporation at its Gary, W. Va., operations, and at Lynch, Ky., and the

SEN. GUFFEY, MR. LEWIS EXAMINE PEN WITH WHICH FDR SIGNED GUFFEY COAL-PRICE BILL

AUGUST 30, 1935, WAS A DAY OF VICTORY FOR THE UMW AS SEN. GUFFEY'S BILL IS SIGNED

Front Row, Left to Right—UMWA Counsel Henry A. Warrum; Walter E. Jones, Pennsylvania attorney; Sen. Joseph Guffey, Rep. David Lewis, Md.; Mr. Lewis, UMWA's Thomas Kennedy, lieutenant-governor of Pennsylvania. Among those in the rear are Charles O'Neill, operator; Sen. Matthew M. Neely, W. Va.; Sen. Alben W. Barkley, Ky.; Rep. Fred M. Vinson, Ky.; and Rep. Dennis Driscoll, Pa., co-author of the Guffey-Driscoll Bill.

remainder of its mines in the coke field of Pennsylvania have been organized. The same is true of the Alabama Fuel and Iron Company, the West Kentucky Coal Company, and other interests in Western Kentucky, as well as the Harlan field of the same state, and the mines of the Phelps-Dodge Corporation at Dawson, N. Mex.

"The records of the United Mine Workers of America show that 95 per cent of all workers in the anthracite and bituminous coal industries are now members of our union.

"Our membership must keep in mind the dangers that constantly beset the United Mine Workers of America, and the trade union movement as a whole, while other great major industries remain unorganized. There can be no feeling of permanent security for trade unions in our country so long as the major portion of the workers of the nation remain unorganized.

"The safety of our nation and the welfare of its people are dependent upon the establishment of true industrial democracy. The country cannot achieve the solution of its economic problems until this has been accomplished. Industrialists are not going to rehire the 11 million unemployed. Their chief interest is the profit motive. Ample opportunity has been given them during the period of the depression to do so. Their obvious interest is mass production through increased use of machinery, the lowering of taxes and the general condemnation of the government's plan to feed the hungry, clothe the naked and shelter the poor.

"Production has reached 95 per cent of the 1923-1925 level, and yet these 11 million people remain unemployed. Profits have increased, while wages are kept at exceedingly low levels.

"In the absence of any relief from the burdens of unemployment, it seems reasonable that the only real remedy for this deplorable state of affairs lies in complete industrial democracy. Unionism of the workers will bring about economic reform. Collective bargaining upon a basis of equality will solve unemployment. It will give human beings an opportunity to control the machine. It will exact an equitable share of the tremendous profits derived by industries through the increased use of mechanical devices. Organization will assist amply in the solution of our political as well as our economic problems."

The miners were ready. The long, lean years of fighting for their own organization, of hard work and self-discipline had prepared them for the job at hand, the biggest job of all—to organize the unorganized.

63

"BOYS, WE'D BETTER GO OUT AND STOP IT!"

THE CIO IS BORN

ORGANIZE THE UNORGANIZED! That was the militant call that John L. Lewis and the United Mine Workers of America sounded to their brother trade unionists in 1935.

The time had come—perhaps it was the only time—when this long-standing ambition of the UMWA could be realized. John Lewis was ready. The miners were ready. And the government, backed by legislation pushed through at the insistence of the mine workers, had given the go-ahead signal.

Seven other unions heeded the call. They, too, believed that the unorganized could only be organized on the basis of large, all-inclusive industrial unions, one to an industry. But the AFL hierarchy insisted that if industry were to be organized, it must be done on a craft-union basis, forgetting that the 1919 steel strike had failed because the industry had been able to deal with each of twenty-seven craft unions separately—dividing and defeating them.

The mine workers' delegates had gone to the 1934 AFL convention with instructions to urge passage of a resolution favoring industrial organization. The year of futile bickering after passage of the resolution is described by Mr. Lewis in a speech to the 1935 AFL convention:

"I was one who came from the San Francisco convention last year under the presumption that the AFL, in the councils of its leaders, had reached a practical compromise upon this question that would enable us to organize these workers without impairment of those organizations already established in certain industries on a craft basis and functioning with great efficiency. For six days and almost six nights, the committee on resolutions at San Francisco wrestled with this problem, and earnest men, in equity and good conscience, applied themselves to the proposition and the problem of compromising what had seemed before to be two extreme viewpoints. There came from that convention a committee report, which has been read here, which provided for the issuance of charters in mass production industries and, as we understood, upon a basis that would permit men in those organizations to have jurisdiction over the workers in that industry. If that was not the understanding at that time, then it is inconceivable that the committee could have worked for six days on the question, because there would have been no question. The convention, adopting the committee's report, gave express direction to the Executive Council of the American Federation of Labor to issue that kind of charter in at least three named industries.

"What happened? When those questions came before the enlarged Council at a meeting held, I think, three months after the convention adjourned, we found that there was a difference there in interpreting the resolution of the convention as to the type and character and scope of the charters and jurisdictions which should be granted those industries. There were those upon the Council who contended that under no circumstances should charters be issued that in any way deprived the right of certain organizations to come into those industries and to have those men in membership and to make contracts for them. After extended consideration and general debate, that idea prevailed on the Executive Council, and a charter was issued in the automobile industry that practically limited the membership of that organization to the men employed in the assembling processes of the plant operations.

"Well, a year ago at San Francisco I was a year younger and naturally I had more faith in the Executive Council. I was beguiled into believing that an enlarged Executive Council would honestly interpret and administer this policy—the policy we talked about for six days in committee, the policy of issuing charters for industrial unions in the mass production industries. But surely Delegate Woll would not hold it against me that I was so trusting at that time. I know better now. At San Francisco they seduced me with fair words. Now, of course,

having learned that I was seduced, I am enraged and I am ready to rend my seducers limb from limb, including Delegate Woll. In that sense, of course, I speak figuratively.

"At San Francisco, as I say, I was younger and more gullible, but I put in some time in the past year attending some meetings of the Executive Council. I am convinced that the Executive Council is not going to issue any charters for industrial unions in any industry."

Then Mr. Lewis made his dramatic last appeal to the AFL delegates, but it was unheeded. He cited the futility of past attempts to organize mass industry workers on a craft union basis:

"Then, as now, practically every attempt to organize those workers broke upon the same rock that it breaks upon today—the rock of utter futility, the lack of reasonableness in a policy that failed to take into consideration the dreams and requirements of the workers themselves, and failed to take into consideration the recognized power of the adversaries of labor to destroy these feeble organizations in the great modern industries, set up in the form of federal labor unions or craft organizations functioning in a limited sphere.

"For twenty-five years or more, the American Federation of Labor has been following this precise policy, and surely in the absence of any other understanding of the question, a record of twenty-five years of constant, unbroken failure should be convincing to those who actually have

AFL PRESIDENT GREEN STARES AT CIO LEADER LEWIS AT A 1935 WASHINGTON LABOR CLINIC

66

a desire to increase the prestige of our great labor movement by expanding its membership to permit it to occupy its natural place in the sun.

"What is the record? Delegate Howard expressed it when he said that we laid claim to a membership of approximately three and a half million, out of an organizable number of approximately 39 million. There is the answer. If we know nothing else on the question, we can at least read the results and in reading the results we surely understand that our influence is less great, that our activities are more circumscribed, and that our power is more limited to achieve our natural and desirable and virtuous objective than it would be if we had those 25 million workers that President Green, in his public address in 1934, talked of organizing. Where are they? Where are those 25 million that in a moment of exuberance we were going to organize? Perhaps President Green's arithmetic was wrong and he meant 25 thousand, because the total results are nearer the 25 thousand than the 25 million.

"On that basis, I submit it to be a reasonable statement that it will be a long time before the AFL organizes those 25 million workers that we are all so anxious to organize. There are others among us who believe that the record indicates a need for a change in policy. This convention floor is teeming with delegates from those industries where those local unions have been estab-

lished and where they are now dying like the grass withering before the autumn sun, who are ready to tell this convention of the need for that change in policy.

"Those of us who have had experience in these mass production industries are ready to stake our professional judgment, for what it may be worth, and say that it is an absolute fact that America's great modern industries cannot be successfully organized, and those organizations maintained, against the power of the adversaries of labor in this country under the policy which has been followed for the last quarter of a century in dealing with that subject.

"The organization I represent has an interest in this question. Our people work in a great base industry, basic in its service to the American people and the economic and commercial processes of the nation. They struggle against great odds and against great influence, and that intensity of their struggle and the weight of their burden is greatly increased by reason of the fact that the AFL has not organized the steel indus-

NOVEMBER 9, 1936, BROUGHT SEVERAL EARLY CIO LEADERS TOGETHER TO TALK ORGANIZING

Seated, Left to Right—M. F. Tighe, Steel Workers; Mr. Lewis; Charles P. Howard, Printers. *Standing, Left to Right*—Sherman Dalrymple, Rubber Workers; Philip Murray, UMWA; Max Zaritsky, Hat Workers; Sidney Hillman, Clothing Workers; Thomas McMahon, Textile Workers; David Dubinsky, Ladies' Garment Workers.

ASSISTANT TREASURY SECRETARY JOSEPHINE ROCHE, MR. LEWIS AT '36 UMWA CONVENTION

try and a few industries similarly situated.

"We are anxious to have collective bargaining established in the steel industry, and our interest in that is, to that degree, selfish because our people know that if the workers were organized in the steel industry and collective bargaining there were an actuality, it would remove the incentive of the great captains of the steel industry to destroy and punish and harass our people who work in the captive coal mines throughout this country, owned by the steel industry.

"I have conferred with the officers of the United States Steel Corporation in relation to our contracts at their private properties, and they frankly admit that they oppose making collective bargaining contracts in the coal mining industry because they do not want that power to follow them and annoy them in the iron and steel industry—and they have no more fear of the iron and steel workers annoying them than they have that the League of Nations will come over and impose a mandate or sanctions upon them.

"We are assured the way is now open for an aggressive campaign of organization in the steel industry. What kind of campaign—a campaign to organize them in '57 varieties' of organ-

izations? You ought to know, without my telling you, how effective that kind of campaign will be. And the several hundred thousands of members of the United Mine Workers of America who understand the position of interests of that character and who also understand the practical problems of organization in these big industries, know that the officers of the AFL might as well sit down in their easy chairs and twiddle their thumbs and take a nap as to conclude that any results will come from that kind of organization in the iron and steel industry.

"I am telling you facts and I am telling you what is in the hearts of my people, and my people down in Alabama tonight are hungry as I stand talking here, because the Tennessee Coal & Iron Co. is daring enough and bold enough to close their mines to them. And I might say to you that because of circumstances in Alabama prevailing in several counties there is no adequate system of public relief there or government relief, and our people are suffering, and they are suffering, in its final essence, by the fact that the AFL for some reason or other, has failed after all these years of experimentation to organize the iron and steel workers and establish collective bargaining in that industry.

"If you go in there with your craft union, they will mow you down like the Italian machine guns will mow down the Ethiopians in the war now going on in that country; they will

SECRETARY OF LABOR PERKINS, MR. LEWIS AT 1936 UMWA CONVENTION IN WASHINGTON

mow you down and laugh while they are doing it and ridicule your lack of business acumen, ridicule your lack of ordinary business sagacity in running your own affairs, because of the cavilling in your own councils and the feebleness of your methods.

"There is more in this proposition than a mere academic discussion of the modus operandi of organization; there is more to this proposition than revolves around the mere acceptance or rejection of the resolution. The economic well-being and the dream of the future of millions of Americans are involved in the question of whether the AFL will be able to devise policies that will permit it to function in a manner that will achieve its own objectives, not the objectives of someone else, but the declared objectives of the AFL since the first day it was organized —the objectives of organizing the unorganized.

"President Green goes down to the White House sometimes to call upon the President of this Republic to discuss the affairs of labor, and the interests of labor and the common people of this country. And sometimes he goes over to the Congressional halls, and he appears there before great committees of the two Houses to make articulate, in a public way, the things for which labor stands. Now, when he goes down there he goes as the representative of perhaps three

and one-half million American working men. How much more powerful and influential would be the silver-tongued President Green if he were able to appear before the Congress of the United States or the President of this Republic speaking, not for three and one-half million specialized craftsmen organized in the AFL, but speaking for 5 million, or 10 million, or 20 millions of workers in American industry who have joined the AFL when you have given them a chance and made them welcome.

"Why not make a contribution toward the well-being of those who are not fortunate enough to be members of your organization? The United Mine Workers of America want to make a contribution and want to do no man and no union ill. We are willing to make a contribution in men and in money to the success of a policy of organizing these industries upon an industrial basis. We are willing to take our young men and send them into these industries to organize them. We have demonstrated that before and we are demonstrating it again. We want to work in cooperation with you, if you can be led

1936 UMWA CONVENTION GIVES FULL SUPPORT TO ITS OFFICERS IN CIO ORGANIZING DRIVE

Left to Right—Vice President Murray, President Lewis, Secretary-Treasurer Kennedy.

CIO LEADERS MEET IN WASHINGTON, JUNE 2, 1936, TO MAP BIG STEEL ORGANIZING DRIVE

Left to Right—Sidney Hillman, Clothing Workers; Mr. Lewis; Philip Murray, named to head Steel Workers Organizing Committee; John Brophy, CIO organization director.

to cooperate. If you hold aloof merely because you suspect the intentions of those who promote this policy to the convention, then I can only say that you do yourselves more of an injustice than you do those of whom you think ill.

"Is it right, after all, that because some of us are capable of forging great and powerful organizations of skilled craftsmen in this country that we should lock ourselves up in our own domain and say, 'I am merely working for those who pay me'?

"And, whereas today the craft unions of this country may be able to stand upon their own feet and like mighty oaks standing before the gale, defy the lightning, yet the day may come when this changed scheme of things—and things are changing rapidly now—the day may come when those organizations will not be able to withstand the lightning and the gale. Now prepare yourselves by making a contribution to your less fortunate brethren, heed this cry from Mace-

donia that comes from the hearts of men. Organize the unorganized! And in so doing you make the AFL the greatest instrumentality that has ever been forged in the history of modern civilization to befriend the cause of humanity and champion human rights!"

Having expounded his beliefs, Mr. Lewis acted immediately. That same night he met with the leaders of seven other AFL unions who believed as he did and who realized the hopelessness of trying to convince the AFL craft union bosses.

They resolved to form a committee within the AFL to be called the Committee for Industrial Organization. The officers' report to the 1938 UMWA convention tells in clipped phrases the story of an event that was to change the economic course of the nation:

"The delegates to the Atlantic City convention of the AFL, in 1935, who espoused the cause of industrial unionism represented more than one million workers in the industries of the nation. Dissatisfied with the action of the convention and convinced of the inherent logic and soundness of the principle of their position, representatives of eight international unions joined together and created the Committee for Indus-

70

trial Organization. The Committee is composed of the following representatives of international unions:

"John L. Lewis, president, United Mine Workers of America;

"Charles P. Howard, president, International Typographical Union;

"Sidney Hillman, president, Amalgamated Clothing Workers of America;

"David Dubinsky, president, International Ladies' Garment Workers Union;

"Thomas F. McMahon, president, United Textile Workers of America;

"Harvey C. Fremming, president, Oil Field, Gas Well and Refinery Workers of America;

"Max Zaritsky, president, Cap and Millinery Department, United Hatters, Cap and Millinery Workers' International Union;

"Thomas H. Brown, president, International Union of Mine, Mill and Smelter Workers.

"The president of the United Mine Workers of America was made chairman of the committee, and Mr. Charles P. Howard, president of the International Typographical Union, was made secretary. John Brophy later was made

director to supervise the activities of the committee. Offices were opened in Washington, D. C., and the committee, since its formation, has functioned in an educational and advisory capacity in the promotion of industrial organization of the workers in the larger unorganized industries of the country.

"Concurrent with this action, the president of the United Mine Workers of America resigned his office as a vice president of the AFL, to which position he had been elected at the San Francisco convention when the council membership was increased."

Immediately after the committee had been formed, ex-coal miner William Green wrote a letter to Mr. Lewis in which he charged the CIO was a dual organization and that "bitterness and strife would inevitably follow." Mr. Lewis replied:

LABOR'S NON-PARTISAN LEAGUE STARTS THE CAMPAIGN OF 1936 FOR FDR'S RE-ELECTION

Left to Right—George L. Berry, Pressmen; Sidney Hillman, Clothing Workers; Mr. Lewis.

"My Dear Green:

"Mr. Charles P. Howard, secretary of the Committee for Industrial Organization, and other members of the committee have replied categorically and conclusively to the statements contained in your public letter. I associate myself with their replies.

"Now of other things: Your official burdens are great; I would not increase them. I do not covet your office; in proof, I submit the record of years of support of your personal and official fortunes. It is bruited about, however, that your private sympathies and individual inclinations lie with the group espousing the industrial type of organization, while your official actions and public utterances will be in support of their adversaries. Such a policy is vulnerable to criticism and will hardly suffice to protect you against attacks from those who may feel rightfully that more is due them than perfunctory support.

"Why not return to your father's house? You will be welcome. If you care to dissociate yourself from your present position, the Committee for Industrial Organization will be happy to make you its chairman in my stead. The honorarium will be equal to that you now receive. The position would be as permanent as the one you occupy. You would have the satisfaction of supporting a cause in which you believe inherently, and of contributing your fine abilities to the achievement of an enlarged opportunity for the nation's workers.

"Sincerely yours,
(Signed) John L. Lewis"

The former secretary-treasurer of the UMWA refused the CIO post and determined to appeal the AFL's case directly to the UMWA convention to be held in Washington in January, 1936. The following account is from the Mine Workers Journal:

"President Green addressed the convention for nearly two hours in an endeavor to induce the delegates to reverse the policy they had previously adopted. He should have known better. He should have known, and no doubt he did know, that he would fail. He used everything he had—voice, oratory, argument and gesture. He pleaded, cajoled, intimidated and practically threatened the convention in his effort to carry

his point. He even gave a history of his life. But it all got him nowhere. He was 'booed' two or three times, but President Lewis stopped the outburst. When it was all over, Green stood a badly defeated and beaten man, and his organization, the AFL, had gone down a little bit further in the estimation of the 1,700 delegates and the hundreds of spectators who filled Constitution Hall. Surely, it was a humiliating experience for the president of the Federation.

"But the climax of the drama came at the conclusion of Green's speech. No sooner had Green said 'Thank you' to the convention than President John L. Lewis arose on the stage amid a great demonstration by the delegates standing in their places. They cheered and applauded President Lewis until the windows rattled. When quiet had been restored, President Lewis spoke, slowly, deliberately, but with intense earnestness. He said:

" 'The President of the United Mine Workers of America will permit the delegates to the Thirty-fourth Constitutional Convention of this organization to render their answer to President Green of the AFL. Let me call upon all delegates in this convention who have changed their minds on this issue on account of the address of President Green to rise to their feet.

" 'The chair sees two delegates.

" 'Again, the question recurs upon the fiat of the Executive Council of the AFL, read to this convention as an ultimatum by President Green. It demands that the president of the United Mine Workers of America, with his associates on the Committee for Industrial Organization, like quarry slaves at night, scourged to their dungeon, dissolve, disband, cease and desist with reference to the CIO. Let those delegates of this Thirty-fourth Constitutional Convention who believe that the president of the United Mine Workers of America should comply with that request rise to their feet.

" 'The chair sees one delegate arise.

" 'Again, let those delegates of this convention who believe that the policies enunciated by this convention should be carried out by the president of their organization and his associate officers rise to their feet.

"(The delegates arose and applauded.)

" 'President Green, you have received the answer of the United Mine Workers of America

THE FUTURE OF LABOR IS THE FUTURE OF AMERICA: JOHN L. LEWIS, LABOR DAY, 1936

MR. LEWIS HEARS A RECORDING OF HIS 1936 LABOR DAY SPEECH AT HIS ALEXANDRIA HOME

to your ultimatum. It is not for the president of the United Mine Workers of America to amplify with mere words an expression of a principle and a conviction so deep seated, so pronounced, and so traditional as exists with reference to this question.

" 'You come as an ambassador from another organization to the United Mine Workers of America. I hope, sir, that you have been treated with all the courtesies and honors due an ambassador, but you have and you may carry back to your organization the answer of the United Mine Workers of America that has just been given by this convention!'

"Never before in any convention of the United Mine Workers of America did anyone witness a scene like this one. Every man in the house was on his feet, clapping hands, cheering and through the medium of noise giving evidence of the depth of his enthusiastic approval of President Lewis' words. In the deep seriousness of the moment, President Lewis, his jaws set and his face a picture of determination and

finality, faced the frenzied enthusiasm of the vast crowd which was thus pledging the support of more than half a million coal miners to their leader. Green, red of face and almost voiceless after his long speech, sat there with his gaze fixed upon the cheering throng. What was passing through his mind can only be surmised. After several minutes of the demonstration, the crowd became quiet, and Green left the hall, and the routine work of the convention was resumed. But no one who was fortunate enough to be present at that historic occasion will ever forget the scene and its significance."

The CIO still preferred to work within the framework of the AFL. But the AFL Executive Council spent the spring and summer of 1936 issuing orders to the CIO to disband. The Council finally decided that a "trial" of the CIO unions should be held on August 3. The members of the Executive Council who voted to suspend represented unions with a total membership of 882,700. The CIO unions had a total membership of 1,000,100. A majority had been suspended by a minority.

When Mr. Lewis heard of the Council's action, he issued a press statement which described it as "an act of incredible and crass stupidity,

CIO LEADERS DISCUSS POSSIBLE PEACE TALKS WITH AFL AT MEETING ON OCTOBER 14, 1936

Left to Right—Charles P. Howard, Printers, first CIO secretary; Max Zaritsky, Hat Workers, and Mr. Lewis.

FDR TALKS TO HARD COAL MINERS AT WILKES-BARRE DURING 1936 PRESIDENTIAL CAMPAIGN

To the left of Mr. Roosevelt is Gov. Earle, Pennsylvania. Directly behind the President is Lt.-Gov. Thomas Kennedy. To the right of Mr. Lewis are Daniel Tobin, Teamsters, and John Kmetz, UMWA. The picture on the rostrum is of John Mitchell, UMWA's fifth president.

an act dictated by personal selfishness and frantic fear." He continued:

"It indicates a total absence of consideration for the well-being of the nation's workers and the requirements of an effective movement of labor. The Executive Council would not trust the judgment of a convention of the Federation which meets in November. It hastened to prejudice the action of the convention by stripping the defendant unions of their voting privilege. The constitution of the Federation contains no warrant for the exercise of such arbitrary power. It amounts to an appalling blunder which Mr. Green and his confederates may continuously rue. We will not disband the CIO."

In a counter action, the president of the AFL was notified to appear before the International Executive Board of his own union, the United Mine Workers of America, on four charges, the most serious of which was that he was supporting and encouraging a dual union, the Progressive Mine Workers of America, which had been chartered by the AFL when the Council sus-

pended the UMWA and the other CIO unions. Mr. Green did not show up. He wrote a letter pleading innocent to the four charges, basing his defense on his past record. His case was referred to the 1938 convention which referred it back to the board for further consideration. The IEB took no further action immediately.

But these things constituted a sideshow. A week after the CIO was formed, Mr. Lewis took to the air waves with a nation-wide speech to emphasize to the American people the aims and hopes of the CIO. He recited the history of organizing failures of the AFL and then went on:

GM SIGNS WITH THE UAW, FEBRUARY 11, 1937, AND CIO LEADERS PLAN THE NEXT CONQUEST

Left to Right—Sidney Hillman, Clothing Workers, and Mr. Lewis.

"The millions of workers in our mass production industries have a right to membership in effective labor organizations and to the enjoyment of industrial freedom. They are entitled to a place in the American economic sunlight. If the labor movement and American democracy are to endure, these workers should have the opportunity to support families under conditions of health, decency, and comfort, to own their own home, to educate their children, and possess sufficient leisure to take part in wholesome social and political activities. How much more security we would have in this country if we had a virile labor movement that represented, not merely a cross-section of skilled workers, but the men who work with their hands in our great industries, regardless of their trade and calling.

"It is for the purpose of enabling them to acquire and enjoy these rights that the eight international unions of the AFL, including the United Mine Workers of America, have formed the CIO. It is our purpose to encourage the formation of industrial unions, equal in economic strength to management, in the steel,

automobile, rubber, glass, textile, radio, and all other basic industries. We have no opposition to craft unions which are established and successfully functioning. We do not believe any craft union, however, as is now the case in the AFL, should be permitted to interfere, through paper jurisdictional claims or otherwise, with the organization of the great majority of American wage and salary workers in our basic manufacturing and mining industries.

"We hope that the significance of our movement will not be misunderstood. It is not a conflict among unions, or a striving for power among organized labor groups. We are working for a future labor movement which will assure a proper future for America, one which will crystallize the best aspirations of those who really wish to serve democracy and humanity.

"There are great influences abroad in the land, and the minds of men in all walks of life are disturbed. We are all disturbed by reason of the changes and the hazards in our economic situation and as regards our own political security. There are forces at work in this country that would wipe out, if they could, the labor movement of America, just as it was wiped out in Germany or just as it was wiped out in Italy. It is our belief that the best security against that menace and against that trend and against that

76

A CALL FOR A LIBERAL SUPREME COURT IN 1937 GETS BOB LAFOLLETTE A HANDSHAKE

tendency is a more comprehensive and more powerful labor movement.

"The years of suffering since the beginning of the depression have brought us the realization of the great fundamental truths that our industries can produce enough for an abundant life for all classes of our people, if all labor groups, however humble, are welded into organizations of sufficient strength to secure a fair share in industrial output. The payment of a living wage to unskilled steel and other mass production workers, with differentials above this level for skilled and trained employees, would make a new America. The very life-blood of industry depends upon the payment of living wages. The heart of industry will stop, or only feebly beat, as at present, if it does not receive the power which comes from the payment of a living wage to the millions of workers, by hand and brain, in our mass production industries."

Mr. Lewis concluded:

"And so it is our conviction that the establishment of industrial unionism involves the real recovery and reform; that shorter hours of work and re-employment of the unemployed are dependent upon its success; that it will secure a living wage for all and not profits for the privileged few; that it offers the only way to emancipation from industrial autocracy—to economic and political freedom to those who work by hand or brain."

The phalanxes of CIO organizers began their sweeping advance. Rubber workers in Akron were among the first to "sit-down" in a strike against Goodyear for union recognition in January, 1936, a strike they won on March 22. The United Automobile Workers joined the march of the CIO in April, bringing in a membership of 35 thousand.

But the No. 1 organizing job was "Fortress Steel." Fully aware of "Big Steel's" history of vicious anti-unionism, the CIO plunged into the drive in June, 1936. The CIO appropriated $500 thousand. Two hundred organizers, most of them miners, were assigned to the job. The UMWA's Philip Murray was named chairman of the Steel Workers' Organizing Committee and David J. McDonald, Murray's assistant, secretary-treasurer, with Clinton Golden placed in charge of the campaign in the Pittsburgh area, the UMWA's Van Bittner in Chicago, John Owens in Ohio and William Mitch in Alabama. On July 6, 1936, John L. Lewis announced the drive to organize steel:

A WASHINGTON LABOR DEPT. CONFERENCE ON THE '37 GENERAL MOTORS SITDOWN STRIKE

Seated, Left to Right—Charles P. Howard, Printers, CIO secretary; Secretary of Labor Frances Perkins; Mr. Lewis; Sidney Hillman, Clothing Workers. *Standing, Left to Right*—George F. Addes, Auto Workers, secretary-treasurer; Leo Krzycki, Clothing Workers; Edward Hall, Auto Workers; Homer Martin, Auto Workers; Wyndham Mortimer, Auto Workers; John Brophy, CIO director of organization, and Lee Pressman, Steel Workers general counsel.

"I salute the hosts of labor who listen. I greet my fellow Americans. I salute the members of my own union as they listen tonight in every mining community on this continent. To them, whose servant I am, I express my pride in their courage and loyalty. They are the household troops of the great movement for industrial democracy and from their collective sentiment and crystallized power I derive my strength.

"In their daily calling the mine workers toil with the spectre death ever at their side, and the women of the mining camps share their Spartan fortitude. Enduring hardship, inured to danger, contemptuous of death, breathing the air of freedom—is there anyone who believes that the men of the mines will flinch in the face of the battle for industrial democracy which now impends in America?

"The American Iron and Steel Institute last week published a full-page advertisement in 375 newspapers, at an estimated cost of one-half million dollars. Its purpose was to justify the outmoded labor policy of the Institute and to announce the determination of the steel corporations to oppose the campaign now in progress for the organization of the workers in the iron and steel industry. That statement is sinister in its implications. It is designed to be terrifying to the minds of those who fail to accept the theory that the financial interests behind the steel corporations shall be regarded as the omnipresent overlords of industrial America. That statement amounts to a declaration of industrial and civil war.

"It contravenes the law! It pledges the vast resources of the industry against the right of its workers to engage in self-organization or modern collective bargaining.

"The American Iron and Steel Institute boasts that it includes 95 per cent of the steel production of the country and represents an associated corporate investment of $5 billion. This gigantic financial and industrial combination announces that its members 'are ready to employ their resources to the full' to prevent the independent organization of their employees. It contravenes the law!

"The Institute says that it favors the right of organization among its employees without coercion from any source. What coercion can the representatives of organized labor exert upon the workers in these plants, and what appeal can they make to them except the appeal that they bring themselves within the organized labor movement for their own protection and for the common good of those who toil? The Institute does not propose to meet that argument; it does not propose to trust the independent action of the steel workers; it does not intend to grant them the free liberty of organization.

"Interference and coercion of employees trying to organize comes from the economic advantages held by the employer. In the steel industry it is manifested in an elaborate system of spies and in a studied discharge of those who advocate any form of organization displeasing to the management. It is shown by confining all yearning for organization to make-believe company unions, controlled and dominated by the management itself. This coercion is finally shown in the implied threat of a blacklist, which attends the announcement of a joint and common policy for all the steel corporations of this country.

"Why shouldn't organized labor throw its influence into this unequal situation? What chance have the steel workers to form a free and inde-

pendent organization without the aid of organized labor? What opportunity will they have to bargain collectively through representatives of their own choosing except by the formation of an organization free from the control of management?

"The statement of the Institute is an open warning to representatives of recognized and firmly established labor unions that if by any legal and peaceful methods—public meetings, personal solicitations, or otherwise—they are so bold as to attempt to persuade steel workers to become members of recognized, standard labor

LABOR LEADERS ENDORSE FDR COURT PLAN IN MARCH 8, 1937, WHITE HOUSE CONFERENCE

Left to Right—Steve Nance, Georgia Federation of Labor; J. C. Lewis, Iowa Federation of Labor; John Horn, California Labor's Non-Partisan League; Mr. Lewis; Judge Michael Musmanno, Pittsburgh; Joseph Obergfell, Brewery Workers; George L. Berry, Pressmen, LNPL president; Charles P. Howard, Printers, CIO secretary; Rose Schneiderman, Women's Trade Union League; Harvey Fremming, Oil Workers; Dennis Lane, Butchers; Sidney Hillman, Clothing Workers; John Kane and Luigi Antonini, Ladies Garment Workers.

unions, the brutal and ruthless forces of the steel oligarchy will be unloosed against them.

"From bitter experience we know what this means. It means that meetings of steel employees will be disrupted by thugs and hoodlums employed by the steel corporations; that the organizers themselves will be brutally beaten; that the police and judicial authorities of steel manufacturing communities, who are designated and dominated by the steel companies, will be used to arrest labor union organizers, to imprison them on false charges, to maltreat them cruelly while imprisoned, and in many cases forcibly to drive them from the community.

"In this connection, I wish to add with all

the full, open gaze of the public; or, in other words, through the radio and the press, the public will be continuously informed.

"We have also taken measures to protect our people. We shall bring to justice anyone in the steel industry who is guilty of lawlessness. This does not mean merely the subordinate officials of the steel corporations, their armed guards, or other hirelings or mercenaries. It means that we shall hold to accountability those who are really responsible—bankers, directors and officials of the steel corporations—those who really formulate policies and methods, from J. P. Morgan & Co., which controls the United States Steel Corporation, down through other bankers, direc-

FEAR IS KING IN GERMANY, MR. LEWIS TELLS NEW YORK ANTI-NAZI RALLY, MARCH 15, 1937

Behind the UMWA leader is Rabbi Stephen S. Wise of the American Jewish Congress.

earnestness at my command, that if any strike, violence or bloodshed occurs as a result of the present effort of our Committee to organize the steel workers, it will not arise from our organizers or their activities. We shall pursue our purpose relentlessly but legally and peacefully.

"I wish also solemnly to warn those who represent the steel industry that their unlawful, ruthless tactics of former years will not be tolerated by our Committee. This organization drive in the steel industry will be conducted in

tors and officials of less powerful, but important, steel corporations, to the lowest member of the hierarchy.

"Although the industry has produced thousands of millionaires among bankers, promoters, so-called financiers, and steel executives, it has never, throughout the past thirty-five years, paid a bare subsistence wage, not to mention a living wage, to the great mass of its workers.

"The industry has constantly sought to give the impression that it pays exceptionally high wages, and so far-reaching and efficient are its means of publicity that this idea is widely accepted.

"Actually, there is no basis for this belief. When comparisons are made between the earnings of workers in the steel industry and the earnings of workers in other industries of a comparable character, the standing of the steel industry is at best no more than mediocre and at worst no less than disgraceful.

"Our Committee would bring to the steel workers economic and political freedom; a living wage to those lowest in the scale of occupations sufficient for the support of the worker and his family in health and modest comfort, and sufficient to enable him to send his children to school, to own a home and accessories, to provide against sickness, death, and the ordinary contingencies of life; in other words, a wage sufficient for him to live as an independent Ameri-

to fight for the prize of economic freedom and industrial democracy."

But before the big organizing campaigns could get under full headway, the UMWA and the CIO wanted to be sure that the federal government was on their side. The best way, it seemed, was to assure the re-election of Franklin Delano Roosevelt.

Mr. Lewis, the miners and CIO made three big contributions to Franklin D. Roosevelt's campaign. The first was cash—$500 thousand donated by the United Mine Workers of America. The second was the formation of a nationwide organization to work for Mr. Roosevelt's re-

can citizen, with hope and assurance in the future for himself and his family. Above this basic wage, our Committee believes that differentials should be paid to other workers according to skill, training, hazard and responsibility.

"There is but one other fundamental motive which the CIO has for unionizing the steel industry. It is simple and direct. It is to protect the members of our own organizations. We know, although we are now free men and women, that so long as millions of other industrial workers are without economic and political freedom, a condition exists which is a menace to our freedom.

"Organized labor in America accepts the challenge of the omnipresent overlords of steel

VICTORY NO. 2 IN THE DRIVE TO ORGANIZE THE AUTO INDUSTRY AS CHRYSLER SIGNS UP
Left to Right—Mr. Lewis, Gov. Frank Murphy, Michigan; Walter P. Chrysler; James Dewey, U. S. conciliator.

election on every level from grass-roots up. This organization, forerunner of the CIO's Political Action Committee and the AFL's League for Political Education, was Labor's Non-Partisan League. The third contribution was the time, energy and eloquence of John L. Lewis. He took to the stump throughout the eastern states, spoke from train observation platforms, in public halls and over the radio, telling the people to vote for Roosevelt.

On October 1, 1936, he told the voters:

81

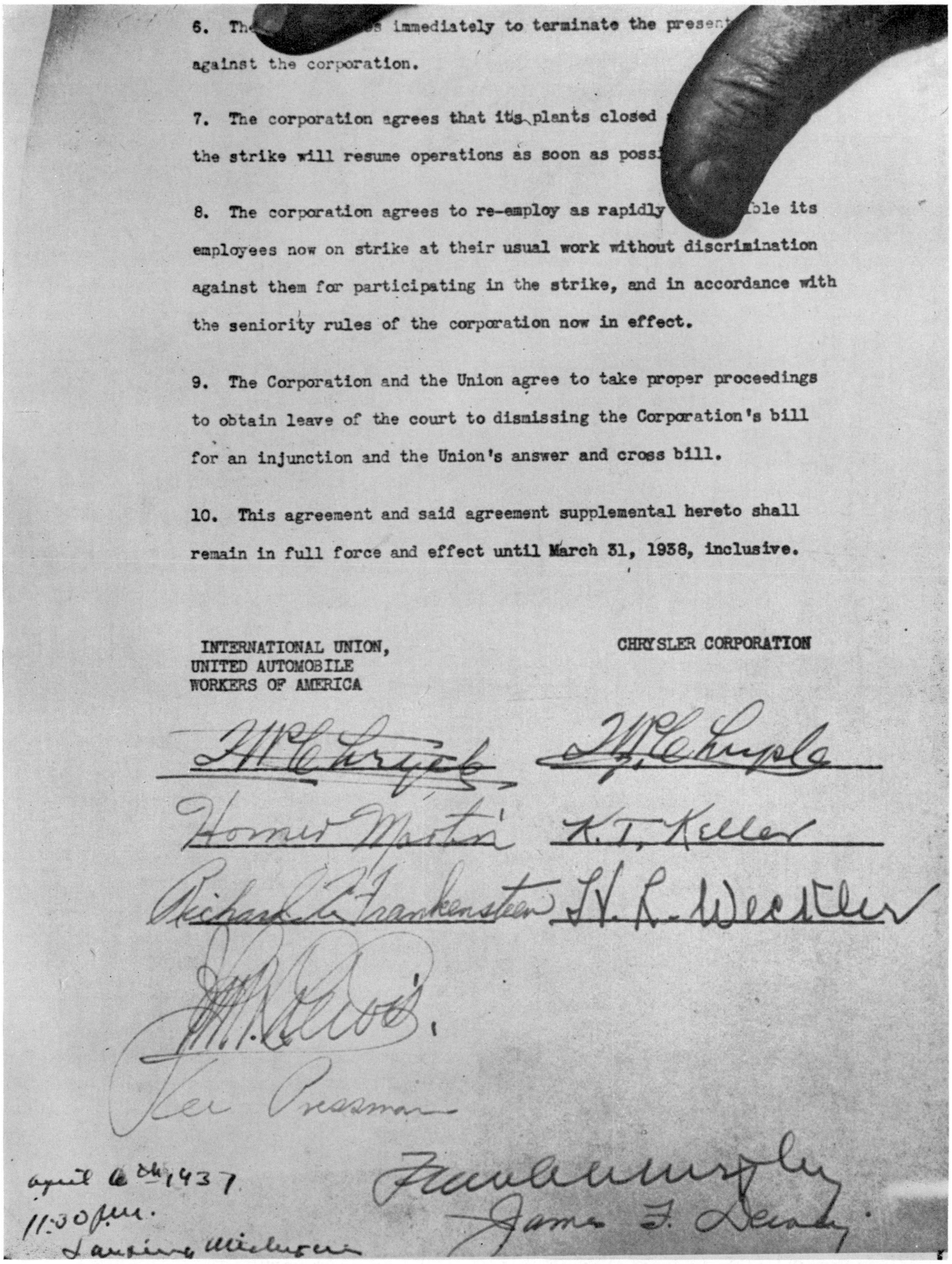

6. The ~~corporation agrees~~ immediately to terminate the presen~~t~~ against the corporation.

7. The corporation agrees that its plants closed ~~during~~ the strike will resume operations as soon as poss~~ible~~

8. The corporation agrees to re-employ as rapidly ~~as possi~~ble its employees now on strike at their usual work without discrimination against them for participating in the strike, and in accordance with the seniority rules of the corporation now in effect.

9. The Corporation and the Union agree to take proper proceedings to obtain leave of the court to dismissing the Corporation's bill for an injunction and the Union's answer and cross bill.

10. This agreement and said agreement supplemental hereto shall remain in full force and effect until March 31, 1938, inclusive.

INTERNATIONAL UNION,
UNITED AUTOMOBILE
WORKERS OF AMERICA

CHRYSLER CORPORATION

[signatures]

Homer Martin

K. T. Keller

Richard Frankensteen

H. L. Weckler

Lee Pressman

April 6th, 1937.
11:00 p.m.
Lansing, Michigan

Frank Murphy

James F. Dewey

SIGNATURE PAGE OF THE HISTORIC 1937 CONTRACT BETWEEN CHRYSLER AND THE UAW

"The issues of the present campaign are clear and apparent to those who will take the trouble to brush aside the thin veil of sham and pretense with which the Republican managers and their financial backers have attempted to conceal their inner purposes.

"This significant fact has been made glaringly apparent to every American voter by the report of the Senate Committee on Campaign Expenditures, especially as to the contributions made to the Republican Party in its recent campaign in the state.

"The bands may play, 'Oh, Suzanna.' You may be asked to join in singing 'Mine Eyes Have Seen the Glory of the Coming of the Lord.' The voices you hear may be the voices of Governor Landon and Colonel Knox. Actually, the strings to this puppet show are being pulled by big business.

"The real progressives of the Republican Party—Norris, LaGuardia, the LaFollettes and hundreds of others—have formed a Conference of American Progressives, to work and vote for President Roosevelt.

HONORING THE "LITTLE GIANT OF THE ANTHRACITE" AT A HARRISBURG DINNER IN '37

Left to Right—Gov. George H. Earle of Pennsylvania, Mr. Lewis and UMWA's Secretary-Treasurer Thomas Kennedy, then lieutenant-governor of the commonwealth.

"New Deal legislation—guaranteeing to labor the right to organize and bargain collectively through chosen representatives, regulating speculative stock exchange activities, prohibiting the issuance and sale of fictitious securities and exploitation of security purchasers and consumers of power companies—has been assailed on constitutional grounds by representatives of the same financial oligarchy which fought the AAA and the NRA and who are now supporting Governor Landon. These cases are now pending in the courts.

"This is why the coming election is the most important and significant in the history of our democracy. It is for this reason that all farmers, farm tenants and farm laborers, and every industrial worker in America—whether he labors in a white collar or in a suit of overalls, whether man or woman, whether young or old, whether a member of a labor organization, or not—should take an active, personal interest in the present political campaign, and thus make sure the overwhelming re-election of President Roosevelt."

In a national broadcast on October 17, 1936, Mr. Lewis told the voters:

"We are faced now with the choice between the malignant and selfish forces of reaction and the sorely beset forces of progress. As a people, we are fortunate to have that choice. We have

ONE CARTOONIST'S VERSION OF THE DRIVE BY CIO TO "ORGANIZE THE UNORGANIZED"

only to look at the desperate, tottering nations of Europe to visualize and understand the price which nations and people inevitably pay for purblindness in economic and political leadership.

"The candidate of the Republican Party is known to you all. You have seen his picture—the picture of a man bewildered by a position which is greater than his understanding. You have heard his voice, as he halts and stumbles over the most simple phrases of our common tongue. Betimes, you have listened to the broadcasting of his diurnal and nocturnal babblements, as with quibble and quirk, he seeks to cozen the American people. His antecedents and his small accomplishments have been blazoned forth to the world. Surrounded by his scribes, a group of modern political sorcerers, he seeks, by complaining, bewailing, lamenting and whining, to chisel an entrance into the White House of the people.

"You know, also, the candidate of the Democratic Party. He has served our country for almost four years. He found it on the verge of an economic and political cataclysm. He found its people in a slough of despond. The policy of patriotic inertia followed by his predecessor, Hoover, who had forgotten that he was born the son of an Iowa blacksmith, had brought the nation to the very brink of ruin and despair. Bankers, industrialists, employers and Republican politicians were despairing of the morrow. Millions of people were starving and homeless; millions were unemployed. One authoritative governmental agency reported to Mr. Hoover that 5 million babies were undernourished and suffering from malnutrition. Mr. Hoover took no action. No doubt he believed that assistance to babies would undermine their initiative and destroy their fortitude. The very foundations of our democratic institutions and our economic system were tottering.

"You know what President Roosevelt has done. His actions speak for themselves. The record book has been opened to the American people. He is daily giving an account of his stewardship. In a blinding white light of publicity and a microscopic examination of his every official act, he stands forth clear and undefiled. The common people have proclaimed him a good and faithful servant and they stand as his

"ORGANIZE," MR. LEWIS TELLS NEW ENGLAND TEXTILE WORKERS AT A MAY 24, 1937, RALLY

protector against the enemies who would assail him by stealth or by boldness. He has succeeded so well in his task of rehabilitating America, that the industrialists and financiers have recovered sufficiently to fight him with malice and venom, defamation and prevarication.

"An American concerned with the future will vote for the re-election of Roosevelt."

Labor's Non-Partisan League offices had been opened for business in Washington on May 11, 1936. John L. Lewis was chairman of the board. Major George Berry of the Pressmen's Union was president and Sidney Hillman was treasurer. The officers' report to the 1938 UMWA convention tells the story of its successful activities during and after the 1936 presidential elections:

R. R. TRAINMEN'S A. F. WHITNEY AND MR. LEWIS AFTER A 1937 WASHINGTON MEETING

"Events of the past eighteen months have not only justified the wisdom of the leaders who established Labor's Non-Partisan League in the summer of 1936, but have also demonstrated that effective labor political organization is a necessary adjunct of industrial organization in gaining for American workers their proper participation in the industrial and political life of the nation.

MR. LEWIS FOUND TIME IN THE HECTIC DAYS OF '37 TO WIN WAGE BOOSTS FOR THE UMWA

Signing the new Appalachian Wage Agreement on April 2 are Mr. Lewis and Charles O'Neill, chief spokesman for the bituminous coal operators.

"Although the immediate purpose of the League was declared to be the re-election of President Roosevelt, its founders announced that the organization would be continued after the 1936 election, to support progressive and labor legislation, as well as to insure labor's recognition in any political realignment which might later develop.

"The unprecedented fury of the attack upon President Roosevelt by the employers represented in the American Liberty League made the wholehearted support of labor essential to the President's re-election. Only the fast and effective work done by the national and state leaders of Labor's Non-Partisan League brought the vitally necessary labor support into the President's campaign. Nothing is more certain now than that the overwhelming character of the Roosevelt victory is attributable to the organization and mobilization of labor in every industrial section behind his candidacy.

"The presidential campaign of 1936 was the first testing ground of the modern labor move-ment in national politics and stimulated League organization on a vast scale. Many of the state leagues expanded their organizations on a county, district, city, ward and precinct basis. In the mining states, especially, Labor's Non-Partisan League was built upon a strong foundation."

With President Roosevelt re-elected, the League broadened its field to include active legislative contact work and laid plans for the 1938 "off-year" local and Congressional elections. The League was the only important organization to support the President in his fight against the conservatives on the United States Supreme Court in 1937.

The Democrats had swept the national elections in 1936. President Roosevelt carried all of the states but Maine and Vermont. Men who had run on platforms favorable to labor were in control of Congress. And among other labor victories, former UMWA President Frank J. Hayes was elected lieutenant governor of Colorado. So CIO organizers, spearheaded by UMWA shock troops, were freed from their political duties and could buckle down to their arduous task of organizing.

ANOTHER STOP ON THE ORGANIZING ROAD; LAWRENCE, MASS., AND A TEXTILE RALLY

In November, 1936, "Big Steel," in an attempt to continue its company union system, offered its employees contracts calling for a 10 per cent wage increase with wages tied to the cost of living. The employees came to Washington to ask Mr. Lewis' advice on the logic of such contracts and he arranged a conference for them with Secretary of Labor Perkins and President Roosevelt. The President advised the workers not to tie themselves to wages based on cost-of-living figures.

Steel was being organized and the infant UAW was trying to negotiate with General Motors Corporation. The company's officials refused to deal with the union and Senator Robert M. LaFollette ordered an investigation of GMC by his Civil Liberties Committee. On December 30, four major GM plants were shut down.

The next day, on an NBC broadcast, Mr. Lewis told of the CIO's plans for the new year:

"The year 1936 has witnessed the beginning of this great movement in the mass production industries. The year 1937 will witness an unparalleled growth in the numerical strength of labor in the heretofore unorganized industries and the definite achievement of modern collective bargaining on a wide front where it heretofore has not existed.

"In the technical, professional and white-collar groups of workers throughout our country are engaged some three and a half million per-

THE REPUBLIC STEEL MASSACRE, MEMORIAL DAY, 1937; CHICAGO POLICE KILLED TEN

JOHN L. LEWIS AND THOMAS KENNEDY AT U. S. HEARINGS ON THE '37 LITTLE STEEL STRIKE

sons. Through the bitter, tragic years of the depression since 1929, they have come to realize that their position in business and industry is no more secure than that of the manual worker. Corporate employers have treated them with the same ruthless lack of consideration universally extended to the workers in production.

"In that field of public service represented by classified employees of the federal government and the inferior political sub-divisions of the nation are again something in excess of 3 million persons, whose need of articulate organization is a paramount necessity to protect them in their status, and to assure them security in the vicissitudes of life.

"There are obvious manifestations that the campaign for organization among industrial workers has aroused the intense interest and sympathy of these employees, and that they also intend to organize and become articulate.

"It is the refusal of employers to grant reasonable conditions and to deal with their employees through collective bargaining that leads to widespread labor unrest. The strikes which have broken out in the last few weeks, especially in the automotive industry, are due to such 'employer trouble.' Modern collective bargaining, involving negotiations between organized workers and organized employers on an industry

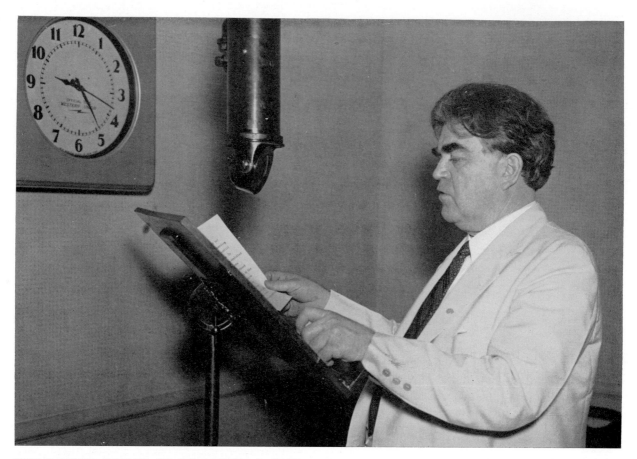

THE FAMOUS SPEECH OF SEPTEMBER 3, 1937, FIRST HINTS OF A BREAK WITH ROOSEVELT

basis, would regularize and stabilize industry relations and reduce the economic losses occasioned by management stupidity. The sit-down strike is the fruit of mismanagement and bad policy towards labor. Employers who tyrannize over employees, with the aid of labor spies, company guards, and the threat of discharge, need not be surprised if their production lines are suddenly halted.

"Mr. Alfred P. Sloan, Jr., president of General Motors Corporation, in his published year-end summary, refers to the possibilities of industrial strife in industry. Is it possible that Mr. Sloan is predicting continued hostility on the part of his corporation towards the demands of its employees for fair consideration? The giant General Motors Corporation is at present pursuing the dangerous course of refusing to answer the request of the United Automobile Workers for a national conference for collective bargaining

purposes. The union has repeatedly requested such a conference, but was told by a vice president that any grievances should be taken up with plant managers or general managers in the various localities.

"It is absurd for such a corporation to pretend that its policies are settled locally. Everyone knows that decisions as to wages, hours, and other conditions of employment are made at a central point for all the plants controlled by General Motors.

"Huge corporations, such as United States Steel and General Motors, have a moral and public responsibility. They have neither the moral nor the legal right to rule as autocrats over their hundreds of thousands of employees.

"The workers in the steel industry are organizing; the workers in the automotive industry are organizing; the workers in other industries are organizing. Any sane concept of industrial relations would indicate that the labor problems of these industries should be settled across the council table.

"The unlicensed and unrestrained arming of

corporations against the workers has no place in any political or industrial democracy. Recent revelations before the LaFollette subcommittee of the Senate have revealed in part the plans of industry to club, gas and cripple workers with the lethal weapons of warfare. Huge stocks of such weapons have been purchased at enormous expense. Over $500 thousand worth of tear and mustard gas has been delivered to industrial plants, and the expenditure necessary for the purchase of these war supplies is charged to the cost of production.

"The time has passed in America when the workers can be clubbed, gassed, or shot down with impunity. I solemnly warn the leaders of industry that labor will not tolerate such policies or tactics. Labor will expect the protection of the agencies of the federal government in the pursuit of its lawful objectives."

The history of the American labor movement in 1937 is crammed so full of memorable events that an impression is created that John L. Lewis was ten men, doing ten different jobs in ten different places at the same time and that the miners and other CIO organizers numbered in the millions. No one book or section of a book could tell the story of the myriad things John

Lewis, the CIO and the UMWA accomplished during 1937. But a short section of Mr. Lewis' report to the first CIO convention entitled, "A Period of Sweeping Advance," touches on the highlights of CIO accomplishments during that year:

"This period was marked by the winning of the General Motors strike, as a result of which the UAW grew almost overnight into a union of 400 thousand members.

"Then followed the winning of the CIO agreement with the United States Steel Corporation, as a result of which the Steel Workers' Organizing Committee became a union of a half million members, with contracts covering the greater part of this basic industry.

"The most formidable barriers to union organization were now removed, and collective bargaining was established in industry after industry by the new industrial unions of the CIO.

"Even the last-ditch stand of the reactionary industrialists which found its most vicious expression in the violent resistance of the inde-

THE LARGEST LABOR DAY RALLY IN HISTORY; 250,000 GATHERED IN PITTSBURGH IN 1937

MR. LEWIS WAITS FOR THE CHEERS TO DIE DOWN AT A MADISON SQUARE GARDEN RALLY

pendent steel companies during the 'Little Steel' strike of 1937, failed to check substantially the onward march of industrial organization.

"Organizing efforts of the CIO expanded in the summer of 1937, and at the very time when Girdler and his brutal henchmen were shooting and gassing the steel workers and claiming that they had 'stopped the CIO,' a million more organized workers were brought into the CIO in other industries.

"At its Atlantic City conference in October, 1937, the CIO was able to report that it had organized more than 3,800,000 workers, that it had thirty-two national and international unions, as well as hundreds of directly affiliated local industrial unions.

"Its organizational achievements were reflected in the winning of more than a billion dollars of wage increases; the winning of shorter working hours for 2 million workers; and innumerable improvements in working conditions,

including vacations with pay for the first time throughout many industries. More than 30 thousand companies had been induced to sign union agreements with CIO unions during this period."

The General Motors stay-in strike lasted forty-four bitter, wintry days. The company's negotiators were adamant in their refusal to sign a contract and their attitude was reflected in the actions of their underlings who made life as miserable as possible for the freezing men and women in the plants and on the picket lines.

President Roosevelt and Secretary of Labor Perkins unsuccessfully tried to conciliate the dispute. William Green tried to break up the negotiations. One of the GM negotiators, William Knudsen, produced a telegram from Mr. Green at one of the meetings, which asked that the AFL be made a party to the talks. Mr. Green's request was overruled when Mr. Lewis suggested that Haile Selassie be invited to participate because he represented the same number of GM workers as the AFL.

But it was the patience of Governor Frank Murphy of Michigan, who refused to listen to "public clamor" for the use of troops against the strikers, which kept the GM officials in contact with Mr. Lewis until they finally realized that the workers were not to be defeated.

The contract granting union recognition was signed in Detroit, February 11, 1937. In a

ANOTHER RALLY, ANOTHER TALK; OCTOBER, '37, AND NEW YORK'S TRANSPORT WORKERS

later description of the end of the strike, Mr. Lewis said:

"At three o'clock in the morning on one of the high floors of the Statler Hotel, Mr. Knudsen, the president; Donaldson Brown, chairman of the finance committee of the board, and John Thomas Smith (the GM negotiating committee) walked into my room, when I was in bed. And they had on their overcoats, and they had their hard hats in their hands, and their gloves on because the room was cold. I didn't get up, and they said that they would sign the contract at eleven o'clock that morning in Governor Murphy's office. And they did."

The financial world was stunned on March 2, 1937, when it read in the newspapers that the United States Steel Corporation had, without a struggle, signed a wage agreement with the CIO. The signs all had pointed toward a long, bitter strike.

The contract was the culmination of a long series of conferences between Mr. Lewis for the CIO and Myron C. Taylor for U. S. Steel. In a press statement issued on the day the contract was signed, Mr. Lewis called it "a fine example of an intelligent approach to a great economic problem."

His statement added: "It has been made possible by the vision and industrial statesmanship of Mr. Myron C. Taylor. From time to time over a period of several months in New York City and Washington, Mr. Taylor and I

MR. LEWIS VISITS PRESIDENT ROOSEVELT AT THE WHITE HOUSE ON SEPTEMBER 15, 1937

have engaged in conversations and negotiations. We were each conscious of the great responsibility and the far-reaching consequence attached to our decisions. Labor, industry and the nation will be the beneficiaries."

Shortly after U. S. Steel had been signed up by the CIO, a month-old strike of 65 thousand workers at several plants of the Chrysler Corporation ended. Walter P. Chrysler, Mr. Lewis and representatives of the UAW signed a contract after several days of conferences. Much credit for the successful meetings went to labor's good friend, Governor Murphy. The agreement ended the company-union, industrial spy system which Chrysler had used in its vain attempts to defeat the auto workers.

CIO organizers were also hard at work in fields other than autos and steel. Packinghouse workers, seamen, quarry workers, electrical workers, office workers and textile workers were flocking into CIO unions. Mr. Lewis travelled all over the country, talking to mass meetings, advising and instructing the young leaders of the infant unions, giving them the inspiration to organize the unorganized.

A FRIENDLY GREETING FOR HEYWOOD BROUN, FOUNDER OF AMERICAN NEWSPAPER GUILD

91

The bloodless winning of the contract with U. S. Steel led many people to believe that the entire steel industry could be organized on a civilized basis. But such optimistic reasoning failed to take into account the hidebound anti-union attitude of the leaders of other steel companies.

Jones and Laughlin, which permitted an election, won by the union, and signed a contract, was a lone exception. The companies were led by men who hated unions and who had reverted to business ethics of pre-depression days. Prices and wages were cut to the bone.

Chief spokesman for the "Little Steel" companies was Tom Girdler, president of the Republic Steel Corporation, who ranted and raved in reactionary cliches pleasing only to the ears of Liberty Leaguers.

The recalcitrance of the companies—Republic, Bethlehem, Youngstown Sheet & Tube, Weirton and Inland—led to the sanguine "Little Steel" strike of 1937.

The 1937 file of Mine Workers Journals tells the heartbreaking story. Eighteen men and women were killed—all unarmed strikers. Hundreds were wounded seriously—all unarmed strikers. And thousands were arrested—all un-

armed strikers. Not a "special policeman," "deputy sheriff," "militiaman," nor any other form of strikebreaker was seriously hurt or arrested.

The most brutal outburst against the steel workers occurred in Chicago on Memorial Day, 1937, when the Chicago police killed ten strikers in cold blood. Eight were shot in the back and another had his brains clubbed out while he was trying to run away from the massacre.

But the violence was not centered in Chicago. In Johnstown, Pa., the mayor, an ex-convict, was actively at work deputizing thugs and buying ammunition at company expense to help Bethlehem Steel break a strike. And he continued his activities until Governor George Earle and Lieutenant Governor Thomas Kennedy threatened him with state troops.

In Ohio, stronghold of "Little Steel," where John Owens directed the strikes, six men were killed. Blood was shed at Youngstown, Canton, Cleveland and Massillon. Governor Martin E. Davey, who had run for election on a labor platform and had been backed by the UMWA, called out militia to break strikes. Mr. Owens, in a radio speech on November 22, called the attention of Ohio voters to Governor Davey's tie-up with Tom Girdler.

The "Little Steel" strike did not end in 1937. It took many months of hardship and litigation

GENERAL HUGH JOHNSON AND JOHN L. LEWIS AT A 1937 ANTI-NAZI RALLY IN NEW YORK

THE LEWIS HOME IN SPRINGFIELD, ILL.;
THE UMWA PRESIDENT VOTES FROM HERE

before the companies stopped fighting. But it demonstrated to American workers that the CIO was strong enough and united enough in 1937 to withstand the lowest punches that the employers were able to throw.

Government handling of the strike widened the small rift between Mr. Lewis and President Roosevelt, which eventually became an unbridgeable chasm in 1940. The first crack in their relationship came during the GM strike when FDR, in spite of his campaign promises to support organized labor, played the part of the benevolent neutral. He also privately applied pressure on Frank Murphy to call out the Michigan state guard during the strike.

But when the President, soon after the Chicago Memorial Day Massacre, said, "a plague on both your houses," in spite of the documented proof being gathered by the LaFollette Civil Liberties Committee that violence in the "Little Steel" strike was management-inspired, the crack became a real break. And the continuing federal policy of awarding government contracts to the "Little Steel" companies who were able to lower prices due to a non-union wage scale did nothing to patch it up.

Mr. Lewis' indignation at repudiation of cam-

paign promises to labor by the White House, the Congress, and state administrations mounted and on September 3, 1937, he told a nationwide CBS radio audience:

"Out of the agony and travail of economic America, the Committee for Industrial Organization was born. To millions of Americans, exploited without stint by corporate industry and socially debased beyond the understanding of the fortunate, its coming was as welcome as the dawn to the night watcher. To a lesser group of Americans, infinitely more fortunately situated, blessed with larger quantities of the world's goods and insolent in their assumption of privilege, its coming was heralded as a harbinger of ill, sinister of purpose, of unclean methods and non-virtuous objectives.

"The workers of the nation were tired of waiting for corporate industry to right their economic wrongs, to alleviate their social agony and to grant them their political rights. Despairing of fair treatment, they resolved to do something for themselves. They, therefore, have organized a new labor movement, conceived

93

REMODELING THE NEW HEADQUARTERS IN '37; THE ROOM IS PART OF MR. LEWIS' OFFICE

within the principles of the national Bill of Rights and committed to the proposition that the workers are free to assemble in their own forums, voice their own grievances, declare their own hopes, and contract on even terms with modern industry for the sale of their only material possession—their labor.

"The Committee for Industrial Organization has a numerical enrollment of 3,718,000 members. It has thirty-two affiliated national and international unions. Of this number, eleven unions account for 2,765,000 members. This group is organized in the textile, auto, garment, lumber, rubber, electrical manufacturing, power, steel, coal and transport industries. The remaining membership exists in the maritime, oil production and refining, shipbuilding, leather, chemical, retail, meat packing, vegetable canning, metalliferous mining, miscellaneous manufacturing, agricultural labor, and service and miscellaneous industries. Some 200 thousand workers are organized into 507 chartered local unions not yet attached to a national industrial union. Much of this progress was made in the face of violent and deadly opposition which reached its climax in the slaughter of workers

paralleling the massacres of Ludlow and Homestead.

"In the steel industry, the corporations generally have accepted collective bargaining and negotiated wage agreements with the Committee for Industrial Organization. Eighty-five per cent of the industry is thus under contract and a peaceful relationship exists between the management and the workers. Written wage contracts have been negotiated with 399 steel companies covering 510 thousand men. One thousand thirty-one local lodges in 700 communities have been organized.

"Five of the corporations in the steel industry elected to resist collective bargaining and undertook to destroy the steel workers' union. These companies filled their plants with industrial spies, assembled depots of guns and gas bombs, established barricades, controlled their communities with armed thugs, leased the police power of cities and mobilized the military power of a state to guard them against the intrusion of collective bargaining within their plants.

"During this strike, eighteen steel workers were either shot to death or had their brains clubbed out by police or armed thugs in the pay of the steel companies. In Chicago, Mayor Kelly's police force was successful in killing ten strikers before they could escape the fury of the police,

94

shooting eight of them in the back. One hundred sixty strikers were maimed and injured by police clubs, riot guns and gas bombs and were hospitalized. Hundreds of strikers were arrested, jailed, treated with brutality while incarcerated and harassed by succeeding litigation. None but strikers were murdered, gassed, injured, jailed or maltreated. No one had to die except the workers who were standing for the right guaranteed them by the Congress and written in the law.

"The infamous Governor Davey of Ohio, successful in the last election because of his reiterated promises of fair treatment to labor, used the military power of the commonwealth on the side of the Republic Steel Co. and the Youngstown Sheet and Tube Co. Nearly half of the staggering military expenditure incident to the crushing of this strike in Ohio was borne by the federal government through the allocation of financial aid to the military establishment of the state.

"The steel workers have now buried their dead, while the widows weep and watch their orphaned children become objects of public charity. The murder of these unarmed men has never been publicly rebuked by any authoritative officer of the state or federal government. Some of them, in extenuation, plead lack of jurisdiction, but murder as a crime against the moral code can always be rebuked without regard to the niceties of legalistic jurisdiction by those who profess to be the keepers of the public conscience.

"Shortly after Kelly's police force in Chicago had indulged in their bloody orgy, Kelly came to Washington looking for political patronage. That patronage was forthcoming and Kelly must believe that the killing of the strikers is no liability in partisan politics.

"The men in the steel industry who sacrificed their all were not merely aiding their fellows at home but were adding strength to the cause of their comrades in all industry. Labor was marching toward the goal of industrial democracy and contributing constructively toward a more rational arrangement of our domestic economy.

"Labor does not seek industrial strife. It wants peace, but a peace with justice. In the long struggle for labor's rights, it has been patient and forebearing. Sabotage and destructive syndicalism have had no part in the American labor movement. Workers have kept faith in American institutions. Most of the conflicts which have occurred have been when labor's right to live has been challenged and denied.

"Fascist organizations have been launched and financed under the shabby pretext that the CIO movement is communistic. The real breeders of discontent and alien doctrines of government and philosophies subversive of good citizenship are such as these who take the law into their own hands.

"No tin-hat brigade of goose-stepping vigilantes or bibble-babbling mob of blackguarding and corporation-paid scoundrels will prevent the onward march of labor, or divert its purpose to play its natural and rational part in the development of the economic, political and social life of our nation.

"Unionization, as opposed to communism, presupposes the relation of employment; it is based upon the wage system and it recognizes fully and unreservedly the institution of private property and the right to investment profit.

"The organized workers of America, free in

THE FORMER WASHINGTON UNIVERSITY CLUB WHICH BECAME UMWA HEADQUARTERS IN '37

their industrial life, conscious partners in production, secure in their homes and enjoying a decent standard of living, will prove the finest bulwark against the intrusion of alien doctrines of government.

"Do those who have hatched this foolish cry of communism in the CIO fear the increased influence will be cast on the side of shorter hours, a better system of distributed employment, better homes for the under-privileged, social security for the aged, a fairer distribution of the national income?

"Certainly labor wants a fairer share in the national income. Assuredly labor wants a larger participation in increased productive efficiency. Obviously the population is entitled to participate in the fruits of the genius of our men of achievement in the field of the material sciences.

"Under the banner of the Committee for Industrial Organization, American labor is on the march. Its objectives today are those it had in the beginning: to strive for the unionization

of our unorganized millions of workers and for the acceptance of collective bargaining as a recognized American institution.

"The objectives of this movement are not political in a partisan sense. Yet it is true that a political party which seeks the support of labor and makes pledges of good faith to labor must, in equity and good conscience, keep that faith and redeem those pledges.

"The spectacle of august and dignified members of Congress, servants of the people and agents of the republic, skulking in hallways and closets, hiding their faces in a party caucus to prevent a quorum from acting upon a labor measure, is one that emphasizes the perfidy of politicians and blasts the confidence of labor's millions in politicians' promises and statesmen's vows.

"Labor next year cannot avoid the necessity of a political assay of the work and deeds of its so-called friends and its political beneficiaries. It must determine who are its friends in the arena of politics as elsewhere. It feels that its cause is just and that its friends should not view its struggle with neutral detachment or intone constant criticism of its activities.

JOHN C. LEWIS AND JOHN L. LEWIS—NOT RELATED—CHAT AT THE 1938 CONVENTION

A FRANK APPEAL TO PRESIDENT ROOSEVELT
FOR AN ACTION PROGRAM ON THE RECESSION

Left to Right—A. A. Berle, Jr., representing New York City; UMWA Vice President Philip Murray, Mr. Lewis, Owen D. Young, board chairman, General Electric; Thomas Lamont, New York banker.

"Those who chant their praises of democracy, but who lose no chance to drive their knives into labor's defenseless back, must feel the weight of labor's woe even as its open adversaries must ever feel the thrust of labor's power.

"Labor, like Israel, has many sorrows. Its women weep for their fallen and they lament for the future of the children of the race. It ill behooves one who has supped at labor's table and who has been sheltered in labor's house to curse with equal fervor and fine impartiality both labor and its adversaries when they become locked in deadly embrace."

At the same time that the thrilling advance of the CIO was taking place, Mr. Lewis was hard at work for the miners. And the miners were hard at work digging the coal, sweating and shedding blood to earn the money that paid the largest share of the cost of the CIO's organization drives.

The 1936 UMWA convention at Constitution Hall in Washington, except for the appearance of William Green, was a happy one. The organization was solidly behind its leaders. The delegates applauded speeches by Senator Burton K. Wheeler of Montana, Secretary of Labor Perkins and Miss Josephine Roche, the Assistant Secretary of the Treasury in charge of public health. And the membership vigorously approved the actions of their leaders in forming the CIO.

"THE BOSS" STUDIES A REPORT AT THE 1938 UMWA CONVENTION IN WASHINGTON

97

THE UMWA PRESIDENT AND THE FIRST LADY AT A WASHINGTON CONFERENCE IN 1938

The first hard chore that Mr. Lewis and his fellow officers performed was the negotiation of a new anthracite contract. An official circular from the International and Tri-District officers told the anthracite membership of the protracted 1936 negotiations:

"More time was devoted to the negotiations than ever before in the history of anthracite wage conferences. Your Scale Committee found the operators in a more determined mood than ever before in their desire to lower wage standards."

At one stage in the slow-moving series of conferences, an exasperated John L. Lewis said:

"We have not even agreed on a semi-colon."

But an agreement was finally reached on May 7, 1936. The circular continues:

"The new contract continues the provisions and awards of the anthracite coal strike commission for the full term of the contract, ending April 20, 1938. Up to May 1, 1937, the hours and working time are on the basis of the present agreement. Starting May 1, 1937, and for the remaining term of the contract, the work day is changed from eight to seven hours per day, and the work week from six days to five days per week.

"Under the new agreement equalization of working time is provided for in principle, to be worked out by the contracting parties in the respective localities. In securing this provision on equalization it would be well to point out that the operators bitterly fought the inclusion of any provisions covering equalization in the contract, and on this issue the conference nearly broke up several times. With the principle of equalization being granted, the organization is in a position to take jurisdiction over the matter and to have equalization problems worked out on a basis that will mean proper distribution of available working time.

"The agreement also provides for the complete standard check-off arrangement to apply in the anthracite region."

The UMWA and Mr. Lewis had to begin again on their efforts for legislative help in stabilization of the coal industry when in May, 1936, the "nine old men" of the U. S. Supreme

98

MR. LEWIS DISCUSSES EFFECTS OF THE '38 RECESSION WITH JOE CURRAN OF THE NMU

Court declared the Guffey Coal Act unconstitutional. Mr. Lewis commented bitterly:

"It is a sad commentary upon our form of government when every decision of the Supreme Court seems designed to fatten capital and starve and destroy labor."

The Supreme Court had based its decision on

AT NEWSPAPERDOM'S EXCLUSIVE GRIDIRON DINNER IN WASHINGTON, APRIL 10, 1938

the labor provisions of the law and Representative Fred Vinson of Kentucky and Senator Joseph Guffey sponsored a coal stabilization bill, similar to the old law, but eliminating its labor provisions and substituting the following:

"It is hereby declared to be the public policy of the United States that employees shall have the right to organize and bargain collectively through representatives of their own choosing, and shall be free from interference, restraint or coercion of employers, or their agents, in the designation of such representatives or in self-organization or in other concerted activities for the purpose of collective bargaining or other mutual aid or protection; and that no employees and no one seeking employment shall be required as a condition of employment to join any company union."

The new bill was supported by a group of operators headed by Charles O'Neill and by the UMWA. At Senate hearings on the bill, Mr. Lewis said:

"I want to put the UMWA, with its entire membership, on record as petitioning Congress

A MOVE FOR UNITY BETWEEN AFL-CIO IS PLANNED IN NEW YORK, MARCH 9, 1938

Frank Hughes, president, UMWA District 3; W. Jett Lauck, UMWA economist; Mr. Lewis.

---

to enact this bill. We do that only as a last resort. We do not think that a pure price-fixing measure is the answer to the basic ailments of the coal industry. We do think that our people in the mining industry are entitled to live until the Congress in its functions and the courts in their judicial meditations can ascertain what solutions are necessary for these problems.

"The Supreme Court, in its judicial majesty, kicked the mine workers and labor from any participation in the Guffey Act. We were faced with the alternative of joining with the forward-looking operators in the industry, in asking the Congress to enact this measure, or to accept the alternative of what Mr. O'Neill has made plain in his testimony before this committee; namely, the convulsion and agony and despair of economic warfare in the bituminous coal industry.

"Now, as the quid pro quo of supporting this bill, the UMWA agrees that the bill should provide for representation of the workers by two members on the commission. We think our people have the right to be heard in the court of last resort affecting this industry. That is the reason we want two representatives of labor on this enlarged commission of seven."

100

The officers' report to the 1938 convention concludes the story:

"The Guffey-Vinson Bill became a law with the President's approval on April 20, 1937.

"In Major Percy Tetlow and Mr. J. C. Lewis the United Mine Workers of America have contributed two able members of the commission

---

A. D. LEWIS, ORGANIZING CHAIRMAN OF THE CIO UNITED CONSTRUCTION WORKERS

CONGRESSMEN CALL ON MR. LEWIS TO TALK
ABOUT PROPOSED WAGE-HOUR LAW IN 1938

and our representatives are upon each of the twenty-three district boards established by the law. It is gratifying to report that while disputes have arisen over the administration of the act, its constitutionality and sound objective have been recognized by the industry and public generally."

A FORMAL PORTRAIT OF THE UMWA LEADER DURING HIS DAYS AS HEAD OF THE CIO

The bituminous negotiations of 1937 began on a sour note. In spite of the fact that the Appalachian Agreement could not be opened by either party until February 15, 1937, Mr. Lewis reported in a radio speech on December 16, 1936, that:

"Prodded and goaded by the financial interests dominant in steel, automobile and other major industries, the coal industry has just taken an amazing action. The coal operators of the Appalachian area, representing three-fourths of the nation's bituminous coal tonnage, on December 15, 1936, formally notified the United Mine Workers of America that they had already met among themselves and decided upon the wages, hours and conditions of employment affecting the mine workers for an additional two-year period. They decided that the seven-hour day would be lengthened to an eight-hour work day, at the same daily wage; they decided that the rates for tonnage workers would remain the same as heretofore; and they decided that the important question of inter-district and intra-district differentials would remain undisturbed until 1939."

In spite of the Appalachian operators' proposals, the UMWA won a contract on April 1, 1937, which called for a daily wage rate of $6.00

101

TIME OUT TO LIGHT A FAVORITE CIGAR AT A HEADLINE-MAKING 1938 NEWS CONFERENCE

in fields north of the Ohio River and $5.60 in the South. The seven-hour day was made universal.

The agreement also provided for the creation of a Mechanized Mining Commission. That section of the contract reads:

"The technological displacement of men in industry is one of our organization's chief problems. With that thought in mind an amendment was written into the last wage agreement, which reads as follows: 'A Joint Commission is hereby created, to be known as the Mechanized Mining Commission, which shall consist of the Appalachian Joint Wage Conference, together with the eight officials of the United Mine Workers of America: John L. Lewis, Philip Murray, Thomas Kennedy, Van A. Bittner, Samuel Caddy, P. T. Fagan, James Mark, John Owens, or their representatives.'

"It shall be the duty of this Commission to make a joint study of the problems arising from mechanization of bituminous coal production by the use of conveyors and mobile loading machines in the area covered by the Appalachian Joint Wage Agreement, including the problem of displacement of employees."

The UMWA members of the commission made a study which showed that 19 per cent

of the production in the United States came from mechanized mines and that the proportion was steadily growing. The conclusion of their report to the 1938 convention stated:

"It may be said that under the far-sightedness of the union, the miners have attained, in a measure, participation in the advantages derived by the owners from mine mechanization.

"From this study certain conclusions can be made which would be pertinent and helpful in the negotiation of the next wage agreement.

"To be specific, the available data can be used to prove:

"1. That there is a wide enough margin in cost reduction due to mechanical loading to allow participation in the benefits;

"2. That a high day rate is inadequate without a guaranteed number of working days per year, or guaranteed annual earnings;

"3. That the displacement of labor is proceeding at a rate necessitating a definite form of protection (insurance, dismissal wage, etc.);

"4. That the problem of safety should be brought under control as in cases of explosives and explosions;

"5. That abuses of various deductions from earnings call for wider activities in group medical service, hospitalization, community housing, co-operative stores, undertaking establishments, bathhouses, etc.;

"6. That the problem of competing fuels, specifically of gas and petroleum, can be mini-

50,000 EAGER WORKERS CAME OUT TO HEAR MR. LEWIS SPEAK IN MEXICO CITY IN 1938

mized by encouragement of coal by-product recovery, etc., etc."

UMWA membership in the Canadian districts grew by leaps and bounds in the 1936-38 period. District 18 (British Columbia) had 8,300 members in 1938 as against only 2,300 in 1926. The miners on Vancouver Island had been organized for the first time since 1912. In District 26 (Nova Scotia) the membership grew from 6 thousand to 12 thousand.

In December, 1937, the International headquarters was moved to its present site from rented office space in Washington. The officers' report to the 1938 convention said:

"About eighteen months ago, the International officers learned that the University Club building, located in the city of Washington at 15th and Eye Streets, was for sale. We secured an option on the building, and in negotiation secured a purchase price offer of $275 thousand. The matter was submitted to the International Executive Board for consideration, and the Board by unanimous vote authorized the purchase of the building and its remodeling so that it might be adapted to the office needs and other requirements of the International Union.

"If we look at the transaction from an investment standing, it is equally commendable be-

AMONG OTHER PROBLEMS, MR. LEWIS HAD TO SETTLE UAW-CIO FACTIONAL FIGHTS IN '38

Seated, Left to Right—Wyndham Mortimer, UAW; Mr. Lewis, Lee Pressman, CIO general counsel. *Standing, Left to Right*—John Brophy, CIO organization director; Richard Frankensteen, Paul Miley, Walter Reuther and Maurice Sugar, all of UAW.

cause the entire cost of purchase and remodeling was $550 thousand, while reputable and responsible real estate experts give as their conservative opinion that the building as it stands today is worth a million dollars."

In addition to the bitterness against President Roosevelt engendered by the Chief Executive's actions during the 1937 strikes, Mr. Lewis had other reasons for his gradual drawing away from President Roosevelt. One was the recurrence of economic depression, the "recession" of 1937-39. Mr. Lewis told the October 15, 1937, CIO conference at Atlantic City:

"The United States of America, economically speaking, is not out of the woods. There are certain fundamental economic questions in this country which need attention from the American people and from the American Congress. In five years of experimentation, no progress has yet been made toward composing what is one of America's greatest economic questions, namely, the question of unemployment.

103

A WHISPERED CONFERENCE BETWEEN FATHER AND DAUGHTER AT 1938 CIO CONVENTION

"President Roosevelt has said that one-third of all Americans are ill-housed, ill-clothed and underfed. Let us do something about that. What has been done about it so far? Nothing! The last Congress adjourned without even enacting that poor, halting, wages-and-hours bill that finally emerged from the committee.

"Americans cannot eat or live on platitudes or musical phrases—they want buying power— they want shorter hours. Give them buying power and shorter hours and they will improve their economic and their social status. They will learn to improve their leisure, to avail themselves of it. They will know what to do with it. No special training is needed for an American citizen who gets only $500 a year, to know what to do with another $100, if he gets it.

"Those people have no one upon whom to depend, except upon a militant, intelligent, well-organized, well-functioning and modern American labor movement. In that fact lies the strength of the CIO."

And, in March, 1938, in a special broadcast to the British people over the BBC network, Mr. Lewis said:

"Thirteen million Americans are now unemployed. Their numbers are steadily increasing, as the nation drifts, with terrifying and deadly sureness, to the never-never realm of financial bankruptcy, economic collapse and human tragedy. This is appallingly true, despite the fact that government has dipped into the public purse to make possible the granting of huge subsidies to industry, agriculture, banking and finance.

"Since 1933 these grants, directly and indirectly, have amounted to the enormous total of $22 billion. Our national internal economy has attained the amazing condition where it appears that practically all of our major enterprises are unable to exist or function on their own resources.

"America is moving in economic reverse. Our consumer goods industries began to slow down in June, 1937, and by October of the same year, our heavy industries began to feel the icy hand of the depression.

"Meantime, cavilling and confusion prevails, and our statesmen, and those carrying the responsibilities of the nation's manifold enterprises, are reviling each other with an anger and bitterness that defiles, sears and destroys. Meantime the population suffers, and a creeping paralysis progressively impairs its functions."

A few days later, Mr. Lewis asked the House Appropriations Committee to approve a bill to alleviate unemployment by creating three and a half million new WPA jobs. He stated:

"On two counts it is important that these three and a half million jobs be provided immediately.

"First, there is terrible need among our people, and on all grounds of humanity and decency these human beings must be provided for.

"The second important purpose of the program is to provide and stimulate purchasing power and recovery. The longer that stimulus is delayed, so much longer do we drift not toward recovery but toward economic disaster.

"Labor is asking that this fund be so appropriated that it can be operated under four main principles.

"The first principle is that all workers should be employed on work suited to their needs and skills.

"The second principle upon which labor makes its demand is that projects should be socially necessary and productive. This means housing and slum clearance, flood control, the building of schools and hospitals, health measures, cultural and white collar projects, and vocational training work.

"The third principle that labor asks is that jobs should be given those who need jobs without requiring honest, decent unemployed workers to degrade themselves as paupers.

"The fourth principle that labor asks is that funds be so appropriated that government will be able to meet current needs wherever and whenever such needs arise. The government should be equipped to meet emergencies.

"One of the proudest boasts of our nation has always been the American standard of living. For those who are on WPA that American standard of living means an average of less than $52 a month income. That is an average of approximately $620 a year. In the Southern wage region workers on WPA receive about

---

DEBATING THE CIO VS. THE AFL AT THE HERALD-TRIBUNE FORUM, OCTOBER 26, 1938

Left to Right—Wendell L. Willkie, Mr. Lewis, Ogden Reid, Herald-Tribune publisher, and Joseph A. Padway, counsel for the AFL, who spoke in the absence of William Green.

**CIO ADOPTS A CONSTITUTION AT PITTSBURGH
AND ELECTS ITS FIRST PRESIDENT IN 1938**

half that amount. Unskilled workers receive as little as $21 a month and 15 cents an hour. Most of the men on these projects have families to support. Government has the obligation of creating decent standards. It now pays at levels below those of sweatshops, below those universally accepted as absolute minimums for American citizens.

"I cannot express in strong enough terms how inadequate these levels of income are to provide livelihood for American families. Such a condition can only bring a deep sense of shame to responsible citizens."

And in his opening speech to the 1938 UMWA convention, Mr. Lewis warned the miners that once again they would have to fight to hold the line against wage cuts as they had done in the '20s.

"There are those in the land at the present time, in the realm of industry and finance, who are saying aloud that the price structure of manufactured commodities is too high and that

prices must be reduced. They then say—and they all say it—that they are losing money in the operation of their plants, by reason of the low volume of production and that if, through circumstance or policy, they are compelled to reduce to the public the price of their goods and their commodities, they expect to make that possible by reducing wages, and placing upon the backs of the workers of this country the economic and financial responsibility of such a policy. Let me say this: In the few short months of the existing depression the volume of production has spiralled downward in all industry more rapidly, in a more devastating fashion and to a substantially lower level than was the case in the same number of months of the depression which began in 1929. All we need now in this country to encompass and insure a complete and most devastating economic, social and political debacle, is to reduce the prices of commodities and reduce the wage structure of this country. I know of nothing that will contribute so much to the economic confusion of this nation or the sum total of the degree of human agony to be endured by the workers and all the people of this country, than to undertake further to reduce their meager earnings on the basis of the small opportunity that exists for them to earn today."

The officers' report to the 1938 convention tells of the birth of a new branch of the UMWA:

"District 50 was formally set up on September 1, 1936, to cover the gas and by-product coke field. It was first interested only in organizing coal process workers. It was soon realized that the men working in the distribution of natural gas had the same problems as those distributing manufactured gas, so it has accepted into membership workers in already established natural gas distribution systems.

"It was found that many chemical products came from coal tar processing and accordingly in June, 1937, the district began a drive to organize the employees in that industry."

By 1940, District 50 had more than 20 thousand members and had been led by some of the ablest organizing talent in the UMWA, including Kathryn Lewis and Ora E. Gasaway.

The drives of John L. Lewis and his co-workers in the CIO to organize the unorganized had been slowed up by widespread unemployment. But Mr. Lewis was able to report to the 1938 CIO convention:

"The success of the CIO in this recent period has made a contribution to the welfare of the whole American people. In every previous depression, unemployment had been accompanied by general wage cutting which had seri-

A UNION ARTIST DRAWS A UNION LEADER; PORTRAIT PRESENTED AT CIO CONVENTION

Left to Right—Mr. Lewis and Morris J. Kallem, member of a New York artists union.

HER PARENTS GREET KATHRYN LEWIS ON HER RETURN FROM LABOR CONVENTION IN PERU

ously impaired the purchasing power of the workers upon which our national welfare depends.

"But in this depression, the CIO has stood as a mighty bulwark against the general wave of wage reduction. When the steel companies reduced prices earlier in the year, the wage cutting which had always accompanied such price reductions was prevented by the organized strength of the Steel Workers Organizing Committee.

"Among the examples of new advances made by the CIO in the period of depression are the winning of a national agreement for the first time with the great General Electric Corporation by the United Electrical, Radio and Machine Workers of America, the winning by the American Communications Association of national agreements with Postal Telegraph, RCA Communications, and other companies, and the organizing successes of the Packinghouse Workers Organizing Committee."

Organized labor in America suffered an irreplacable loss when Charles P. Howard, a militant and fearless trade unionist, president of the International Typographical Union and secretary of the CIO, died July 21, 1938. He was succeeded as CIO secretary by youthful James B. Carey, president of the United Electrical, Radio and Machine Workers of America.

Carey was elected at the first CIO Constitutional Convention at Pittsburgh in November, 1938. Having failed in its efforts to bring about labor unity, the CIO changed its name from the Committee for Industrial Organization to the Congress of Industrial Organizations. In his report to the convention, Mr. Lewis said:

"This is a historic occasion. Today we fit the rooftree in a mighty new house of labor. Where three years ago there was only an idea in the minds of a few men, there now stands a structure as solidly built as if of stone and steel."

John L. Lewis was elected first president of the CIO. Sidney Hillman and Philip Murray were elected vice presidents and Mr. Carey was elected secretary-treasurer.

Successful organizing campaigns continued. In Chicago, on July 16, 1939, the Packinghouse Workers Organizing Committee held a mass meeting during the drive on the "Big Four" meat packers—Armour, Wilson, Swift and Cudahy.

The meeting marked the first appearance on

MR. LEWIS READS FDR NOTE DECLINING BID TO FIRST CIO CONSTITUTIONAL CONVENTION

"The organized packinghouse workers of the nation are now serving notice on Armour & Co. that their patience is nearing an end, and that if the company continues to refuse collective bargaining, it must accept the consequences of its own action.

"The packinghouse workers have at all times followed the orderly procedure prescribed by the National Labor Relations Act. They have taken, and they plan to take, no action which is not fully in accord with the law. All they ask is that the packinghouse corporations be similarly law-abiding and negotiate with them in good faith as required by the law."

And on August 1, 1939, the CIO formed the United Construction Workers Organizing Committee with A. D. Lewis of the UMWA as chairman. Other members of the committee were James B. Carey, Philip Murray, Sherman Dalrymple, president of the Rubber Workers, and R. J. Thomas, president of the Auto Workers. The committee is now affiliated with the UMWA and A. D. Lewis is still chairman.

a CIO platform of a member of the Catholic hierarchy, the Most Rev. Bernard J. Sheil, Senior Auxiliary Bishop of the Catholic archdiocese of Chicago. He told the packinghouse workers of the encyclicals of Pope Leo XIII and of the duty of Catholic workers to join trade unions. Mr. Lewis told the meeting:

One of John L. Lewis' duties as head of the CIO was to attend the Latin-American Labor

TWO FIGHTERS FOR THE RIGHTS OF WORKING MEN MEET AT A 1939 PACKINGHOUSE RALLY

Mr. Lewis is shaking hands with the Most Rev. Bernard J. Sheil, senior auxiliary bishop of the Catholic archdiocese of Chicago.

Conference in Mexico City in September, 1938. In a speech before 50 thousand people in the Mexico City bullring, Mr. Lewis echoed the concern of people the world over at the rise of nazism and fascism:

"In the United States the reactionary employers have always opposed the right of workers to organize and take concerted action on their own behalf.

"When employers use spies and provocateurs, form company unions, spread lies and false propaganda, form 'law-and-order' and vigilante committees against workers, and corrupt public officials to use the forces of the state against workers, then they are using the weapons of fascism against workers.

"We have had Silver Shirts, the Ku Klux Klan, the Black Legion and Nazi Bunds. We have seen a congressional committee lend itself to the lies and false propaganda of these agents. Organized labor stands ready to overcome these various groups just as it has triumphed over spies, provocateurs, vigilantes, law-breaking offi-

---

NEW YORK MAYOR LAGUARDIA WAS WORRIED ABOUT A POSSIBLE COAL SHORTAGE IN 1939

cials and company unions. Reactionary employers and their satellites would welcome the triumph of fascism in Latin America. For this reason the workers of America rejoice at the preservation of democracy in Latin America."

The 1938 UMWA convention was held at the Rialto Theater, Washington, the Daughters of the American Revolution having refused to let the miners use their Constitution Hall. Speakers included Miss Josephine Roche, Senator Joseph Guffey, Homer Martin and Richard Frankensteen of the Auto Workers Union, and the Rev. Francis Haas, professor of social science at the Catholic University of America.

The delegates praised the tremendous work done by the LaFollette Civil Liberties Committee in documenting the vicious practices of employers during the GM, Chrysler, "Little Steel" and Harlan County strikes. The resolution stated:

"The investigations of the LaFollette Civil Liberties Committee revealed, insofar as the Committee's survey extended through industry, an annual expenditure by designated and identified corporations of between 10 and 11 million dollars annually for espionage in furtherance of

THERE WERE NO SMILES DURING 1939 FIGHT TO WIN UNION SHOP FOR SOFT-COAL MINERS

Left to Right—John D. A. Morrow, president, Pittsburgh Coal Co., Mr. Lewis, UMWA Vice President Murray.

agents provocateur. On the basis of those figures it is estimated American industry annually expends a sum of at least $80 million for espionage, secret service, the payment of informers and agents in order to keep the workers in the employ of these corporations from organizing into unions to bargain collectively, and in order to bring confusion, disorder, and turmoil into the ranks of established labor organizations. A tremendous sum! Eighty million dollars of annual expenditures or a lesser sum is capable of bringing an intense degree of confusion into a human institution. The practice is abhorrent

THE GOVERNMENT INTERVENES IN THE 1939 SOFT-COAL DISPUTE OVER THE UNION SHOP

To the right of Mr. Lewis is Philip Murray, UMWA vice president. To his left are John Owens, District 6 president; Walter L. Robison, operator chairman of the joint conference; John R. Steelman, director, U. S. Conciliation Service; Charles O'Neill, chief operator spokesman; James Dewey, federal conciliator.

UMWA NEGOTIATORS AT THE WHITE HOUSE TO SEE PRESIDENT ROOSEVELT, MAY 9, 1939

Front, Left to Right—Van A. Bittner, District 17 president; Philip Murray, UMWA vice president, and Mr. Lewis. *Rear, Left to Right*—John Owens, District 6 president, and David J. McDonald, assistant to Mr. Murray.

---

to every lover of liberty, of free speech, of free assemblage, or one who believes in protecting the principles written into the Constitution of this democracy."

In 1938, Thomas Kennedy, the UMWA's beloved "little giant of the anthracite" ran for the Democratic nomination for governor of Pennsylvania. He polled more than 500 thousand votes but was defeated in a close race. His defeat was another blow at the UMWA by the Democratic Party. The party machine had thrown its weight and money behind Mr. Kennedy's opponent in the primary and, as a result, the Democrats were defeated by the Republicans in the fall elections.

Political defeats notwithstanding, the miners won an important trade-union victory the following spring. The Appalachian Agreement expired on April 1, 1939, and the operators determined to cut wages. But wages were not cut and the UMWA won a union shop in soft coal for the first time in history. The story is told in excerpts from the officers' report to the 1940 convention:

"Basic wage proposals were:

"A standard six-hour day, thirty-hour week; 15 cents a ton advance in mining rates; 50 cents a day increase in day rates, and the establishment of a $5.00 a day minimum; 25 per cent increase on yardage and deadwork rates; an adjustment of mechanized mining rates designed to provide an amount in wages commensurate with increased productive efficiency; double time for Sundays and holidays; elimination of reject clauses; a guarantee of 200 working days a year; vacations with pay; establishing of seniority rights; a plan for improved hospitalization; elimination of discrimination in physical examinations; inspection of mines by United States Bureau of Mines; financial responsibility of operators' associations for defalcation of payrolls or checkoff; elimination of inequitable differentials; establishing of a joint commission to study the problems of mechanized mining; clarification of the recognition clauses of all agreements; a checkoff clause for the Appalachian Agreement; and a series of miscellaneous provisions providing: operators' compliance with the National Bituminous Coal Conservation Act; protective clause in leases; equitable adjustment of house rents; payment of wages in cash or par check; delivering of cars to and from working places; use of only union-made supplies, tools and explosives; elimination of foremen performing work of mine workers; arrangements for the employment of umpires; and expiration of agreements on March 31, 1941.

"The National Policy Declaration, later presented to the Appalachian Conference as the United Mine Workers' wage proposals, was the most comprehensive document of its kind ever prepared by the organization. It can well serve as a guide in the drafting of future proposals and stand as a bill of particulars for the aims of the union."

The operators and mine workers assembled in New York, March 14, 1939, and Walter L. Robison was elected chairman, replacing D. C. Kennedy, chairman of all previous Appalachian Conferences. The officers' report continues:

"After the formal arguments had been presented, President Lewis, on March 15, suggested that the conference guarantee to the industry and to the consuming public that there will not be any suspension of production in 1939. No formal action was taken on this proposal and it soon became evident that it would be impossible to gain any concessions which would add to the cost of production. Throughout the conference, outside interests, closely allied with important non-union steel producers, had maintained a lobby group which brought every possible pressure upon the operators in order to prevent them from granting any concessions. The general watchword was, 'If you stop the United Mine Workers, you stop the CIO.'

"When it became evident that no wage increase could be obtained, and there was no pos-

sible chance of contracting for a thirty-hour week or instituting any other changes which might cost money, the mine workers decided to stand firm on one final proposition; that was to eliminate the penalty clause from all existing district agreements. When the operators refused that concession, the miners then proposed, in lieu of removing the penalty clauses, that the wording of the enacting clause of the Appalachian Agreement be rewritten so as to provide a union shop.

"The 1937 agreement expired on Friday, March 31, and when no decision had been made and no contract existed on Monday, April 3, the bituminous mines in the Appalachian area remained closed.

"As the month of April wore along, the operators submitted several open-shop propositions, but the mine workers would not waver from their position. The Department of Labor assigned Dr. John R. Steelman, director of its conciliation bureau, to attend the conference and

MR. LEWIS ARGUES THE UMWA CASE AT 1939 BITUMINOUS COAL CONTRACT NEGOTIATIONS

Left to Right (around table)—Secretary of Labor Frances Perkins, James Dewey, federal conciliator; Mr. Lewis. *Left to Right (in background)*—John Owens, District 6 president; Van A. Bittner, District 17 president; UMWA Secretary-Treasurer Thomas Kennedy.

attempt to break the deadlock. The operators had decided to starve out the miners and so on April 19 the Scale Committee empowered the International officers to notify the outlying districts that they should advise the operators that work-pending-settlement agreements would expire within fifteen days. This was done, and at midnight, May 3, practically all the bituminous mines in the United States ceased operating."

On May 7, with the conference still deadlocked, Mr. Lewis wrote to Dr. Steelman:

"You have personal knowledge that the following are facts:

"a. Responsibility for the present stoppage of coal production in the Appalachian area does not lie with the mine workers. Four times between March 14 and April 1 they proposed an extension of the status quo of the industry beyond April 1, either to a fixed date or until a new agreement had been negotiated. Acceptance of either of these proposals by the operators would have resulted in no stoppage of production and no public inconvenience, either as to supply or price. Failure of the Roosevelt administration to approve or sustain the mine workers' offers to keep the industry in operation caused many coal operators to believe that they had carte blanche from the government to disembowel the mine workers' union if they could. In consequence, your department must accept responsibility for its own administrative blunder.

"b. Contrary to published reports, the mine workers do not demand the so-called 'closed shop' with restrictions upon employment and managerial policies. The mine workers ask the acceptance in the agreement of the 'union shop,' legalized by an act of the federal Congress, or alternatively they offer, in lieu thereof, the elimination of the automatic, unilateral penalty clauses, so obnoxious in principle to any thoughtful citizen.

"c. You have knowledge of the parliamentary control of the machinery of the Appalachian Joint Conference by operators producing a minority of coal tonnage in any one of the twenty-one mining districts embraced in the Appalachian Conference. You know further that between 70 and 80 per cent of the bituminous tonnage now estopped from produc-

duction are willing immediately to sign such a contract with the United Mine Workers of America and terminate forthwith the progressively increasing national emergency.

"If the foregoing statement of facts, in whole or in part, is incorrect, I should be glad to have you publicly refute it. By the same token, if my averments are true, I submit that you, sir, in the position you occupy, should publicly sustain them."

The following day Secretary of Labor Frances Perkins arrived at the sub-committee meeting and insisted that a settlement be made. Later in the day an invitation was received to call on President Roosevelt at the White House on the following day. The report goes on:

"Accordingly, at noon on May 9 the negotiating sub-committee and the officers of the conference called upon the President. He

---

➤

MORE DIFFERENCES THAN THE EYE CAN SEE: MR. LEWIS AND COAL OPERATOR O'NEILL

John L. Lewis and Charles O'Neill, chief management spokesman, in identical poses (*above*) at a Washington parley and (*below*) in a hotel corridor conference in New York.

➤

---

stated that he wanted an answer by midnight of May 10.

"Back in New York the operators made another open-shop offer on May 10. Like all its predecessors, it was unacceptable to the United Mine Workers of America. It was evident that a large portion of the operators' group, approximately 80 per cent by this time, was in accord with the union shop proposal of the mine workers. So, on that evening, Dr. Steelman summoned the negotiating sub-committee and read to them the following statement:

"'Speaking as the government representatives, we are asking that such companies and associations as are in agreement with the United Mine Workers of America sign contracts and begin operations immediately in order to relieve the grave crisis facing the nation.

"'We are asking such operators and representatives of the United Mine Workers as are not in agreement to continue negotiations with the assistance of officials of the federal govern-

A SIX WEEKS' SHUTDOWN ENDS AS THE UMWA WINS THE 1939 FIGHT FOR THE UNION SHOP

Left to Right—Charles O'Neill, chief operator spokesman; U. S. Conciliation Chief John R. Steelman, Mr. Lewis.

---

ment until amicable and fair contracts can be completed.'

"The next morning outlying districts were notified to execute union shop agreements with the operators' associations. That afternoon the sub-committee again met and drafted a report and recommendations for submission to the Appalachian Joint Conference. The pertinent sections of this report read:

" 'Witnesseth: It is agreed that this contract is for the exclusive joint use and benefit of the contracting parties as heretofore defined and set forth in this agreement. It is agreed that the United Mine Workers of America is recognized herein as the exclusive bargaining agency representing the employees of the parties of the first part. It is agreed that as a condition of employment all employees shall be members of the United Mine Workers of America, except in those exempted classifications of employment as provided in this contract.'

"The report and recommendations were accepted by all except Big Sandy Elkhorn Coal Operators, Hazard Coal Operators, Kanawha Coal Operators, Southern Appalachian Coal Operators, Harlan County Coal Operators, and Virginia Coal Operators. These six associations then withdrew from the conference.

"Five out of the six operators' associations which withdrew from the conference returned to their fields and met with the respective district organizations of the United Mine Workers of America. Within ten days after adjournment of the conference, all had signed the Appalachian Agreement, with the exception of the Harlan County Coal Operators' Association. However, on July 19, 1939, this association signed an agreement exact in details with the Appalachian Agreement, except that instead of writing in the union shop provision it eliminated the penalty clause section from the district agreement.

"It is gratifying, indeed, for your officers to report to this Fiftieth Anniversary Convention of the United Mine Workers of America, that after dark days and bright days—days of suspense and terror—days of brilliance and great achievement—through which your Union has passed since its inception in 1890, a lofty pinnacle of success has been reached in establishing a union shop contract for the bituminous coal industry."

The 1939 anthracite negotiations were protracted but a settlement was made without work stoppage. The new agreement continued the old wage scale for two years. The only clause in the contract which was changed dealt with the selection of an umpire to arbitrate disputes on interpretations of the contract. The new clause specified that if the Anthracite Board of Conciliation could not agree on an umpire, then the choice should be made by one of the judges of the Third Judicial Circuit of the United States.

One of the most able, loyal and conscientious

↑
A THOUGHTFUL SCRUTINY OF LAFOLLETTE'S BILL TO END OPPRESSIVE LABOR PRACTICES

ANOTHER TRY FOR LABOR UNITY IN 1939; MR. LEWIS ALSO WAS BUSY WITH COAL TALKS

To Mr. Lewis' right is John Owens, District 6 president and founder-director of the first state CIO industrial union council in Ohio.
↓

1890-1940: FOR THE GOLDEN ANNIVERSARY A PORTRAIT OF THE FIRST UMWA OFFICERS

Left to Right—Mr. Lewis and John H. Rae, son of John B. Rae, first president of the United Mine Workers of America.

members of the staff of the International Union, Judge Henry Warrum, died during the 1939 coal negotiations. He was seventy-one years of age and had been UMWA chief counsel since 1898, representing the organization ably through its most trying days.

The signing by the Harlan County Coal Operators' Association of the 1939 Appalachian Agreement brought an end to an operator reign of terror which had lasted for almost ten years in "Bloody Harlan" County, Ky.

The story of Harlan County is grim but it is also inspiring. It is a tale of men who died for something bigger than themselves: their union, their fellow workers and their belief in freedom.

It is a story filled with the sound of bullets screaming through the rocky Kentucky mountains and of shotguns blasting through open windows at union organizers.

It is a saga of names—names of union men, some dead, who died brave and unafraid—of other names such as William Turnblazer, George Titler, Paul Reed and John Saxton, brave UMWA organizers who fought the weary battle until the miners got a contract. It tells of T. C. Townsend, the UMWA lawyer who fought for his men both in and out of the courtroom.

It is also filled with names such as Ben Upthank and Theodore Middleton, who killed and clubbed in the name of "law and order" for their bosses, the Harlan County Coal Operators.

It is a story told in gruesome detail in the reports of the LaFollette Civil Liberties Committee and in the courthouse records at Harlan County, a courthouse outside of which hung a sign: "ALL PERSON MUST BE SEARCHED BEFORE ENTERING COURT ROOM. CHECK GUNS IN SHERIFF OFFICE."

AN AUDIENCE OF ONE: POSTMASTER FARLEY AT A PRESS CLUB DINNER IN WASHINGTON

It was the bravery and militancy of the miners themselves that brought about the signing of the first contract with the Harlan County operators on August 27, 1938. The agreement was patterned on the Appalachian Agreement and called for a daily wage of $5.60 and the seven-hour day.

Except for a brief outburst of shootings and wholesale arrests of union men after the Harlan operators walked out of the 1939 negotiations, murder on a wholesale basis had ended in notorious "Bloody Harlan" County of Kentucky.

On the political front, Labor's Non-Partisan League reported with pride to the 1940 UMWA convention of its activities during the 1938 elections. The biggest successes had been gained in Ohio where "Strikebreaker" Martin E. Davey had been defeated as governor and labor had been victorious in many local elections in campaigns led by John Owens, president of District 6. Additional victories had been won all over the country, from New York to California.

But many of these same politicians forgot who had helped to elect them and, as a result, the League had to spend much effort in defeating reactionary legislation.

Mr. Lewis spent a great deal of his time in 1938 and 1939 opposing such legislation. On June 3, 1938, he wrote a letter to Secretary of Labor Frances Perkins which said:

"Some days ago, a representative of your department inquired whether a Committee for Industrial Organization representative, now in Europe, could act upon a departmental commission to secure information on British labor laws. Presumably, this information was for the use of your department. The answer was affirmative.

ABOUT GARNER: A LABOR-BAITING, POKER-PLAYING, WHISKY-DRINKING, EVIL OLD MAN

A VICTORY FOR NEW YORK TRANSIT WORKERS AND A FRIENDLY HANDCLASP FOR THE MAYOR

Left to Right—Allan S. Haywood, CIO national director; Sidney Hillman, Clothing Workers; Mr. Lewis; Mrs. Anna M. Rosenberg, Social Security Board; Mayor LaGuardia; Michael Quill, president, Transport Workers Union.

"Newspaper stories today indicate that the information will be used as a basis for modification of the Wagner Labor Relations Act. The CIO cannot sanction such an enterprise, nor permit its representative to serve on such a commission. It will oppose amendment or modification of the Wagner Act."

On November 30, 1938, Mr. Lewis testified against a bill which would allow employers to substitute profit-sharing schemes for wage increases:

"Testimony has been adduced before this committee urging a policy that labor accept as part of its just compensation a participating share in profits which are completely beyond its control or influence. Labor's disillusioned experience in regard to profit-sharing plans has been that they have been used as a device to avoid the payment of an immediate decent wage and make labor dependent upon haphazard industrial and financial policies of management.

"We believe if any industry or a concern is making profits that would permit them, if they desired, to share those profits with the employees, that they will have no difficulty at all under collective bargaining practices in making the necessary adjustments of the wage structure so as to permit the employees to have a higher wage. In fact, I think the unions will cooperate at all times on any suggestion from the corporations that they wanted to modify the wage structure upward."

On July 15, 1939, Mr. Lewis denounced a drastic cut in WPA appropriations just voted by Congress:

"Labor does not forget that in the 1936 campaign the Democratic platform promised work for the unemployed.

"The relief bill which was passed is a clear repudiation of that platform pledge. The measure will throw out of WPA employment a million WPA workers in the fiscal year. Five hundred thousand of these will be thrown out by the end of July. This happens at a time when there are at least 11 to 12 million employable unemployed.

"The bill seriously discriminates against a number of groups of our citizens, especially the

120

artists, musicians and theatrical workers.

"The total effect of this bill upon the economic situation cannot help but be depressive. There are grounds for the fear that such a terrible cut in WPA jobs and wage rates will touch off a definite downward movement."

Efforts to kill the Wage-Hour law were made in August, 1939. Vice President John Nance Garner had gathered around him a powerful group of reactionaries who were prepared to vote for amendments. Mr. Lewis had some well-chosen words on the matter. They were most effective, for all efforts to change the law were abandoned at that session. Mr. Lewis said:

"I come before the committee today to say that the CIO is opposed to the amendments to this act.

"He who proposed in this Congress to amend this act must have known that he was opening up the floodgates of complaint and lamentations and propaganda and sinister political influence which have revolved around the discussion of this proposition ever since this committee began to sit upon it.

"Why, certainly, the Amalgamated Association of Porch Climbers and Sneak Thieves would like to get together and have the various state

A HANDSHAKE FOR MRS. ROOSEVELT FOLLOWS A 1940 DENUNCIATION OF THE PRESIDENT

acts covering their professions amended so that they might take ladies' purses with impunity.

"It all runs to the point that the Congress of the United States believed that this act was vitally necessary when it was enacted; that the act would run against certain industries and certain peoples and give protection to certain workers in industry, to the extent of many millions in the United States.

"We want this act to have a chance. We do not understand the necessity for this spectacle that has recently confronted the Republic, in the House of Representatives, where the Republican minority aided by a band of 100 or more renegade Democrats, have conducted a war dance around the bounden, prostrate form of labor in the well of that House, whirling like dervishes, and dancing with glee when that extraordinary combination is able to do something to hamstring labor in the United States.

"You know, the genesis of this campaign against labor in the House of Representatives is not hard to find.

"It is within the Democratic party. It runs across to the Senate of the United States and emanates there from a labor-baiting, poker-playing, whiskey-drinking, evil old man whose name is Garner.

"I am against him officially, individually, and personally, concretely and in the abstract, when his knife searches for the heart of my people.

"I object to Mr. Garner putting his foot upon the neck of millions of Americans by conducting this intrigue that he has been conducting in recent weeks in this Congress on every proposal that protected the rights of labor or sought to give labor increased or additional privilege.

"I say to this committee that all of these amendments should be laid aside in this session of Congress. And the people against whom this act is directed should come to know that the Congress of the United States and the Republic require and expect them to comply with the law.

"If the House of Representatives wants to do something, let it set aside some hours of debate, so that its great intellects can tell the American people where 12 million workers can get jobs. There is a job for them.

"Do not tinker and chisel away at acts that were passed with enthusiasm and great majorities and never given a chance to prove themselves."

Almost immediately after the Executive Council amputated the CIO unions from the AFL, efforts were made to bring about unity of the labor movement in America. Amateur "surgeons," including Secretary of Labor Perkins and President Roosevelt, tried to bring about a CIO-AFL amalgamation. But the "great brains" of the AFL, always fearful of their own job security, angrily demanded unconditional surrender by the CIO.

In October, 1937, at the first CIO conference, Mr. Lewis said:

"This movement must go on. We are 4 million strong today after less than two years of organizing effort. When two years more elapse, we will have more millions of members in our great movement. If the AFL chooses to lay aside its prejudices and join the CIO in working out a program of unity, it is well. If they elect not to do so, the responsibility for that decision will be upon their own heads and their own shoulders. But the CIO will go on. It will go on working out its own destiny—to make true some of the dreams of its millions of members."

Mr. Lewis delivered his valedictory on labor unity as CIO president at the 1940 convention in response to a resolution for exploring further possibilities of peace with the AFL:

"It must not be forgotten by those who preach peace, when there is no peace, that a large number of these organizations represented in this convention were expelled from the AFL, as was related by John Owens, without a trial for the crime and high offense of undertaking to organize these workers in the modern industries into membership in the AFL. And, keep in mind, that action has never been rescinded or revoked. And if the AFL were sincere or believed the words it sometimes utters, then the AFL should rescind the infamous action by which it expelled and drove from its own doors a million members in good standing who throughout the years had contributed of their strength and energy, their money and their services towards the upbuilding of an instrumentality that they hoped some day would come to represent their true labor.

"There is no peace because you are not yet strong enough to command peace upon honorable terms. And there will be no peace until you possess that strength of bone and sinew that will make it possible for you to bargain for peace on equal terms.

"The resolution read here this afternoon by one of the speakers said that we should go into a peace conference, or explore the mind, or explore the possibilities. We have explored every proposition. What have we all been doing? I have been an explorer in the AFL. Explore the mind of Bill Green? Why, Bill and I had offices next door to each other for ten years. I was a member of the same executive council that he was for one year. I have done a lot of exploring in Bill's mind and I give you my word there is nothing there. Explore Matthew Woll's mind? I did! It is the mind of an insurance agent.

"Waste more time on unprofitable explorations? Well, after all, I think there is a limit to which the membership of my organization should permit me to waste my time and their money.

"We have had numerous offers of peace. The

President called both sides down to the White House and said he would like to have peace. The CIO put forth a plan that there should be an assembly under the auspices of the President, a great peace conference composed of accredited representatives of the CIO, AFL and the Railroad Brotherhoods and form in one mighty organization of labor these great groups of millions of men and women.

"Mr. Green and his associates said the suggestion was outrageous because they knew that the Railroad Brotherhoods never before had been members of the AFL and that it was absurd and they said the plan would not be feasible.

"Later, in several public addresses throughout the country, I offered to recommend to the CIO another plan, if it were acceptable to the AFL, that on any given day of the week in any month I would recommend that the affiliates of the CIO would march into the AFL and become members thereof, with the understanding that a certificate of affiliation for charters would be issued to each unit of the CIO, after which a convention should be called of both organizations to work out details and select the leadership. It was denounced forthwith by the officers of AFL.

"Under those circumstances, I think it would be a waste of time to raise the hopes of millions of people in this country by making it falsely appear that there is any possibility of peace."

The unity controversy did not divert Mr. Lewis from his constant battle for mine safety. At Monongah, W. Va., where the worst mine disaster in American history took the lives of 361 coal miners in 1907, Mr. Lewis, on April 1, 1940, told of attempts to push the Neely-Keeler Mine Safety Bill through Congress:

"The United Mine Workers of America now, with the cooperation and with the help of West Virginia's great statesman in the Senate, United States Senator M. M. Neely, are trying to have enacted by the federal Congress a law that will provide for the federal inspection of coal mines by representatives appointed by the federal government, in order that the question of life or death in the coal mines may be raised higher than the mere plane of partisan political policies, and the question of enforcing the law of safety in the coal mines may not be left to the disposition of a man who, though a state inspector, or in charge of state inspectors, may be more responsive to the political influence which created him, than his desire to avoid the killing of men in the coal mines of America.

"When the Bartley explosion occurred, I called this matter to the attention of every Congressman and Senator, and urged that they

MR. LEWIS ON '40 TOWNSENDITE NATIONAL CONVENTION PLATFORM WITH SEN. WHEELER

Left to Right—Mr. Lewis, Sen. Burton K. Wheeler of Montana, Dr. Francis Townsend, Mrs. Lewis.

MR. LEWIS WITH LEADERS OF THE NAACP AT 1940 CONVENTION IN PHILADELPHIA, PA.

Left to Right—Arthur P. Spingarn, president of the National Association for the Advancement of Colored People; Mary White Ovington, NAACP founder; and Mr. Lewis.

make a contribution toward the enactment of this legislation. When the Willow Grove explosion occurred, we again called their attention to it. Through the good offices of Senator Neely, and many other honorable men in the United States Senate, that bill has passed the Senate of the United States, and is now pending in the House of Representatives."

It died in the House.

The UMWA convention of January, 1940, in Columbus, Ohio, observed the fiftieth anniversary of the founding of the United Mine Workers of America in that city. John Owens, president of the Ohio miners, made the keynote speech and introduced Mr. Lewis, who said:

"What a feeling of pride there must come to every delegate here attending in his representative capacity as an official representative of this union, to be able to participate in the deliberations of a convention as historical and as fraught with the potential implications of the future as the Thirty-sixth Constitutional Convention of the United Mine Workers of America!

"What a feeling of pride there must come to those delegates, to the wives and the members of their families who accompany them, and to the membership of our union at large when they realize that throughout all dangers and vicissitudes of a half century of struggle, effort and progress, that this union which was formed fifty years ago has reached one of its historic milestones! Who among us can lay claim to the wisdom that we can see ahead for fifty years or visualize for that length of time the conditions that might obtain or the instrumentalities that might then exist?

"And yet that little band of less than 200 men who met in this city fifty years ago must have had the vision and the foresight and the prescience to have seen in some way in some manner that their handiwork would last and endure for that period, would grow in influence and power through the years and eventuate in that wholesome, magnificent institution represented by this great union of ours."

The tenor of the convention changed when Mr. Lewis made a short speech on UMWA endorsement of presidential candidates in the coming national elections:

"As the current year opens, the Democratic Party is in default to the American people. After seven years of power, it finds itself without solution for the major questions of unemployment, low national income, mounting internal debt, increasing direct and consumer taxation and restricted foreign markets. There still exists the same national unhappiness that it faced seven years ago.

"I am one who believes that President Roosevelt will not be a candidate for re-election.

"The Republican Party can be prevented from winning only by an accord between the Democratic Party and organized labor, and the adoption of an intelligent and rational program to be written into the platform of the Democratic Party and placed before the American people as the issues of this election.

"In view of these facts and the attendant conditions, it would be unwise in my judgment for this convention at this time to bestow its endorsement upon any candidate for the presidency of the United States."

Mr. Lewis and the President had drifted a long distance apart since the fall of 1936. Campaign promises had been broken. FDR had promised to support labor. At best he had been neutral. He had promised to end unemployment. In spite of a pick-up in military spending, unemployment was almost as bad as it ever had been. And lesser promises had not been kept. In spite of platform pledges to poor people in the South, particularly, their economic and social position had not improved substantially during the years of the New Deal. At a UMWA eight-hour day celebration on April 1, 1940, in Monongah, W. Va., Mr. Lewis said:

"Between now and July 4 I expect to address two conventions of great Negro organizations in this country. And I am going to say to those representatives of the Negro race that it is an outrage and a shame that 8 million Negroes in America are prevented from voting in eight Southern states, because they do not have enough money to pay their poll tax for one year or for the accumulated years which

IT'S FUNNY TO MR. LEWIS, BUT ALF LANDON AT 1940 GOP POLICY MEETING ISN'T SURE

125

the taxes run in those states. In addition to those 8 million Negroes, there are millions of white Americans in the same situation who are disfranchised in the same manner, in order that they might be prevented from expressing themselves at the polls, as to who should represent that population in public offices of the state and federal government. Why, in some of our Southern states only 26 per cent of the population vote. In others of our Southern states only 24 per cent of the population vote, and in one Southern state only 18 per cent of the population are able to pay the price to vote through the iniquitous poll-tax arrangement. Talk about minority representation and a dictatorship of politicians! These are startling examples of how Americans are prevented from casting their vote on public questions because they are poor. Because they are poor! And being poor, they should not be permitted to express an opinion about what their master may desire. What a damnable condition!"

A third major issue on which Mr. Lewis' differences with President Roosevelt were irreconcilable further widened the gulf that separated them. In addition to FDR's broken promises to labor and his failure to solve the unemploy-

ment problem, Mr. Lewis was convinced that the President was leading the nation toward war. In a 1939 NBC Labor Day broadcast, Mr. Lewis said:

"Let us consider the plight into which incompetent industrial and political leadership has led this nation. Where does labor stand? Where does the nation stand as the year 1939 enters its final months? Of the many grave economic and political problems confronting us, that presented by our millions of unemployed workers is still by far the most serious. For ten years we have been struggling in the swamp of the great depression. We have sometimes climbed a little nearer solid ground, and at times we have slipped deeper into the mire. But the net effect of all the efforts that have been made is to leave the number of unemployed not far less than at the worst period of the depression. There has been some resumption of industrial activity in 1939, but it is scarcely enough to absorb the advance guard of the army of our unemployed.

UMW HEAD TELLS SENATE LABOR COMMITTEE OF PROPOSED 1940 WAGNER ACT REVISIONS

Left to Right—Sen. Robert A. Taft, Ohio; Sen. Allen J. Ellender, Louisiana; Mr. Lewis; and Sen. Elbert D. Thomas, Utah.

"In the face of the economic deal in America many of our statesmen are more concerned and agitated over the political quarrels in Europe. War has always been the device of the politically despairing and intellectually sterile statesman. It provides employment in the gun factories and begets enormous profits for those already rich. It kills off the vigorous males who, if permitted to live, might question the financial and political exploitation of the race. Above all, war perpetuates in imperishable letters on the scroll of fame and history, the names of its political creators and managers.

"Labor in America wants no war nor any part of war. Labor wants the right to work and live, not the privilege of dying by gunshot or poison gas to sustain the mental errors of current statesmen."

Despite Mr. Lewis' aversion to war, he recognized that the power lust of Hitler and Mussolini might force us to fight against Germany and Italy. In his opening address to the first CIO convention, Mr. Lewis said:

"We stand appalled today at what we witness in Europe. Whose heart can fail to become anguished as he reads in the daily press of the terrible abuses and atrocities and indignities and brutalities that are now being inflicted by the German government and some of the German people on the Jews of that nation? One of the most appalling events in history, shameful indeed to our concept of the ethics of our modern civilization, of which we boast, and harking back to the practices of the mediaeval ages, is the torture and debasement of a great race of people who only ask the right to live.

"The United States of America is under increasing pressure in the realm of foreign affairs. The United States of America may one of these days face a great external crisis. When this mad, blood-thirsty wolf of the German government inflicts its will upon the defenseless people of Germany, of Austria and of Czechoslovakia, and incites individuals in other countries to perpetrate the same atrocities in Europe, then it is possible that we will have to meet the German dictator as he tries to extend his domain into the realm of the Western Hemisphere. If that day comes, who is going to sustain the United States of America? Who is going to man its industries? Who is going to send its

JOHN L. LEWIS TELLS A NETWORK AUDIENCE IN 1940 HIS CHOICE IS WENDELL WILLKIE

young men to military ranks to engage in war? Labor! Labor! Who is going to protect the institutions of this country, those that are meritorious? Labor! Who is going to protect the titles to property and great wealth down through the generations in America? Labor!

"In consideration of all of these things; in consideration of the fact that we are Americans, and that we believe in the principles of our government, that we are willing to fight at any time to maintain that flag, we are going to ask from those who are the beneficiaries of that service and that attitude and that policy and that loyalty, we are going to ask proper treatment ourselves. Proper treatment ourselves! And I have every confidence that our government and our State Department will make emphatic representations to the German government, protesting the actions of that government in permitting these atrocities to be inflicted on the Jewish people. I say to the government of the United States if it takes that action, the 20 million members of the CIO and their dependents will support the government and uphold its hands."

And in a later speech at the same convention, he said:

"Labor is not blind to the facts of Europe's problems. It has a major stake in those problems. In war, labor must perform most of the

127

SIGHT OF CIO PRESIDENT LEWIS LAUNCHED
THIS DEMONSTRATION AT 1940 CONVENTION

work and do most of the dying. Upon labor always is inflicted most of the agony and the tragedy of war. Labor demands and must be accorded its rightful consideration in any emergency which affects national interest.

"So we meet under the shadow of the grave conditions which hang like a pall over civilization, under conditions where the voice of labor and the ill-treated in our own country become weaker because the air is filled with reverberations ensuing because of the involvement of civilized nations in war. And war, in all of its terrible forms and aspects down through the ages, has always operated to suppress the voice of those who are imposed upon. Under those circumstances, and under those conditions there is but one thing for the men and women of labor to do and that is, through the recognized instrumentality of labor organizations, to undertake to expand their numerical strength and organize the unorganized, and build up a modern labor movement here in America to such proportions that its voice may never be ignored here in our homeland whether it be for peace or whether it be for war."

Mr. Lewis lamented the coming of war because he knew that wars brought with them inevitable peril to individual liberties. In an address before a convention of the International Union of Mine, Mill and Smelter Workers

on September 1, 1940, Mr. Lewis declared:

"With the questions now confronting labor in this country, labor cannot be too strong, because its adversaries are powerful and influences are abroad in the world and in the nation; and they run to the question of whether or not your union is to be permitted to live and as to whether or not you, as a citizen, will continue to enjoy those privileges and those civil liberties that you have been taught to believe are inherently right and legal, and to which you are, as a man or a woman, inherently entitled.

"Why, already, if you read the papers this morning—concurrently with this threat to enact a bill for conscription of American citizens—in the Senate of the United States, Congressman Sabath has introduced a bill providing for twenty-one years in the penitentiary to any citizen who might do any one of a great number of things. Twenty-one years in the penitentiary!

"I thought that the principle of free speech and the expression of each man's opinion was an inherent right in this country, guaranteed by the Constitution, that the legislature or the Congress could not modify. And yet the press dispatches this morning say that a great Congressman of the United States wants to enact a bill that will prevent Americans from expressing

DISPLEASED? IMPATIENT? MR. LEWIS PACES PLATFORM AT ATLANTIC CITY CONVENTION

A DRAMATIC MOMENT AS THE GUARD CHANGES AT 1940 CIO CONVENTION IN ATLANTIC CITY

Left to Right—Philip Murray, Mr. Lewis, and Tom Kennedy, UMWA secretary-treasurer.

opinions! Opinions! As to the wisdom of any strategy or any policy! Why, Hitler could not do any worse than that, no matter how long he worked at it.

"Is it that in our feverish desire to protect ourselves against a Hitler, or a philosophy that is obnoxious to Americans, we utilize the same methods that were utilized by that dictator or by that totalitarian nation, which, in turn, will circumscribe and limit the freedom of Americans and break down those liberties which they now enjoy?"

Finally, the day came which organized labor had dreaded. The break between John L. Lewis and Franklin D. Roosevelt was made final by these words, spoken from Mr. Lewis' heart, in September, 1940.

In a nation-wide broadcast he said:

"I address all Americans. Our country is at one of the crossroads of its political destiny. The issues run deep and will inevitably affect the well-being and lives of every American. They will also affect the population of every other civilized country, and may well determine the stability or instability of all the free institutions of our present-day culture.

"The words I utter tonight represent my mature convictions. They are expressed because I believe that the men and women of labor, and all other Americans, are entitled to know the truth as I see it.

"I think the re-election of President Roosevelt for a third term would be a national evil of the

first magnitude. He no longer hears the cries of the people.

"It is obvious that President Roosevelt will not be re-elected for the third term unless he has the overwhelming support of the men and women of labor. If he is, therefore, re-elected, it will mean that the members of the Congress of Industrial Organizations have rejected my advice and recommendation. I will accept the result as being the equivalent of a vote of no confidence, and will retire as president of the Congress of Industrial Organizations, at its convention in November. This action will save our great movement, composed of millions of men and women, from the embarrassment and handicap of my leadership during the ensuing reign of President Roosevelt.

"President Roosevelt is asking the American people to contribute to him at least four more years out of their individual lives. What will he do with those lives and this nation in the next four years, and how does he propose to do it? He has not said, and he asks from the people a grant of discretionary power that would bind him to no course of action, except the unpredictable policies and adventures which he may later devise.

"After all, Americans are not a nation of guinea pigs, constantly subject to the vicissitudes of the economic and political experiments of an amateur, ill-equipped practitioner in the realm of political science.

"If not Roosevelt, whom do I recommend to do the job of making secure our nation and its people? Why, of course, I recommend the election of Wendell L. Willkie as the next President of the United States.

"He is a gallant American. He has opened his heart to the American people. He is not an aristocrat. He has the common touch. He was born in the briar and not to the purple. He has worked with his hands and has known the pangs of hunger. He has had experience in various fields of American enterprise and is an administrator and an executive.

"Wendell Willkie has said that he will put the

"MR. CIO" RESIGNS AT 1940 CONVENTION; BAGPIPES SALUTE INCOMING PHIL MURRAY

JOHN L. LEWIS AND MRS. LEWIS IN 1940
AFTER HE PICKED MURRAY TO HEAD CIO

unemployed to work; that he will abolish pauperism. He has said that he will increase the national income by working to increase the wages and incomes of those unemployed.

"He says that he will enlist the representative brains of the nation to do this job. He says that he will take the representatives of labor into his cabinet and into the policy-making agencies of government, to assist and cooperate in the economic rehabilitation of America.

"He has said that he will reduce the cost of operation of our government and thus reduce the taxes imposed upon individual citizens.

"He has said that he believes in, and will enforce the right of labor to organize, and will promote collective bargaining between industry and labor.

"He has said that he will preserve and maintain all social legislation previously enacted for the protection of labor and any other citizen.

"Wendell Willkie has given his guarantee to the American people that if elected President he will not send the sons of American mothers and American fathers to fight in foreign wars. He avers that he will not use the power and influence of this mammoth nation to promote or create war, but rather exercise that power and

that influence to abate war and promote and maintain peace between nations.

"This statement of principles and objectives entitles Mr. Willkie to the support of every thoughtful citizen."

When President Roosevelt was swept into office for a third term in the November, 1940, elections, John L. Lewis, true to his word, stepped aside as CIO president. Philip Murray, vice president of the UMWA, was chosen to succeed him.

At Mr. Lewis' first appearance on the platform at the CIO convention in 1940, the delegates' cheers for him lasted forty minutes. Mr. Lewis, at the conclusion of the demonstration, delivered his presidential farewell address to the CIO, the organization he had founded as the answer to the unrealized dreams of the millions of unorganized working men and women:

"Now, my friends, I came to this convention to make a report of my stewardship as your president. I have done my work. In just a day or two I will be out of this office, which

131

AS MR. LEWIS' DAUGHTER, KATHRYN, WEEPS HE ENDS HIS HISTORIC ERA AS CIO CHIEF

at the moment I occupy. I shall hope that whoever you elect as my successor, you will give him your support without stint. Tomorrow is yesterday gone and tomorrow also a day. I am concerned with tomorrow; and I care not what happened yesterday except insofar as the events of yesterday may bring wisdom to us to guide our steps tomorrow.

"We cannot stop to weep and wear sackcloth and ashes because something that happened yesterday did not meet with our approval or because we did not have a dream come true. Tomorrow is the day that always faces men and women; and among the masses of this country are those who would be workers if they had jobs and a right to participate in our internal economy.

"In their homes always is the problem of tomorrow. Will the family eat tomorrow, and will they have shelter from the inclemency of the weather? And tomorrow, as they go down the years of life's brief existence, there falls on every man and woman the shadow and the menace of the tomorrow that brings the evening of life and whether they will become public charges, or perhaps just be one of those people who die on a pallet without medicine or a physician.

"There is a dark cloud that hovers over the minds of men and women of America. And this movement of ours can do something to remove that menace by being brave and being forthright, by being diligent and by demanding consideration for those human requirements that we all know, by every method and means, are virtuous and justifiable.

"Keep your organization alive and strong! And you can perhaps do more on those things than any other instrumentality in American life, because after all you represent the common people of this country who, without you, are inarticulate and a subject of constant exploitation—to the point of life itself.

"While I have served you, I have told you the truth as I saw it, according to my light and understanding. I have been doing that for a long time; I don't think I shall change. You know when you first hired me I was something of a man, and when I leave you in a day or two I will still, in my own mind, be something of a man. So thank you, my friends, thank you for the reception you gave me. I appreciate it."

132

COAL AND BAYONETS

EVERY YEAR IS A "year of destiny" to politicians and Fourth of July orators, but no oratory was required for Americans to recognize 1941 as one of the fateful years in world history.

By the end of that year, the civilized world was immersed in war. The American Navy had been struck a deadly blow by Japanese air power at Pearl Harbor. The German Army was overrunning Russia as fast as its transportation could carry it. Great Britain, armed mostly with spirit and Spitfires, was fighting with her back to the wall.

As 1941 opened, the United States was still at peace. But signs of imminent war were growing. American men were being drafted into the army and aid to the British had become material as well as moral.

John L. Lewis had resigned as president of the CIO because he had given his word that he would do so if President Roosevelt were reelected and also because, as he has since drily remarked, "I had some chores to perform for the organization that pays me, the United Mine Workers of America." He realized that his "chores" would have to be done quickly because war would mean an end to labor's advances and would mark the beginning of an era when unions could expect oppressive legislation and a desperate fight to hold their own.

In speaking of his resignation as head of the

CIO, Mr. Lewis later told a miners' meeting:

"I don't think I need to say in a meeting of the United Mine Workers of America that when I retired from the CIO presidency I was glad to get out. I had wanted to get out the year before, because I could see—I believed I could see—some of the things that were coming in the future and some of the problems that would be facing us, and I was weary and worn from five or six years of bitter struggle and controversy.

"I wanted to be a one-union man for a while. I had in my mind's eye plans and suggestions to make to our people that would mean more bread and butter on the kitchen table of every coal miner in America and would bring the UMWA into the position of security of which its founders and its supporters had dreamed for a half century of time."

The first fruit of the individual effort of the miners' "one-union man" came in March, 1941, when Congress passed a mine inspection law. The two-year drive to push the act through was spearheaded by Mr. Lewis and John T. Jones, District 16 president and newly appointed head of Labor's Non-Partisan League. The officers' report to the 1942 UMWA convention briefly tells the law's provisions:

"The new law requires the Secretary of the Interior to investigate the causes of mine explosions and mine accidents and to recommend

measures for improving the health and safety conditions in the coal mines of the nation."

The biggest "chore" to be done in 1941 was to negotiate new wage agreements in the anthracite and bituminous industries.

The bituminous negotiations of that year were long and bitter. They opened on March 11 and the final contract—another battle won by the UMWA—was not signed until July 5. The UMWA, with elimination of the 40-cent differential, became the first union to wipe out the wage differential between North and South. The universal basic daily wage became $7, a token annual vacation payment of $20 was obtained, and the union shop became universal in the commercial mines, even in Harlan County.

After three weeks of unsuccessful bargaining in March, the miners stopped work. Dr. John R. Steelman, head of the U. S. Conciliation Service, intervened and found that the Southern operators were balking at the UMWA proposal, supported by the Northern Appalachian operators, that the 40-cent differential be eliminated.

THE PENNANT TELLS A DRAMATIC STORY OF UMWA CONTRIBUTION TO THE ARMED FORCES

On April 11, the Southerners withdrew from the conference and later appealed to President Roosevelt to have their case referred to the National Defense Mediation Board.

After the departure of the Southern operators, Charles O'Neill, spokesman for the Northern operators, and Mr. Lewis held a joint press conference at which Mr. Lewis said:

"Obviously, there can be no agreement here while these Northern economic carpetbaggers,

WORKING OUT TERMS OF A NEW BITUMINOUS AGREEMENT IN NEW YORK CITY, MARCH, 1941

Seated, Left to Right—Mr. Lewis, Ezra Van Horn, operator chairman of the joint conference; Charles O'Neill, chief operator spokesman; L. T. Putnam, operator. *Standing, Left to Right*—Percy Tetlow, UMWA technical adviser; William Hynes, District 4 president; John Owens, District 6 president; John Hatton, District 24 president; J. B. Morrow, L. C. Gunter, operators.

MR. LEWIS: "BEST DEFENSE FOR AMERICA IS FAIR AND JUST TREATMENT OF ITS WORKERS"

Seated—Ezra Van Horn, operator, chairman of the 1941 bituminous joint wage conference.

who call themselves Southern coal operators, are holding up the coal industry by the thumbs."

On April 19, Secretary of Labor Frances Perkins recommended that mines belonging to operators with whom the UMWA had reached an understanding should reopen, but both operators and the union rejected her request.

Two days later, the President recommended

that talks be resumed. The Southern operators went back to New York City, negotiated briefly and returned to Washington.

As a result of this second walkout, Secretary Perkins certified the case to the National Defense Mediation Board. A panel of the board recommended that the mines reopen on April 28 on the basis agreed to by the Northern operators, eliminating the differential.

The Northern operators signed a temporary agreement on that basis on April 29; the Southerners followed on April 30. At resumed negotiations on May 12, however, the Southerners again balked and the mediation board reopened hearings. The board findings were made public by Chairman William H. Davis and, in the main, they were favorable to the UMWA.

The Northern Appalachian operators signed the new agreement on June 19 and the Southern operators signed on July 5.

While Mr. Lewis was negotiating with two

DISTRICTS 1, 7, 9 PRESENT PROPOSALS TO THE ANTHRACITE OPERATORS, APRIL 8, 1941

From left around rear of table—W. W. Inglis, operator; John T. Kmetz, District 1 board member; Hubert Farrell, UMWA; Michael Kosik, District 1 president; Peter M. Flyzik, UMWA; Hugh Brown, District 7 president; Joseph Kershetsky, District 7; Mart F. Brennan, District 9 president; UMWA Secretary-Treasurer Thomas Kennedy; Mr. Lewis; John Boylan, Anthracite Board of Conciliation. *From left in front of table*—L. R. Close, J. B. Warriner, James Prendergast, C. A. Garner, H. J. Connolly, Ralph E. Taggart, James H. Pierce and Santo Volpe, all anthracite operators.

groups of soft coal operators during the spring of 1941, he also had to meet with the anthracite operators. Anthracite negotiations opened in New York City on April 8. Again, the officers' report to the 1942 convention tells what happened:

"The conference was in session six weeks. During the course of the negotiations, the old agreement, expiring April 30, was extended several times with the provision that, when a new contract was eventually written, it would be retroactive to May 1. On May 17, which was the expiration date of the last retroactive extension, it was impossible to conclude an agreement within the allotted time and a suspension of work occurred as of midnight, May 17. Negotiations, however, were continued and on Sunday, May 18, the operators agreed to write a contract on the basis of a wage increase of 7½ per cent dated from May 1, 1941, to and including September 30, 1941, with said increase to become 10 per cent October 1, 1941, and continuing for the balance of the contract, until April 30, 1941, and a token payment of $20 to each person for a vacation period. A new contract was written and under date of May 24, 1941, was submitted to our anthracite membership for approval or rejection by referendum vote. It was approved by a vote of 59,663 to 8,208."

The contract was signed at Hazleton, Pa., on June 20, 1941.

The last big company to be organized by the CIO before the war also signed a contract on June 20. Rugged individualist Henry Ford signed an agreement which included union shop and check-off clauses after an intensive five-year organizing drive led by the UMWA's Michael Widman.

In 1940, a UMWA-sponsored production allocation program for the anthracite industry was started. It was designed to equalize working time for all anthracite miners. By the spring of 1941, it was operating successfully. In their report to the 1942 convention, the UMWA's International officers explained how the plan was administered:

"The production control plan for the anthracite industry is a voluntary plan whereby production is related to market demand. The plan functions under an act of the Pennsylvania leg-

---

A CIGAR SMOKER AND A PIPE SMOKER CONFER ON THE APRIL, 1941, SOFT-COAL STOPPAGE

Mr. Lewis and Van A. Bittner, UMWA representative.

EMPHASIZING OBJECTIONS TO THE PROPOSED ST. LAWRENCE SEAWAY ON JULY 28, 1941

---

islature and is administered by the Anthracite Committee, which is made up of three representatives of labor, the presidents of Districts 1, 7, and 9, UMWA; three representatives of the State, the Attorney General, the Secretary of Commerce and the Secretary of Mines; and three operators elected by the cooperating producers."

A bill to create a St. Lawrence Seaway was first introduced during the 1934 session of Congress. Its proponents, including Presidents Roosevelt and Truman, have tried to push it through every session since that time. It was last defeated in July, 1952.

Thomas Kennedy has led the UMWA's fight against the "Iceway," but in July, 1941, Mr. Lewis, himself, appeared before the House Rivers and Harbors Committee to present a definitive outline of the miners' objections to the bill:

"The UMWA insists that electricity generated by the project will displace coal. We contend that for every 2 thousand kilowatt hours produced by this project, one ton of coal will be displaced.

"Steam generated plants can be constructed at a cost of $68 million that will provide the power proposed by the St. Lawrence develop-

ment, which would in the end cost more than a billion dollars and subject all of our American markets to tramp ship delivery of slave-produced foreign commerce.

"Rejected in 1934 as being totally unnecessary for either power or commerce, it is here again in a new dress—patriotism. It is being propelled by all the adjectives known to the seasoned campaigner, plus all of the wartime facilities of an over-recruited, high-powered publicity staff.

"Since we have failed to make any assured permanent progress in solving our unemployment problems, I cannot understand how, in the name of common sense, even though disguised in the new dress of defense and progress, this committee can act favorably on this proposal, which in the end means a graduated, mounting scale of unemployment that in time will displace 50 thousand, and maybe more, American workingmen."

Immediately after the Southerners had signed the Appalachian Agreement in 1941, a fourth dispute commenced, the famous "captive mines dispute" of that year.

Its story is told in the words of the officers' report to the 1942 convention:

"After the new Appalachian Agreement had been signed by Northern and Southern commercial mines, as well as by the captive mines of 70 per cent of the public utilities, railroads, steel manufacturing and other companies, eleven of the large steel corporations operating captive mines, employing approximately 50 thousand workers, refused to accept the agreement because of its union shop provisions. Of the large steel companies, the Jones & Laughlin Steel Corporation, alone, entered into an agreement with the mine workers.

"Prolonged but unsuccessful efforts were made by representatives of the UMWA to secure agreements with these recalcitrant companies. Finally, President Lewis, under authorization by the National Policy Committee, recommended a strike of captive mine workers September 15, 1941. More than 45 thousand immediately ceased work. For the first time in the history of these steel corporations, their mines were completely closed down.

"On the same day that more than 45 thousand men responded to the strike order, September 15, Chairman William H. Davis, of the

National Defense Mediation Board, claimed that the board had jurisdiction over the case and called upon the striking miners to return to work immediately pending a hearing by the board in Washington two days later."

The board's hearings opened on September 17 and, on September 19, the UMWA agreed to a thirty-day truce, during which the captive mines would be operated under the terms of the Appalachian Agreement, with the exception of the union shop clause, provided that collective bargaining sessions would be carried on during the truce.

President Roosevelt then suggested that Mr. Lewis meet with Myron C. Taylor, former U. S. Steel board chairman. On October 25, Mr. Lewis wrote the President that he would be glad to meet with Mr. Taylor, but added that the mediation board had evaded its duty when it failed to rule on the union shop issue.

The story continues from the officers' report to the 1942 convention:

"On October 26, President Roosevelt again wrote President Lewis, insisting that he confer with Mr. Taylor and that the mine workers resume work in advance of the meeting.

"On the next day all captive mines where wage agreements were not in effect were closed down. President Lewis also replied to President Roosevelt's letter of the preceding day, telling him that Mr. Taylor had already advised him that he (Mr. Taylor) did not possess authority to speak for the steel industry.

"On the same day that President Lewis' letter was written and received by President Roosevelt, the latter replied with another request that the captive mines be reopened unconditionally.

"On the morning of October 29, President Lewis and Mr. Taylor entered into conference at the latter's hotel. Several hours later, Chairman Davis of the mediation board joined them. The three later visited the White House to confer with President Roosevelt.

"As a result of this meeting, President Lewis agreed to recommend that the mines be reopened pending a decision on the captive mines controversy by the full mediation board, such decision not to be binding on either party to the dispute.

"On the afternoon of the next day, President Lewis and Mr. Taylor received representatives of the press, and President Lewis praised Mr. Taylor for his constructive attitude and assistance. He said: 'The entire basis of this agreement was the conference between Mr. Taylor and me yesterday. It may be recalled that seven years ago Mr. Taylor and I settled the captive mine controversy. In 1937 we substantially negotiated the contract covering present relations in the steel industry. At that time, I stated in a public statement that Mr. Taylor was an industrial statesman of far-seeing vision. I reiterate that today.'

"As Chairman Davis had advised President Roosevelt that in his opinion the board could render a decision within a week, it was announced by President Lewis that unless the board reached a decision by November 15 the strike would be resumed.

"All intelligent sources of opinion indicated that the UMWA would receive favorable action from the board. But on November 10, when the decision of the board was announced, all appraisers and forecasters were unprepared for the astounding revelation that the decision was nine to two against the union shop.

"On the day following the decision, Vice President Murray and Secretary Kennedy resigned from the board. All UMWA and CIO alternates on the board also resigned. Moreover, John Owens, president of District 6, UMWA, and of the Ohio Industrial Union Council, also resigned as labor adviser of the OPM. He stated that he could not continue to serve a governmental agency which accepted the open shop as a declared policy. Thus, the infamous captive mine decision finally culminated in the liquidation of the National Defense Mediation Board.

"On November 19, President Roosevelt made the following offer to UMWA representatives and steel officials:

" 'I am asking all of you, as patriotic Americans, to accept one or the other of the following alternatives:

" '(a) Allow the matter of the closed (sic) shop in the captive mines to remain in status quo for the period of the national emergency, or

" '(b) Submit this point to arbitration, agreeing in advance to accept the decision so made for the period of the national emergency.'

"The President's proposal was submitted to the Policy Committee and it was decided that the union would agree to arbitrate.

"President Roosevelt then wrote Mr. Lewis

and informed him: 'I am appointing a board of three members consisting of Dr. John R. Steelman, as the public representative; Mr. Benjamin Fairless, representative of the steel industry; and Mr. John L. Lewis, representing the mine workers.

" 'Dr. Steelman possesses the qualifications essential to the task of public representative and is of unquestioned integrity.'

"The arbitration board, as thus constituted, met and conducted its proceedings in New York City. On December 7, 1941, it handed down an award granting the union shop signed by John R. Steelman and John L. Lewis, with Benjamin F. Fairless dissenting."

The miners had won their struggle for the union shop in the captive mines, the last open-shop section of the coal industry. The strike

---

HARD-COAL MINERS WIN WAGE BOOSTS IN ANTHRACITE AGREEMENT OF MAY 20, 1941

With Mr. Lewis is Maj. W. W. Inglis, operator chairman of the joint conference.

that had been emblazoned in banner headlines all through the autumn of 1941, the strike that had brought jingoist vituperation on John Lewis' head for three months was settled.

But the news of the settlement was buried under small headlines in the back pages of the morning papers on Monday, December 8, 1941. The Japanese had struck on Sunday. America was at war. Americans began to read of their beleaguered garrisons in faraway places—Wake Island, Guam, Bataan and Corregidor.

The entire nation girded itself for a bloody conflict. John L. Lewis, like all patriotic Americans, pledged unstinting effort until the war was won. Immediately after Pearl Harbor had been attacked, he said:

"When the nation is attacked, every American must rally to its defense. All other considerations become insignificant. Congress and administrative government must be supported, and every aid given to the men in the combat services of our country.

"Each true American will cooperate and unified effort becomes a living reality. With all other citizens, I join in the support of our government to the day of its ultimate triumph over Japan and all other enemies."

And the miners, themselves, pledged at their 1942 convention:

"The war must be won by America and won at any cost. No sacrifice is too great for any one of us to make in this death struggle for a free life for our children and their children, for all time to come.

"The United Mine Workers of America, from its International officers down to the trapper boy at the most remote wagon mine in the country, stand ready and willing at all times to answer our country's call for service in this great struggle, regardless of the form in which that call may come or from what source it may be heard. We are Americans, first, last, and always."

The mine workers lived up to that pledge. While miners were being killed and injured at home, their sons and brothers were fighting and dying all over the world in the armed services of their country. The miners expected no reward except a free United States of America to live in after the war.

The officers' report to the 1946 convention tells statistically the magnificent story of the UMWA's contribution to the war effort:

UNITED STATES OF AMERICA
Inducted into the Armed Services.... 162,136
Killed, Died, Missing in Action...... 3,345
Wounded 10,125
War Savings Bond Purchases... $175,000,000
Contributions to War Relief
    Agencies $5,000,000

DOMINION OF CANADA
Inducted into the Armed Services.... 8,123
Killed, Died, Missing in Action...... 299
Wounded 500
War Bond Purchases.......... $10,693,000
Contributions to War Relief
    Agencies $450,000

GRAND TOTAL FOR BOTH NATIONS
Serving in the Armed Forces........ 170,259
Killed, Died, Missing in Action...... 3,644
Wounded 10,625
Value of War Bond Purchases.. $185,693,000
Contributions to War Relief
    Agencies $5,450,000

Even more of the men who stayed home to mine coal were killed and injured. The following figures, taken from Bureau of Mines reports, show the number of American coal miners who were killed and hurt in mining accidents during the war years:

Year	Killed	Injured
1941	1,266	63,465
1942	1,471	69,564
1943	1,451	64,594
1944	1,294	65,900
1945	1,079	59,350
Total	6,561	322,873

The record speaks for itself—more than 10 thousand miners killed and more than 333 thousand hurt, fighting in the mines at home and on the battlefronts abroad. The United States Treasury wrote a letter after the war which said that the United Mine Workers of America had made the largest financial contribution per capita of any organization in the country. The mine workers' war record was not surpassed by any other organization in the United States.

Immediately after Pearl Harbor, the federal government took steps to insure wartime labor-management cooperation. The inadequacy of its effort is told in these excerpts from the officers' report to the 1942 convention:

"On December 17, 1941, there assembled, at the request of the President, a conference of labor, employer and government representatives to formulate means for eliminating serious disputes in the war industries. President John L. Lewis was among the labor members of the conference. President Lewis, conscious of the reasons for the failure of the National Defense Mediation Board, urged upon the conference the adoption of a code of principles and policies to govern the work of any new mediation or arbitration which might be set up."

President Roosevelt rejected Mr. Lewis' proposals, but on December 23, 1941, accepted the three-point report of the conference that there be no strikes or lockouts, that all disputes be settled by peaceful means, and that the President set up a war labor board to handle these disputes. FDR said: "The particular disputes must be left to the consideration of those who can study the particular differences and who are thereby prepared by knowledge to pass judgment in the particular case."

The officers' report goes on:

"On January 12, 1942, the President provided for the establishment of a National War Labor Board composed of twelve members.

"In setting up this new board, there was again an utter failure to provide any basic principles for the guidance of the board. The board, however, was given the necessary authority to set up principles of its own.

"It is clearly apparent that the WLB cannot hope to be effective if it bases its procedure and decisions upon such arbitrary formulae as the 15 per cent formula developed in the 'Little Steel' case."

But the WLB took the easy way out. To avoid the trouble of judging each case on its individual merits, it froze wages at the arbitrary "Little Steel" level—15 per cent above the wage level of January, 1941. That particular date was selected with the UMWA in mind. The board knew that the mine workers had received a pay boost in the spring of 1941 and would thus be ineligible for any further increases for the duration. So, in exchange for its no-strike pledge, labor was given a wage strait jacket and a War Labor Board mainly composed of "psuedo-intellectual nitwits" who had been "public" members of the unsuccessful National Defense Mediation Board.

The year 1942 saw a rift come between the CIO and the UMWA which culminated in the removal of Philip Murray as vice president of the UMWA on May 28, and the UMWA's formal withdrawal from the CIO on October 7. It was a breach which was started by Mr. Murray's objections to Mr. Lewis' renewed efforts to bring about unity in the labor movement.

On January 17, 1942, Mr. Lewis wrote identical letters to Mr. Murray and William Green, AFL president, which asked that representatives of both the AFL and CIO meet to discuss organic unity. Mr. Lewis believed that labor could best battle wartime restrictions if it presented a united front.

MYRON C. TAYLOR, FORMER U. S. STEEL HEAD, AND MR. LEWIS MEET, OCTOBER 29, 1941

President Green's reply to President Lewis accepted the peace proposal in behalf of the AFL.

President Murray replied that the proposal would be referred to the CIO Executive Board meeting on January 24 in New York. It added:

"As you are well aware, all arrangements in behalf of the CIO with reference to unity with the AFL will necessarily have to be initiated through the office of the president of the CIO."

But the 1940 CIO convention had authorized a standing labor-unity committee, empowered to initiate unity talks at any time. Mr. Lewis was chairman and the other members were Mr. Murray and Sidney Hillman. The chairman had been authorized to act for the committee. Mr. Lewis immediately wrote the CIO president:

"Your letter dated January 19 states, in effect, that all future negotiations between the AFL and the CIO will have to be initiated by you, and you alone.

"Such an assumption on your part constitutes an astonishing error.

"Your letter and public statements imply that I have taken it upon myself to assume the authority to blueprint some plan for labor peace between the CIO and the AFL and that, in addition, I have tentatively agreed to certain leadership that might in the end dismember the CIO if such a coalition were formed. Nothing could be further from the truth. I have made no commitments of any character to anyone that affect any phase of this problem."

There were other signs of a split. The UMWA, financial pillar of the CIO, also had money differences with the CIO during the early months of 1942. The officers' report to the 1942 convention gives the bare facts:

"The financial assistance of the UMWA to the CIO, up to February 1, 1942, amounted to $7,249,303.84. Of this amount, $1,685,000 was in the form of negotiated loans to the CIO. Twenty thousand dollars was later repaid, leaving a balance due the United Mine Workers of America of $1,665,000.

"The officers of your union made no formal

THE ARBITRATION BOARD THAT SETTLED THE 1941 CAPTIVE MINES UNION SHOP DISPUTE

Left to Right—Benjamin Fairless, president, U. S. Steel Corp.; John R. Steelman, director, U. S. Conciliation Service; Mr. Lewis.

demand upon the CIO for repayment of this loan. In February, 1942, the secretary-treasurer of the UMWA requested the comptroller of the CIO to credit the UMWA with payment of two months' tax, amounting to $60 thousand, and deduct this item from our loan account. The officers of the CIO refused this request and disavowed their obligation to the UMWA. In consequence, since that time your officers have made no further payment of per capita tax to the CIO until such time as a report could be made to this convention."

Early in May, 1942, Mr. Murray visited his home district in the Pittsburgh area, the UMWA's District 5, and unsuccessfully tried to arouse sentiment against Mr. Lewis among the miners. He also took a $20 thousand dollar a year job as president of the United Steelworkers of America, constituted in 1941. The UMWA officers reported to the 1942 convention:

"In May, 1942, the vice president of the International Union accepted an elective office with another union. This action was in violation of definite provisions of the constitution of this organization, and the International Executive Board, with the International Policy Committee concurring, declared the office vacant.

"Mr. John O'Leary, previously a member of the board from District 5, was designated to fill the vacancy. His nomination was confirmed by the board, with the Policy Committee concurring. He assumed the office of vice president of the UMWA on May 28, 1942."

In June, 1942, the CIO stepped up its anti-UMWA propaganda and launched organizing raids against the UMWA's District 50.

In July, John Owens, president of the Ohio CIO Industrial Union Council, sent the following telegram to Philip Murray:

"Returning commission as representative of the CIO. Your obnoxious attacks upon a gentleman, a great labor statesman and a great American, John L. Lewis, make it impossible for me any longer to cooperate with you. I am resigning as president of the Ohio CIO."

Other mine workers followed suit. Thomas Kennedy in Pennsylvania, William Mitch in Alabama, and the vast majority of miners resigned their CIO positions and again became "one-union men."

At the opening of the October, 1942, UMWA convention, UMWA-CIO relations had reached the breaking point. The officers recommended to the convention that:

"The United Mine Workers of America now officially withdraw from the CIO and direct

143

their subordinate units and members to withdraw from any official participation in the affairs, or affiliation with any unit, of the CIO until such time as the CIO sees fit to correct its errors, desist from its policy of denunciation and antagonistic attitude toward the United Mine Workers of America and recognize its valid financial obligation."

On October 7, 1942, the UMWA convention confirmed the action. Virtually all of the mine workers severed their CIO connections. Notable exceptions were Van A. Bittner, president of District 17, and P. T. Fagan, president of District 5. Mr. Bittner resigned his UMWA post. Mr. Fagan, after a campaign in which he bitterly denounced Mr. Lewis, was defeated in the election for the presidency of District 5 by John P. Busarello. Joseph Yablonski was elected District 5 International Executive Board member despite efforts of Fagan and Murray to defeat him.

DECEMBER 15, 1941—BILL OF RIGHTS DAY— SEES STEEL INDUSTRY SIGN UNION SHOP PACT

Left to Right—Mr. Lewis and Harry M. Moses, president, H. C. Frick Coal & Coke Co.

The Mine Workers Journal got a new editor in 1942. The officers' report to the 1942 convention said:

"The period since the last convention has witnessed the retirement, because of age and ill health, of Mr. Ellis Searles, who for twenty-three years has been editor of the United Mine Workers Journal. During that time, Mr. Searles has served the organization with loyalty to its ideals and efficiency in the administration of the managerial and editorial work of the Journal.

"The position of editor has been assumed by Mr. K. C. Adams, whose association with the UMWA covers a thirty-year period."

Mr. Searles, a fine, old-school Hoosier journalist, died on February 13, 1945, at the age of seventy-eight.

On June 2, 1942, Mr. Lewis sent a commission, headed by Major Percy Tetlow and including Curtis Mundell, Charles Funcannon, Frank D. Wilson and John Ghizzoni to investigate contract violations by the operators in District 17.

The commission recommended that the district, largest in the UMWA, be divided in two. On July 9, 1942, the International Executive Board, re-established District 29, with headquar-

JOHN O'LEARY OF DISTRICT 5 BECOMES UMWA VICE PRESIDENT ON REMOVAL OF MR. MURRAY

ters at Beckley, W. Va. The new district included all mines producing smokeless coal in West Virginia.

Its officers were George J. Titler, president, and D. M. Stamper, secretary-treasurer. Paul K. Reed succeeded Mr. Titler as secretary-treasurer of District 17.

The anthracite industry took another step forward through the Anthracite Coal Research Bill, which was passed by Congress and signed by the President on December 18, 1942. It authorized $450 thousand for building and equipment and $175 thousand annually for the maintenance and operation of a laboratory in the anthracite region of Pennsylvania for research in mining and utilization of anthracite coal.

This law was about the last good legislation the UMWA got for the duration. In January, 1943, Mr. Lewis wrote an article for the Scripps-Howard newspapers in which he told of his disillusionment over the government's attitude toward labor. He said:

"Army, Navy and procurement buying on a cost-plus basis puts a premium upon inefficiency, extravagance, war brokers' fees and black market operations—the higher the manufacturer's costs, the greater his unit profits and financial rewards.

"The government's attitude toward organized labor is diametrically opposite. An arbitrary formula has been devised, known as the 'Little Steel' formula, which deprives labor of any wage increase in excess of 15 per cent, subsequent to January, 1941. This formula is an outrageous breach of the no-strike agreement between labor and the government, made in December, 1941. At that conference, labor abandoned the right to strike for the duration, contingent upon the government's creating an agency that would judiciously determine labor's complaints against management. The WLB violates the government agreement with labor each day that it operates.

"In March, the coal industry wage negotiations will begin. At that conference, the men who mine the nation's coal will ask for bread.

145

MICHAEL WIDMAN OF UMWA, WHO ORGANIZED
FORD MOTOR CO. WORKERS, WITH MR. LEWIS

They will hope that a government bureaucrat
will not hand them a stone."

The War Labor Board could offer only the
same old, buy-no-groceries "Little Steel" formula. The board's pettiness and political chi-
canery gave reactionary elements the chance to
bait labor they had been waiting for and provoked the stalemate which prevented negotiation
of a contract.

The anti-union propaganda that was un-
leashed in 1943 and 1944 has seldom been
equalled. Southern Democrats and right-wing
Republicans in Congress hurled their choicest
epithets at Mr. Lewis and the miners. They
combined to pass the infamous Smith-Connally
Act. Newspaper columnists, led by the one Mr.
Lewis calls "Peg-leg Wesler," used their complete file of nasty adjectives to villify the mine
workers. Editorial pages in the press were wide-
open to labor-baiters. Soldiers were told in their
newspaper, "Stars and Stripes," that John Lewis

was another Benedict Arnold. President Roosevelt threatened to send soldiers into mining
communities to see that the coal was mined.

But the miners and John L. Lewis stood firm.
They knew they were right. They listened
grimly to the wild talk and rallied themselves
with the cry, "You can't mine coal with bay-
onets."

The best account of that tense time was an
article, "Not Guilty," written by John L. Lewis
and published in the July 15, 1944, issue of
Collier's Magazine. Mr. Lewis wrote:

"For a year and more, I have been branded
Public Enemy No. 1, and the 600 thousand
members of the United Mine Workers have been
stigmatized as malcontents who put mean greeds
above the welfare of their country. No other
labor executive or union has been subjected to
any such bitter, cruel and sustained attack.

"Fortunately, there is a record that gives the
lie to every charge leveled against our patriotism.
In 1943, when our work stoppages were alleged
to have cut production down to the danger
point, we mined 9 million more tons of bituminous coal than in 1942 and with 25 thousand
fewer men. For the first four months of 1944,

146

we produced 10,244,000 tons more than in the comparable period of 1943, and with 45 thousand less men.

"Inspired propaganda is responsible for a general belief that the United Mine Workers took advantage of the national emergency to make exorbitant wage demands—blackmail, to put it plainly. Nothing is further from the truth. On March 10, 1943, twenty-one days before the expiration of our contract, we sat down with the operators to argue out an agreement that would cover another two-year period.

"At the outset of the conference, we asked for a wage adjustment that would lift the daily rate from $7 to $9. As an answer to the cry of blackmail, let me cite some of the reasons behind our request.

"Under our contract, the miners worked a five-day week. Not that this was our choice. Always, and particularly at the outbreak of war, we had urged a longer working time. Assuming employment for 260 days at $7 a day, that would be an annual wage of $1,820. But due to accidents, shutdowns, and repairs, the average for the year was 231 days, and the average annual wage $1,617. Does that seem a princely sum for a man with a family?

"Even this amount, however, was not his 'take home' pay. Tonnage men were required to pay for their tools, blasting powder, fuses, blacksmithing, the upkeep of pit lights, the rental of their electric caps, and the salary of a checker. In addition, they had to buy special safety clothing, not the least item being three or four pairs of expensive boots during the year. By reason of these deductions, the net annual wage of a coal miner ranged from $1,000 to $1,700.

"These wages, poor enough in peacetime, fell below a decent subsistence level in wartime. Mines, unhappily, are not located in or near populous centers, but in remote places where competition does not operate to keep down prices. Of the 4,200 'company stores' in the United States, 3,500 are in the coal regions, and all are a source of rich profit to the companies. By 1943, prices in these stores had increased as much as 100 per cent, entailing actual privation.

"In 1938, the Fair Labor Standards Act stated specifically that travel time in a mine should be regarded as working time. A United States Circuit Court had upheld the law in a case involving iron-ore miners, and in 1941 the Fifth Cir-

AT THE START OF THE FIGHT AGAINST THE "LITTLE STEAL" FORMULA, JANUARY 15, 1943

Front, Left to Right—Secretary-Treasurer Thomas Kennedy; Percy Tetlow, District 17 president; Mr. Lewis. *Rear, Left to Right*—Robert Howe, UMWA representative; Welly K. Hopkins, UMWA counsel.

cuit Court of Appeals sustained the decision. I might add, parenthetically, that the Supreme Court of the United States, in May of this year, ruled that portal-to-portal time constituted 'compensable work.'

"When, therefore, we faced the operators on March 10, the $9 day was not regarded as a wage increase by us, but as compensation commanded by law and upheld by two judicial decisions. Even so, it was not put forward as a demand, but as a basis for bargaining. Instead of facing us as a body, however, willing to work out a wage agreement that would cover the nation, the Southern companies split off from those of the North, forcing us to run from one to the other.

"Worse still, it soon stood apparent that neither group had any thought of bargaining in good faith, both rejecting our proposals without a single counter-suggestion. Secretary Ickes, looking back over the record at a later date, stated flatly that the operators went into conference 'determined to block agreement.'

"By March 22, when no progress had been made, President Roosevelt asked that negotiations be continued beyond the time of contract expiration. We agreed at once to an extension

until April 30, but the attitude of the operators remained unchanged. Their secret purpose was soon revealed, for on April 22 Madam Perkins certified the case to the WLB. I said then, and I say now, that it was a brazen breach of faith; for our agreement to the thirty-day extension was based on the explicit understanding that negotiations would continue. But that was not our only reason for refusing to acknowledge the jurisdiction of the board. Our other principal objections were these:

"An utter lack of confidence in the board, proceeding from the deep conviction that it was a hodge-podge body whose decisions went by

---

UMWA'S '43 ANTHRACITE NEGOTIATORS MEET ON CONTRACT IN SCRANTON, MARCH 4, 1943

Left to Right—Mart F. Brennan, District 7 president; UMWA Secretary-Treasurer Thomas Kennedy; Mr. Lewis; Michael Kosik, District 1 president.

UMWA TEAM HEADS FOR LABOR DEPARTMENT TO TELL WLB ABOUT STRIKES IN HARD-COAL

Front, Left to Right—Michael Kosik, District 1 president; Mr. Lewis; Mart F. Brennan, District 7 president. *Rear, Left to Right*—Joseph Kershetsky, District 9 president; John J. Mates, District 9 International Board member; John T. Jones, District 16 president.

---

favor. Bitter experience had taught us that we were not among the elect. The fact is that the board was on record with an opinion that the $2 increase was not an adjustment, ordered by law and upheld by the courts, but a wage raise, consequently forbidden by the 'Little Steel' formula. What we were asked to do, therefore, was plead our cause before a tribunal that had decided against us in advance.

"The decision to ignore the summons of the board, I may point out, was not my own fiat. It pleases politicians, press and radio to paint me as a dictator, but nothing was ever more false. The striking characteristics of coal miners are intense individualism and fierce independence. They are men who resent any departure from democratic procedure. The actions of the organization are determined by a Policy Committee of 225 men, drawn from every section of the country, each one of them a miner or a man who has been a miner.

"It was the Policy Committee, by unanimous vote, that rejected the jurisdiction of the WLB and demanded the resumption of collective bargaining. The demand was not heeded, and when the thirty-day extension ended on April 30, the miners laid down their tools. This is our historic procedure. For fifty-three years a contract has been our protection against rapacity and ill-faith. No contract, no work. No stoppage order ever goes out. If a new agreement has not been signed before the expiration of the old, the men quit. Nevertheless, we were not careless of the national interest, for we knew that there were 79 million tons of bituminous coal in storage.

"On May 1, Secretary Ickes took over the coal mines in the name of the United States. At once I asked for a conference, and, on May 2, I sat in conference with him in his capacity as Solid Fuels Administrator. He asked for an immediate resumption of production and my agreement to this was sustained by the Policy Committee the same day. Nevertheless, President Roosevelt went on the radio that very night and, in utter disregard of our action, appealed to the coal miners to get back on the job.

"On May 17, another extension of fifteen days was arranged with the Secretary, a total of thirty days during which miners produced as never before, hopeful that a contract would be negotiated. Let me say that there was no time that Mr. Ickes did not exhibit good faith, but at every turn his hands were tied by the petty vanity of the War Labor Board.

"On May 25, lo and behold, the WLB came out with a 'decision' in our case, and one based, incredibly enough, on the findings of a panel of three, not one of whom had ever been in a coal mine. And what was the mouse that the mountain brought forth? The vacation compensation of coal miners was raised from $20 to $50, and the companies were ordered to assume the costs of safety devices, blacksmithing, lamps, explosives, etc.

"But did the board order the operators to resume collective bargaining? Not by so much as a whisper! With contract negotiations suspended for a second time, the miners laid down their tools. Straightway the President commanded a return to work by June 7, and Secretary Ickes wired a request that I 'direct' such return. I answered that I had no power to 'direct,' but that I would be glad to recommend.

JUNE 22, 1943, BROUGHT A NEW TRUCE IN THE BATTLE WITH WLB AND THE OPERATORS

Left to Right—Mr. Lewis; John Owens, District 6 president; John O'Leary, UMWA vice president

---

"At a stormy meeting, the Policy Committee voted a return to work at once, but on these two conditions: (1) that the government order the operators to obey the law of the land and enter into conference with us; (2) that the government retain control of the mines until a contract could be drawn and signed.

"Grudgingly enough, the operators sat down with us on June 5, but before a mouth could be opened, the WLB ordered an adjournment. And the reason? Because the miners were not yet back on the job! Not important, perhaps, although it lost two days, but it showed the animus of Chairman Davis and his strutting little men. Permitted to assemble on June 7, the operators presented their usual sullen, stubborn front, dominated by ex-Senator Edward Burke, the $25 thousand-a-year spokesman for the Southern Coal Producers Association.

"In mid-June, the first timid ray of light broke through our gloom. The Central Pennsylvania operators, tiring of the intransigeance of their associates, broke away from the combine and offered us a contract. By its terms, portal-to-portal pay was fixed at $1.25 a day, to which was added the increased vacation compensation authorized by the WLB, free tools, safety devices, etc., making a total of $1.50.

"And then, before the contract could be signed, 'Hell broke loose,' to use the words of one unhappy operator. Railroads, steel companies and other principal customers of the Central Pennsylvania group kept the wires hot with threats and, under this compulsion, the offer was withdrawn.

"On July 21 came a second break in the phalanx formation of the operators. The Illinois operators, frankly confessing a desire for litigation, presented a contract much the same as that offered by the Central Pennsylvania group: $1.25 for travel time, plus the extra 25 cents permitted by the WLB. In addition, however, there was a pledge to work the six-day week. And once again the WLB took upon itself the responsibility of continuing strife, forbidding signatures to the contract on the ground that it provided for wage increases in violation of the 'Little Steel' formula.

"July gave way to September and October, and still the operators sabotaged every approach to agreement. Many of them crept to our doors with expressions of regret and dissatisfaction, but Senator Burke and the Southern operators held them in line by assurances that the WLB stood behind them, and would never surrender to John Lewis and his gang. On October 1, Secretary Ickes, doubtless sick of trying to administer under the burden of handcuffs and leg chains, turned back the mines to private operation.

"Now for the capsheaf to bureaucratic meddling and sly malice. On October 26, two months after its rejection of the Illinois contract, the WLB pontificated the reasons for it. There is no point in discussing details, for I myself, after repeated readings, am unable to make head or tail of its tortuous, hair-splitting legalism.

"On November 1, 530 thousand bituminous and anthracite miners 'took a holiday' of their own accord. It was the unanimous protest of men who were tired of serving as guinea pigs for Washington's campus theorists, and sick of sabotage and double-crossing. More than that, it was the answer of the rank and file to the repeated charge that they were not behind their elected leaders, and that our demands were 'purely political,' put forward by me to embarrass the Roosevelt administration.

"Again the government took over the mines, but this time with a difference. The President's order authorized and directed the Secretary of the Interior 'to offer to the duly constituted representatives of the workers' own choosing a contract or contracts governing the terms and conditions of employment for the period of the operation of the mines by the government.' Here, at long last, was what we had been fighting for! The chance to sit down at a table and work out an agreement by collective bargaining. It was what Secretary Ickes had urged in May, and what the War Labor Board had blocked out by vanity and venom.

"Two days of conference followed—frank, vigorous discussions, but with both sides searching for agreement—and on November 3 a contract was signed between the United States and the United Mine Workers of America. Well knowing that the WLB, backed by the White House, would stand on the $1.125 a day authorized in its Illinois decision, we accepted that dishonest

MR. LEWIS PRESENTS THE TRAVEL-TIME PAY DEMAND TO COAL INDUSTRY, MARCH 10, 1943

151

figure, but upped it to $1.50 by consenting to take fifteen minutes away from lunch time and add it to 'productive time.'

"On November 5, the WLB approved the contract, but in language so grudging that it opened the door for further contention by the Southern operators. As a consequence, this group persisted in recalcitrance and refused to join with other operators—representing 70 per cent of coal production—when a contract was drawn up between the UMWA and the employers. This 70 per cent, however, hailed the terms as fair and expressed regret that the agreement had not been reached months before.

"But did the WLB take quick action on this contract? No, indeed! Although the contract was signed by both parties on December 17, it was not until May 20 of this year that approval was finally given. For five months, the board sat on the agreement with all the dull persistence of a hen trying to hatch a porcelain egg.

"With what result? The Southern group was encouraged to balk, boggle and muddle, and the operators as a whole were permitted to welch on an acknowledged obligation. On October 26, Secretary Ickes, with the unreserved approval of the War Labor Board, had fixed on the payment of $40 to each miner as settlement in full for travel time between March 31, 1943, and June 20, the date when we waived payment by the government. Taking advantage of the WLB's procrastination, the operators withheld the payments, and at this writing are still retaining possession of $18 million of our money.

"There, then, in brief, is the story of our 'treason'—the fight of more than half a million Americans, working in the world's most dangerous and arduous industry, to win a daily wage

---

Top

WAR LABOR BOARD HAS "BEFOULED ITS OWN NEST" AND SHOULD RESIGN, MR. LEWIS SAYS

Center

APRIL 11, 1945, AND A WAGE BOOST, OTHER BENEFITS FOR BITUMINOUS MINE WORKERS

Harry M. Moses, representing captive mine operators, and Mr. Lewis.

Bottom

PLANNING LABOR'S STRATEGY AT THE 1945 LABOR-INDUSTRY CONFERENCE, WASHINGTON

AFL President William Green and Mr. Lewis.

152

THE INTERNATIONAL OFFICERS AT A MEETING OF UMWA NATIONAL POLICY COMMITTEE, 1943

that is above subsistence level! A fight carried on against political power and employer sabotage, aided by press and radio with their campaigns of misrepresentation! A fight to uphold collective bargaining as opposed to bureaucratic fiat! And, tragically enough, a fight settled on terms that could have been had at the very beginning but for malign interferences that put the destruction of the UMWA above the national interest."

The 1943-1944 anthracite wage negotiations dragged through the same tortuous months as did the bituminous conferences.

Negotiations opened in March, 1943, and a new agreement was not reached until June 17, 1944. WLB obstruction delayed a contract that could have been settled in two weeks of free collective bargaining.

The contract gave the anthracite miners a 37.8 cents increase in daily wages, with the annual vacation payment increased from $20 to $50.

Like the soft coal miners, the anthracite mine workers were completely dissatisfied with their wage increase, which would buy little or no food. The hard coal miners directed much of their bit-

terness against the Office of Price Administration, because it was failing not only to control the sky-rocketing cost of living, but also was hurting the anthracite industry by refusing to grant hard coal price increases sufficient to keep the industry solvent.

In the late spring of 1943, at the height of the anti-UMWA hysteria, the House and the Senate passed the Smith-Connally Bill, an act which, in effect, nullified the Norris-LaGuardia Act and the Wagner Labor Relations Law.

President Roosevelt vetoed the bill, but his veto message contained a recommendation which even Representative Howard Smith and Senator Tom Connally, labor-haters of the old school, had not thought fit to include in the bill—a provision to conscript strikers into the Army.

Both Houses of Congress passed the bill over FDR's veto within two and a half hours after his veto message had been received and it became the law of the land on June 5, 1943.

The officers' report to the 1944 UMWA convention tells of some of the oppressive features of the act:

"For the first time in the history of the American Republic, the foes of labor, paced by the poll-tax congressmen of the South, succeeded in having placed upon the statute books of this country a federal law restricting labor in its basic

153

rights. Scrapping the voluntary code of labor relations based on fifty years of experience, the Congress enacted punitive and repressive legislation which places the power of government on the side of the employers in labor disputes.

"The section outlawing strikes in plants seized by the government establishes penalties of $5 thousand fine or a year in jail, or both, for any labor official who encourages or incites or instigates a strike. Language of this section is so sweeping as virtually to handcuff any union executive from guiding or taking any action in a strike situation.

"There is a tricky clause which Representative Smith admits is to prevent the WLB from approving any maintenance of membership or other union-security clause. Subpoena powers to require attendance of union spokesmen and

SHORTLY AFTER 1946 UMWA REAFFILIATION WITH AFL IN NEW EFFORT FOR LABOR UNITY

Left to Right—Mr. Lewis; John Owens, District 6 president; Henry Allai, District 14 president; Frank Hefferly, District 15 president; Percy Tetlow, technical adviser; Ed. J. Morgan, District 23 president; John T. Jones (standing), District 16 president; John P. Busarello, District 5 president; Louis Austin, District 11 president; Sam Nicholls, District 10 president; John Hatton, District 24 president; Abe Vales, District 19 president; John J. Mates, District 9 International Board member.

enforcement of WLB orders by federal district courts are also contained in the act.

"In the case of plants not seized by the government, labor is prohibited from strike action until after a thirty-day cooling-off period and secret ballot in which a majority vote to walk out. During this period the plant might be seized by the government.

"Another section prohibits contributions by unions to political campaigns. This is obviously intended to make labor ineffective in federal election contests, while wealthy individuals may continue to raise slush funds to elect anti-labor politicians."

Section 8a of the Smith-Connally Law became as despised by American workers as Section 7a of the NIRA had been admired. Section 7a, briefly and clearly, wrote into law a right which belonged to labor. Section 8a, however, told labor at great length what it could not do.

On May 17, 1943, the UMWA applied for reaffiliation with the AFL, enclosing a check for $60 thousand as evidence of good faith. The AFL craft union leaders would not readmit the mine workers until the question of what to do with District 50's membership had been settled. Mr. Lewis insisted that questions concerning jurisdiction could be settled after the UMWA had

154

been taken back into the fold. The AFL leaders stalled for a year and, finally, on May 8, 1944, an exasperated John L. Lewis wrote the AFL Executive Council:

"The UMWA, a year ago, filed its application for reaffiliation, with your council. Throughout this period of a year, the majority of the members of your Executive Council have lacked the courage to vote either 'Yes' or vote 'No' on the question of acceptance. Instead they have constantly muttered and mumbled and indulged in fearsome incantations over the fallacious and hoary question of jurisdictional rights. It is an amazing exhibition of base hypocrisy approximating moral turpitude.

"It is publicly known that certain members of the Executive Council have been given imperative instructions to refuse admittance of the UMWA to the AFL by the New Deal politicians who are opposed, for political reasons, to unity in the ranks of labor.

"Every well-informed person in Washington knows the identity of the New Deal executives and the members of its Palace Guard, as well as the identity of the individual members of the council, who from time to time during the past year have clandestinely counseled together to insure the consummation of their shameful plans

to betray the interests of the men and women of labor. The members of the Executive Council by their dishonorable intrigue have permitted the AFL to become the puppet of a political organization and, in fact, to achieve the status of a political company union.

"Will you please, without further procrastination or hypocrisy, return to the UMWA the application for reaffiliation dated May 17, 1943, together with check for per capita tax which accompanied the application."

By October, 1944, America's full armed strength had been thrown into the European battle fronts. Victory was in sight. And in October, 1944, the miners were in convention at Cincinnati. They were justly proud of the contribution they were making toward winning the war. The officers' report said:

"An effort has been made to create anti-labor sentiment in the armed forces and among the workers on the home front by the consistent efforts of the Office of War Information, by statements of high military officials and, in effect, by

PARTICIPANTS IN THE LABOR-MANAGEMENT-GOVERNMENT CONFERENCE OF NOVEMBER '45

155

DISCUSSING DEMANDS OF MINE FOREMEN FOR UNION REPRESENTATION IN OCTOBER, 1945

Left to Right—Ezra Van Horn, representing bituminous coal operators; Secretary of Labor Lewis B. Schwellenbach; Mr. Lewis.

---

the President himself, despite the record-breaking production of coal during 1943 by the mine workers of the country of 649 million tons, a tonnage that has never been equaled in the history of coal mining."

And, in his opening speech to the convention, Mr. Lewis said:

"Coal production in 1944 is proceeding at a rate that will produce a combined tonnage of anthracite and bituminous coal in this year of nearly 700 million tons. Seven hundred million tons is 45 million tons more than was produced in the great war year of 1918, and those 700 million tons will be produced with nearly 300 thousand less men than worked in the mining industry in 1918.

"The 700 million tons that will be produced this year is more coal than will be produced in 1944 by all the combined countries of the world. So, what's the matter with coal production?

"In 1943, the Secretary of the Interior issued a statement saying that the casualties in the coal mines up to the month of October, 1943, exceeded numerically the casualties in the armed forces since Pearl Harbor. And yet there are

those who hold that the coal miner is a hewer of wood and a drawer of water and is not entitled to the treatment that should be accorded other men."

The officers reported to the membership on results achieved under the Mine Inspection Law of 1941. The report noted that the federal inspectors had initiated many improvements without interfering with the work of state inspectors, but added:

"It is a physical impossibility for the present inspection force properly to cover the 6,500 relatively large producing mines in the United States."

The officers' report to the 1944 convention also had a question and an answer on the ever-present skeleton at the feast—death and crippling injuries in the mines:

"Why is it that we kill and maim more mine workers than any other coal mining country in the world? Not because mining here is more hazardous; not because of financial stress; not because we lack in science or research; but due in the main to placing production problems first, and the complete lack of organization among the mine owners for concerted action to attack the basic ills of the industry which bear directly upon the underlying causes.

"Your International officers recommend that the International Union be empowered to create a general safety council within the organization itself, for such research, investigation and safety recommendations to the various state mining departments, the United States Bureau of Mines, the state legislatures, and the Congress of the United States that may bring about improved safety conditions in the coal-mining industry."

The winter of 1944-1945 brought bitter weather to America. Coal consumption was already at an all-time high due to the requirements of the war economy, and the unusual demand created the illusion of a coal shortage similar to the "shortage" which Mr. Lewis disproved during World War I.

Six New England governors wired Mr. Lewis, urging UMWA cooperation in maintaining maximum coal production. He replied:

"The mine workers are in no manner responsible for shortages of coal in Northeastern and other Northern states. Interruption to transportation from various weather conditions has been frequent during the months of December and January. In addition, the recent embargo for several days on shipments of coal was a blunder of major magnitude on the part of government bureaucrats. Hundreds of mines were compelled to shut down from one to three days as a result. Our mine workers are working a fifty-four-hour work week, which is a longer basic shift than is worked in any other war industry.

"I know that you will appreciate these facts,

which will enable you to replace the responsibility where it properly belongs."

The "Battle of the Bulge" gave Americans a temporary scare in December, 1944. Reactionary forces in Congress were quick to shout "emergency," and introduce a bill calling for the conscription of labor. On January 20, 1945, Mr. Lewis wrote the following letter to Senator Elbert Thomas of Utah, who had asked for the UMWA's opinion of the proposed bill:

"Complying with your request, I advise that the United Mine Workers of America are unalterably opposed to a labor draft.

"A manpower service act will not overcome the mistakes of our government. It cannot rectify the miscalculations of the Army and Navy. It will not improve the management in private plants. Enforced labor will reduce morale of present working forces. Regimentation, such as provided in the service act, will destroy incentive and reduce efficiency. In the end, the sum total of coerced manpower will count for naught in increased output."

The 1945 bituminous negotiations officially began when the UMWA, as required by the Smith-Connally Act, notified the Secretary of Labor that a "labor-management dispute" existed. This provision of the law was particularly

PEN BETWEEN THE INDEX AND THIRD FINGER IDENTIFIES THIS SIGNER OF THE 1945 PACT

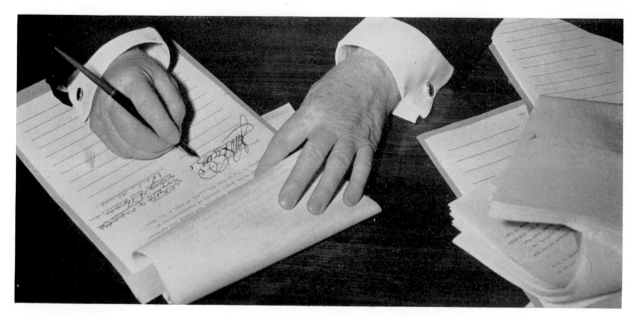

obnoxious to the miners because it sometimes required unions to certify a dispute that didn't exist. In the miners' case in 1945, it merely meant that the industry's wage agreement expired in thirty days.

Secretary of Labor Perkins offered to mediate the differences and the War Labor Board tried to get into the act but the contract was arrived at by collective bargaining.

The new agreement, signed April 11, was for one year instead of the usual two. Both parties recognized that rapidly changing economic conditions made more frequent negotiations desirable. The basic hourly wage rates were retained but a new overtime arrangement increased the pay of the $7-a-day inside men from $57.06 to $63.50 a week. A long-delayed equalization of rates in unit mechanized production gave drillers and shooters a larger share of the benefits of mechanization.

An important contract proposal during the 1945 bituminous negotiations, however, was one the miners did not win. Mr. Lewis did not push for it too hard. With the war still being fought on a two-front basis, he knew a battle for the proposal then would be ill-timed in the face of a hostile administration.

But he laid it on the conference table and the operators knew he would be back with the same proposal next year. Mr. Lewis was resolved that he would get what he asked for next time because it was an ever-recurring dream—his dream and the dream of every coal miner in America— and he knew that the time had arrived for the dream to come true.

The proposal:

"For each ton of coal mined, for use or sale, the producer thereof, by agreement, shall pay to the UMWA in behalf of its members a participating royalty of 10 cents per ton.

"Such royalty shall be deemed partial compensation in equity to the mine worker for the establishment and maintenance of his ready-to-serve status, so vital to the profit motive of the employer and so imperatively essential to public welfare.

"Funds resultant from accrued royalties will be available to the union to provide for its members modern medical and surgical service, hospitalization, insurance, rehabilitation and economic protection."

158

THE SYMBOL OF AN ALMOST SINGLE-HANDED STAND FOR LABOR'S RIGHTS FROM 1941-1945

CHAPTER SIX

1946-1952

GOD BLESS THE DAY

THE REAL BATTLE for the United Mine Workers of America Welfare and Retirement Fund began on March 12, 1946, the date the bituminous contract negotiations began. The miners had resolved to win that battle, no matter what it cost them in time or money.

In 1946, conditions seemed much more favorable for a winning fight than they had been in the spring of 1945, when the fund had been proposed and then dropped in the interests of a quick settlement.

The war was over. Veterans were returning to civilian life. There was a new president in the White House. Franklin Delano Roosevelt had died in Warm Springs, Ga., on April 12, 1945, just prior to the end of the war in Europe. His successor, Harry S. Truman, an apparently amiable, humble man, ex-Senator from Missouri, seemed to be more friendly to labor than Roosevelt had been during the war.

Other omens, however, were not so auspicious. Commodity prices were skyrocketing. The OPA seemed powerless to control food prices. The government still had a law on its books which the miners called the "Smith-Connally Slave Statute." And the coal operators, as usual, were in a pessimistic, poverty-pleading mood.

Conferences began March 12. After preliminary discussions lasting three days, the miners presented their proposals to the operators on March 15. They asked for higher wages and shorter working hours, but President Lewis significantly devoted his entire speech at the opening session to the Welfare Fund. In his talk, he said:

"The conference should note that the mine workers propose the creation of a health and safety fund for mine workers. May I say that throughout the years, since coal mining began in the United States, a huge toll of life has been snuffed out annually as a result of inadequate safety provisions, lack of thorough mine inspection and proper ventilating facilities. Statistically, every man was injured during that period twice, and he took his own statistical chances whether his injury was one that enabled him to return to work in a few days or a few weeks, or whether he was crippled for life and permanently incapacitated, with his back broken or his eyes shot out or his limbs gone. I submit that there is no other industry in the world that has paid that price in blood and bone and human flesh, in the lives of men and the tears of women, as has our own bituminous coal industry.

"Despite all efforts to achieve compensation legislation commensurate with the injuries and permanent disabilities, as well as outright death, today's payments are totally inadequate. There is not a single coal mining state that provides

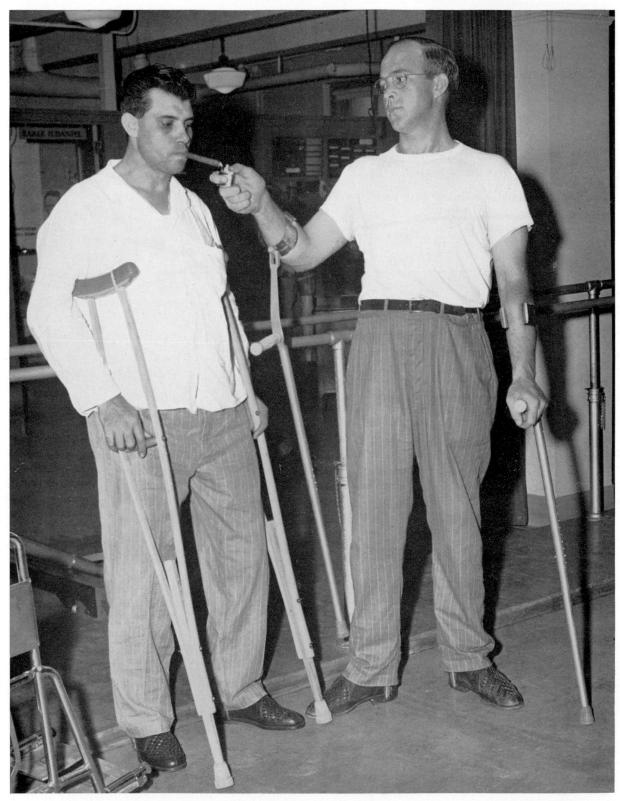

EVERETT BOGGS *(left)*, CUMBERLAND, KY., AND RUFUS SMITH, CROSSVILLE, TENN.

compensation payments adequate to maintain a widowed family or fairly compensate the injured."

The UMWA then presented the results of a survey of medical conditions in mining areas which had been conducted by a miners' committee, headed by Harrison Combs, UMWA associate counsel. The survey showed the degraded condition of sanitation and medical facilities in mining towns. At the conclusion of the committee's report, on March 18, Mr. Lewis said:

"Let me read that indictment, lest ye forget.

"We accuse, by the record, that the management and stockholders of the bituminous coal industry in a period of fourteen years have, through mismanagement, cupidity, stupidity and wanton neglect, made dead 28 thousand mine workers.

"We accuse, by the record, that in the same period the same management and stockholders have, for the same reasons, violently mangled, crushed, and shattered the bodies of 1,400,000 mine workers.

"We accuse, by the record, that the industry does not bury its dead or bind up the shattered bones and the mangled flesh of its victims in any adequate, humane, or modern sense.

"We accuse, by the record, that the management and stockholders of the bituminous coal industry indulge in systematic and widespread financial exploitation of the families of the dead and practice commercial extortion upon the yet living victims of its industrial violence.

"We accuse, by the record, that the industry extorts, annually, from the pay envelope of the mine workers $60 million for pseudo, hypothetical and sub-standard medical service, hospitalization and insurance of an actual value of less than one-third of the aforesaid $60 million.

"We demand abatement of this slaughter.

"We demand cessation of the accompanying extortion.

"It may be noted that the United Mine Workers of America have only made two demands on this conference. Everything else they presented was in the form of suggestions. We have made two demands, and I will read them to you again; I do not want you to forget them:

"We demand abatement of this slaughter.

"We demand cessation of the accompanying extortion.

"These are the demands. What do you want? Peace? Or do you prefer war? We await your reply with interest on those issues."

The operators, with Charles O'Neill acting as chief spokesman, refused all of the mine workers' suggestions and demands, laying particular emphasis on the fact that they would not agree to a welfare fund to be financed by the operators with a royalty per ton of coal mined.

On March 26, therefore, the International officers, Mr. Lewis, John O'Leary and Thomas Kennedy, wrote the following letter to Ezra Van Horn, operator chairman of the joint conference:

"Reference is made to existing National Bituminous Wage Agreement, executed in Washington, April 11, 1945. Exercising its option, the UMWA terminates said agreement as of 12:00 o'clock, midnight, March 31, 1946."

And the officers simultaneously wrote the membership:

"The Bituminous Coal Wage Agreement terminates Sunday, March 31, 1946. No agreement will be in existence after the above given date until present negotiations are completed. Each member will be governed accordingly."

MARCH 26, 1946: EMPHASIZING THE UMWA'S DETERMINATION TO WIN THE WELFARE FUND

The soft coal miners stopped work on April 1. The negotiations dragged on, day after weary day, until April 10. The miners' representatives presented resolutions to the joint conference asking the operators to locate adequate washhouses near mine entrances, asking them to remove urinals and privies from the vicinity of wells and company houses, requesting the operators to provide garbage disposal systems. All of these resolutions were designed to provide sanitation in company-owned communities roughly equal to that in a fairly clean cattle barn. All were voted down by the operators.

Mr. Lewis watched the operators' indifferent reaction to the story of the sordid surroundings in which many miners lived as time and again they voted down the UMWA's proposals. His angry disbelief at such callousness waxed greater each day.

During the negotiations on April 10, while participating fully in the discussions, he was apparently "doodling" on a large scratch pad on the table in front of him. When he had finished his "idle scribbling," he arose and read to the conference a statement he had written on the pad. It said:

"For four weeks we have sat with you; we attended when you fixed the hour; we departed when weariness affected your pleasure.

"Our effort to resolve mutual questions has been vain; you have been intolerant of suggestions and impatient of analysis.

"When we sought surcease from bloodletting, you professed indifference. When we cried aloud for the safety of our numbers, you answered, 'Be content—'twas always thus!'

"When we urged that you abate a stench, you averred that your nostrils were not offended.

"When we emphasized the importance of life, you pleaded the priority of profits; when we spoke of little children in unkempt surroundings, you said, 'Look to the State!'

"You aver that you own the mines; we suggest that, as yet, you do not own the people.

"You profess annoyance at our temerity; we condemn your imbecility.

"You are smug in your complacency; we are abashed by your shamelessness; you prate your respectability; we are shocked at your lack of public morality.

"You scorn the toils, the abstinence and the perils of the miner; we withhold approval of your luxurious mode of life and the nights you spend in merriment.

"You invert the natural order of things and charge to the public the pleasures of your own indolence; we denounce the senseless cupidity that withholds from the miner the rewards of honorable and perilous exertion.

"To cavil further is futile. We trust that time, as it shrinks your purse, may modify your niggardly and anti-social propensities."

Mr. Lewis then walked out of the meeting. As he reached the door to the conference room, he turned to the operators and said: "Good day, gentlemen. It's been nice knowing you."

There were no further meetings until the latter part of April. The operators were busy building up their case in the newspapers and Representatives Howard Smith and Willard Robertson of Virginia were quick to introduce bills into Congress which would outlaw royalties on coal for welfare fund purposes.

After conversations with both miners and operators, Secretary of Labor Lewis G. Schwellenbach brought the disputants together again on April 29. He called in Edward F. McGrady, former Assistant Secretary of Labor, and Paul Fuller, a Labor Department conciliator who had been a UMWA member, to assist in the negotiations.

The new series of meetings accomplished little until May 10, when the UMWA Policy Committee voted to reopen the mines for a two-week period beginning May 13 to supply coal to hospitals, utilities, railroads and essential industries. At 4 P.M. on the same day, Mr. Lewis and Charles O'Neill met with President Truman and three of his top advisers: Dr. John R. Steelman,

MR. LEWIS THANKS SEN. PEPPER FOR HIS 1946 FIGHT AGAINST ANTI-LABOR LEGISLATION

John W. Snyder and Secretary of Labor Schwellenbach. After the meeting, the White House announced that Mr. O'Neill had agreed to "the acceptance of a health and welfare fund in principle."

Mr. Lewis, the next day, issued a statement telling what the money from the proposed fund would be used for:

"1. To furnish adequate and modern medical service to the coal miners and their dependent families with a choice of physicians, which in many areas, particularly in the South, they do not now have. We plan to do away with the company-doctor scourge.

"2. To provide adequate hospitalization under proper standards.

"3. To provide insurance, life insurance and health insurance, for the miners, which they cannot now purchase. Life insurance now costs the mine workers about 277 per cent of what it costs people in sedentary occupations. Obviously, they cannot purchase it at that price. Obviously, they have no insurance, as a result, and the family is unprotected in case of death by violence in the mines or from natural causes. This fund can provide insurance on a mass basis much more cheaply than the individual can buy it himself, even if he is capable of buying it, which he is not.

"4. The fourth reason is rehabilitation. Men who are injured and disabled in the mines through the loss of limbs, blindness, or other major physical injuries, need rehabilitation. There are no facilities available to the mine workers now and there are probably living 50 thousand men who have been incapacitated from mining who have received no assistance in rehabilitation or training for other vocational employment.

"5. The fifth reason is economic aid in distress or hardship cases. Families have become impoverished because they have not received compensation provided by the states due to the manipulation of the company-doctor system and by reason of testimony of the company doctor, which is the only medical testimony available because no other doctor is permitted to attend the victim. The mine worker cannot secure other medical testimony to refute the claims of the company doctor. In consequence, his award for total disability may be cut to as low as 30 per cent and his family become impoverished. There are thousands of such cases.

"6. If any money is left in the fund, we propose to use it for cultural and educational work among the mine workers."

THE INTERNATIONAL OFFICERS AT A UMWA POLICY COMMITTEE MEETING, MAY 8, 1946

**"THE POLICY COMMITTEE WILL BE IN ORDER:"
MR. LEWIS IN THE CRUCIAL 1946 DISPUTE**

On May 15, however, the operators' group repudiated Mr. O'Neill's statement and the negotiations were back where they had started—nowhere. An article in the June 1, 1946, Mine Workers Journal describes the next events:

"The week beginning May 22 and ending May 29 was one of the most hectic weeks in the history of coal controversies, as well as government labor policies. The government seized the coal mines on May 22. The railroad strike immediately followed. On May 25, President Truman proposed his ill-advised legislation to take over industry and draft manpower and force men to work under the strong arm of the Army and Navy. Then came the capitulation of the engineers and trainmen and the calling off of the railroad strike.

"While all this was in progress, President Lewis, Vice President John O'Leary, Secretary-Treasurer Thomas Kennedy, and John Owens, president of District 6, were conferring, first at the Department of the Interior and then at the White House. Almost daily, conferences were being held with Secretary of the Interior J. A. Krug and his deputy, Admiral Ben Moreell. At the White House, President Truman, John Steelman and John Snyder participated.

"The climax came when a contract, the terms of which were agreed upon the night before, was signed by Secretary of the Interior Krug for the government and John L. Lewis for the UMWA in the President's office. The coal strike was over. The movie and news photographers were lined up in rows five deep to photograph the principals, as Secretary Krug, accompanied by Admiral Moreell, and President Lewis, with Mr. O'Leary and Mr. Owens, president of District 6, emerged from the White House office."

The salient points of the "Krug-Lewis" agreement of May 29, 1946, are shown in the following digest of the contract, taken from the June 1, 1946, issue of the Journal:

"1. Hours:

"(a) Mines are to be operated nine hours per day as heretofore, with overtime to be paid after seven hours.

"(b) Work performed on the sixth consecutive day is optional but, when performed, shall be paid for at time and one-half or rate and one-half.

"(c) Holidays, when worked, shall be paid for at time and one-half or rate and one-half. Holidays shall be computed on arriving at the sixth and seventh day of the week.

**MR. LEWIS AND OPERATOR CHARLES O'NEILL
AFTER A WHITE HOUSE VISIT, MAY 10, 1946**

"2. Wages:

"Basic hourly increase of 18½ cents, which, with overtime, means a daily increase of $1.85. The foregoing increases are retroactive to May 22, the date of government seizure of bituminous coal mines.

"3. Mine Safety Program:

"The Federal Mine Safety Code to be issued by Director of Bureau of Mines, Interior Department. Periodic inspections by federal inspectors. Local unions to select mine safety committees at each mine to report violations.

"4. Workmen's Compensation and Occupational Disease Laws:

"Coal Mines Administrator will direct operating managers to comply with state laws, whether elective or compulsory.

"5. Health and Welfare Program:

"(a) A Welfare and Retirement Fund financed by 5 cents a ton on coal produced for use or sale. Tax to be used for payments for sickness, disability, death or retirement. To be managed by trustees, one appointed by the union, one by the administration and the third by the other two.

"(b) A Medical and Hospital Fund financed from deductions now made from miners' pay for such purposes. To be administered by trustees appointed by the president of the union.

"(c) The two funds to be used to complement each other.

"6. Survey of Medical and Sanitary Facilities:

"A comprehensive survey of hospital and medical facilities, medical treatment, sanitary

FURTHER EFFORTS TO BREAK THE DEADLOCK OVER MINERS' WELFARE FUND, MAY 13, 1946

Left to Right—Harry M. Moses, representing steel industry captive mines; Mr. Lewis, Percy Tetlow, UMWA international representative.

and housing conditions in coal mining areas to determine improvement necessary to bring these up to recognized American standards."

The anthracite miners, also, demanded a welfare fund. They held a Tri-District Convention on April 24, 1946, and Mr. Lewis told the delegates at the opening session:

"Without question, the anthracite operators will come into the conference when we meet them and say that they cannot accept A, B, or C proposed by the mine workers because the increase in freight rates is going to raise the cost to the consumer, and that they must be constantly on guard to protect the relationship of anthracite in the consuming market against rival substitutes.

"Well, like the anthracite mine workers, I am rather tired of having the priority of profits pleaded, constantly in the forefront, and before any consideration is given to the human requirements of an industry such as our own. I say, as an economic, as a social, and as a humane policy, as between men, the first application on the production of a commodity such as our own is fair treatment to those who go down into the anthracite mines and produce this commodity for the benefit of society."

166

The anthracite operators used the arguments Mr. Lewis had predicted they would, but the mine workers had their Welfare Fund after less than a month of meetings. The conference opened in New York City on May 10, 1946, and the contract was signed on June 7. The new agreement included these gains, as reported in the Journal:

"Work week: The basic work week will be seven hours a day, five days a week. The voluntary six-day work week agreement of January 1, 1943, is rescinded.

"Holidays: Annual holidays increased from six to eight, the additions being February 12, Lincoln's birthday, and October 29, John Mitchell Day, the latter having been observed in the anthracite industry but not heretofore provided for in the contract as a holiday.

"Wage Increase: Basic wages increased $1.295 a day. Travel time increased from $1.135 for a forty-five minute period to $1.339.

"Overtime: Time-and-one-half for hours worked over seven and the sixth day, and double time for Sundays when worked as the seventh consecutive day.

THE SIGHT-SEEING GUIDE APPARENTLY DID NOT HEAR WHAT K. C. ADAMS SAID TO HIM

Left to Right—Mr. Adams, editor, United Mine Workers Journal; an unidentified Washington guide, Mr. Lewis.

"Health and Welfare Fund: A Health and Welfare Fund is provided by the assessment of 5 cents per ton on each ton of coal mined for sale or company use. The fund will be administered by three trustees, two of whom shall be selected by the International president of the United Mine Workers of America and one by the anthracite operators.

"Vacations: Vacation payment increased from $75 to $100.

"Compensation and Occupational diseases: The contract provides that the anthracite industry accepts as a whole, full compliance with the compensation laws of Pennsylvania and the occupational disease law, which has been elective and heretofore only a few companies have subscribed to.

"Mine Safety: Anthracite operators agree to accept recommendations of the Federal Bureau of Mines. Presently established mine committees shall have the right to inspect and report unsafe conditions affecting mine operation and equipment."

Negotiations for the Anthracite Health and Welfare Fund had been bitter but brief. The government had not intervened during the meetings and the operators, in contrast to the bituminous operators, had negotiated fairly and honestly.

On July 23, 1946, John O'Leary and Thomas Kennedy were selected by President Lewis as

A PICTURE FOR THE HISTORY BOOKS: UMWA WINS WELFARE FUND FIGHT, MAY 29, 1946

Seated, Left to Right—President Truman, Secretary of the Interior Julius Krug, Mr. Lewis. *Standing, Left to Right*—Adm. Ben Moreell, John O'Leary, UMWA vice president; John Owens, District 6 president and assistant to Mr. Lewis.

UMWA trustees of the Anthracite Fund. R. L. Birtley, president of the Anthracite Operators' Wage Negotiating Committee and of the Hammond Coal Co., was chosen to represent the operators. Medical and death benefit payments out of the fund began early in 1947, while the bituminous operators and the government still prevented operation of the bituminous fund.

On January 23, 1946, the UMWA and Mr. Lewis took what they hoped was a real step toward unifying the labor movement when the UMWA reaffiliated with the AFL and Mr. Lewis was named thirteenth vice president. On January 29, in Miami, Mr. Lewis sat in an AFL Executive Council meeting for the first time in more than ten years. At that time, he said:

"Obviously, the pooling of the collective strength of the UMWA and the AFL makes the Federation the most representative and dominant labor organization in America. I think the American people will recognize that fact.

"Unity of labor's policies in America is desirable. Attainment of that unity is labor's task and obligation."

As a symbol of this new unity Mr. Lewis presented to Mr. Green a paid-up dues card in the UMWA, disposing of the charges of dual unionism which had hung over Mr. Green for a decade.

Soon after the signing of the Krug-Lewis agreement on May 29, the government began to put some terms of the soft coal contract into force. Admiral Joel T. Boone, former head of the Navy's medical bureau, initiated a comprehensive survey of medical and sanitary conditions in bituminous mining communities. And, on July 24, Secretary of the Interior J. A. Krug promulgated an industry-wide mine safety code. The operators resisted it because they were opposed to any government safety codes. It was objected to by the UMWA because it lowered Bureau of Mines safety standards. It went into effect anyway.

Early in September, Admiral Ben Moreell,

acting administrator of mines for the federal government, asked the mine workers and the operators to meet to discuss return of the mines to the owners. The operators were playing a waiting game, content, for the present, with government operation, but Mr. Lewis, on September 11, told reporters:

"The UMWA has a contract with the government and is producing coal in ample quantities for national needs. The UMWA has preferred all along to have a collective bargaining agreement with the operators. We are not in favor of government operation of the mines. We were not consulted when the mines were seized by the government. It would be agreeable to the mine workers if the mines were returned to private ownership at any time the government wants to do so—tomorrow, if the government so wishes.

"The UMWA has been forced to await the time when the operators found themselves in a position where they could take affirmative action. Without agreement among the operators, there has been nothing that the UMWA could do.

"If the government does not want to return the mines until a new agreement is made, then

1946 COURT FIGHT KEPT PHOTOGRAPHERS ON CONSTANT WATCH FOR PRESIDENT LEWIS

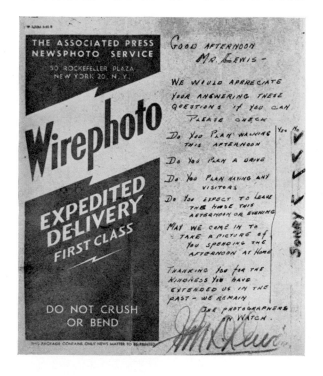

MR. LEWIS CALLS ON SECRETARY KRUG TO HONOR CONTRACT WITH UMWA, OCTOBER '46

the responsibility falls upon the operators to say under what conditions they will employ the mine workers."

Admiral Moreell suggested that negotiations be resumed on the following basis:

1. That the contract run until April 1, 1948.

2. That the mine safety clause in the Krug-Lewis Agreement be amended to allow for revisions in the mine safety code.

3. That trustees for the Welfare and Retirement Fund be appointed, one by the president of the UMWA, one by the operators, and the third chosen by the other two.

4. That the Boone medical survey be completed regardless of any action by the negotiators.

5. That the still unresolved question of pro rata vacation payment to miners who shifted from one company to another during the year be resolved.

Some of the operators were willing to resume negotiations on that basis, but the "retromingent" Southerners again refused, hoping that they could delay settlement until Congress reconvened and could be propagandized into passing a substitute for the Smith-Connally Act, which ran out in June, 1947. They succeeded only too well. Their excuse for not negotiating in September, 1946, was that they could not accept the idea of the 5 cent royalty per ton of coal for the Welfare Fund.

The negotiations recessed without accomplishment and Admiral Moreell resigned as Coal Mines Administrator, effective September 30. His place was taken by Captain N. H. Collisson, USNR, who had been deputy administrator.

The recess continued through the UMWA's Thirty-ninth Constitutional Convention, which was held in Atlantic City, N. J., from October 1 to 4. Four days before the convention was scheduled to open, Mr. Lewis was stricken with appendicitis and taken to Emergency Hospital in Washington for an operation. It was the first convention he had missed since becoming president of the International Union.

Mr. Lewis recuperated quickly and, on Oc-

COAL OPERATORS SAY: "NO, NO" TO UMWA AT NOVEMBER '46 CONTRACT DISPUTE MEETING

Left to right (from head of the table)—Operator Ezra Van Horn, conference chairman; John T. Jones, District 16 president and conference secretary; Secretary-Treasurer Thomas Kennedy, Vice President John O'Leary, Mr. Lewis, Welly K. Hopkins, senior UMWA counsel; John P. Busarello, District 5 president; James Mark, Sr., District 2 president.

tober 19, 1946, in a conference with Secretary of the Interior Krug, asked that the mine workers' grievances against some features of government operation of the mines be eliminated.

Results of the Krug-Lewis conference were not satisfactory, so Mr. Lewis, on October 21, 1946, sent the following letter to Mr. Krug, giving notice of termination of the miners' contract with the government:

"On Saturday, October 19, 1946, you, in conference with me, again refused to correct the unilateral misinterpretations you have heretofore issued of the Krug-Lewis agreement of May 29, 1946. Your interpretative bulletin concerning pro rata vacation payments and your bulletin setting up railroad weights rather than tipple weights upon which to compute the payments due the Welfare and Retirement Fund remain outstanding and uncorrected. They and other similar unilateral misinterpretations constitute a breach of the said Krug-Lewis agreement. That agreement is an integrated instrument and its respective provisions are interdependent. A breach of any of its provisions breaches the whole.

"For ninety days our representatives have protested these breaches of contract which have led to the loss of millions of dollars due to the mine workers. Your adamant refusal to correct these errors continues unabated. The question of pro rata vacation payments has, upon the request of

the Illinois Coal Operators Association, been referred to arbitration and an award was made therein on August 6, 1946. We have called upon you for its enforcement. You have refused. In addition to these breaches of the contract, significant changes in the government wage policy have occurred.

"Under the contract reopening provisions of the National Bituminous Coal Wage Agreement, dated April 11, 1945, specifically carried forward into the Krug-Lewis agreement, either party may give ten days' notice in writing of a date for a negotiating conference upon the matters outlined in said notice. The other party agrees to attend said conference. At the end of fifteen days after the beginning of such negotiating conference, either party may give to the other a notice in writing of the termination of the agreement, to be effective five days after the receipt of such notice.

"The Krug-Lewis agreement, having thus been breached by you and significant changes in government wage policy having occurred, you are accordingly hereby officially notified that the United Mine Workers of America requests a joint conference of the accredited representatives of the joint contracting parties to the Krug-Lewis agreement of May 29, 1946, for the purpose of negotiating new arrangements affecting wages, hours, rules, practices, differentials, inequalities, and all other pertinent matters affecting or ap-

pertaining to the national bituminous coal industry. It is suggested that a convening of the conference at 10 o'clock A. M. Friday, November 1, 1946, in Washington, D. C., would be appropriate."

Upon receipt of a copy of the letter, Captain Collisson issued a statement in which he said that the mine workers' interpretation of the vacation payment clause, which had been backed up by an order of the wage board, was acceptable. Secretary Krug, however, in Amarillo, Tex., on a cross-country trip, issued a statement in which he said that the UMWA's complaints were "technical in nature." He asserted that the government had not breached its agreement and that the contract could not be reopened to discuss "questions of wages and hours." Thereupon, Mr. Lewis, on October 22, wrote Mr. Krug another letter:

"This will reply to your telegram from Amarillo and Collisson's letter from Washington of October 22.

"The existing Krug-Lewis agreement expressly provides that both parties to the agreement are bound to meet within a ten-day period upon formal request of either party.

"Such formal request was filed yesterday by

PHOTOGRAPHERS AND CROWDS WATCH MR. LEWIS LEAVE COURT, NOVEMBER 25, 1946

NOT TO BE OUTDONE BY THE U. S., VIRGINIA JOINED IN HARASSING MR. LEWIS IN 1946

Sgt. J. F. Moriarity tacks a summons on Mr. Lewis' door.

The miners' convention had demanded that their negotiators renew their efforts to secure an immediate reduction in the wartime fifty-four-hour work week. Mr. Krug suggested that such talks with the operators should be for a sixty-day period, which, coincidentally, allowed just enough time for the talks to end during the opening days of the first session of the newly-elected, reactionary Eightieth Congress.

The UMWA refused Mr. Krug's suggestions in a formal statement in which it pointed out that: 1. the Secretary of the Interior delayed twenty-five days after receiving formal notice of the mine workers' intention to terminate the Krug-Lewis agreement before making proposals of any kind; 2. the operators were divided and could not negotiate on a unified basis; 3. Mr. Krug presumed to set the length and subject matter of the negotiations, despite a contract provision that all such matters were to be decided by mutual consent; and, 4. Mr. Krug had no authority to deny the UMWA its "legal and moral" right to reopen the contract. The UMWA's statement closed by saying:

"The government of the United States seized the mines and entered into a contract. The mine workers do not propose to deal with parties who have no status under that contract. We do not propose to be driven like dumb beasts to the

the United Mine Workers of America. Failure on your part to honor this meeting will constitute another breach of the contract and will void the Krug-Lewis agreement."

Mr. Krug invited the mine workers' representatives to meet with him at a vacation resort at Tule Lake, Calif., on November 1, but the invitation was declined. Instead, a series of sub-committee meetings was held, beginning November 1. Mr. Lewis, Vice President John O'Leary, Secretary-Treasurer Thomas Kennedy, John Owens, president of District 6, and Senior Counsel Welly K. Hopkins represented the mine workers in talks with Captain Collisson and members of his staff.

Finally, on November 11, Mr. Krug, the man Mr. Lewis called "a modern Hercules with a number twelve shoe and a number five hat," returned to Washington and "graced the conferences with his presence" for precisely three hours and fifty-eight minutes in the next five days. On November 14, he asked Mr. Lewis to resume talks with the operators about wages and hours.

THEY SAID MR. LEWIS WAS ON THE SPOT IN '46; BUT THE WELFARE FUND IS A REALITY

172

UMWA COUNSELOR HOPKINS AND MR. LEWIS DURING THE '46 CONTEMPT OF COURT TRIAL

slaughter of slow strangulation envisioned by your proposal and the operators' well-known and long-used tactics of evasion and delay. We call upon you to honor your contract."

On November 15, Mr. Lewis wrote to Mr. Krug and informed him that, inasmuch as fifteen days had elapsed since the beginning of their conferences, the UMWA was terminating the Krug-Lewis agreement as of midnight, November 20, 1946.

Mr. Krug replied immediately and said that the UMWA had no right to terminate the agreement. He enclosed a letter written by U. S. Attorney General Tom Clark which backed up his position. He urged the miners to reconsider and resume negotiations with the operators.

On November 17, Judge T. Alan Goldsborough of the U. S. District Court in Washington, D. C., issued a restraining order, without a hearing, directed against Mr. Lewis, the International Union and "all persons in active concert with them"—in other words, all the members of the United Mine Workers of America. The government had seized the property of the mine owners, and now it also armed itself with the operators' favorite weapon, the "yellow dog" injunction.

On November 19, President Truman ordered the Department of Justice to push contempt of court action against Mr. Lewis and the International Union if the work stoppage was not called off. But the miners, relying on their legal right to terminate the contract, and also on the Clayton and Norris-LaGuardia Acts, which forbade the use of ex parte restraining orders in labor disputes, left the pits on schedule. At the time they stopped work, there were more than 50 million tons of coal above ground, amply safeguarding consumers against any hardship.

Judge Goldsborough directed the UMWA to show cause why it should not be held in contempt of court. The hearing was held on November 27. In obedience to the terms of the judge's severe edict prohibiting the union's giving any support to the strikers, there was no December 1 issue of the United Mine Workers Journal. It was the only edition omitted in the Journal's history.

On December 3, Judge Goldsborough found the UMWA and John L. Lewis guilty of civil and criminal contempt of his court and the next day announced that the United Mine Workers of America had been fined $3,500,000 and that Mr. Lewis personally was fined $10 thousand. In anger and indignation, Mr. Lewis told the judge:

"Speaking and acting in my official capacity as president of the United Mine Workers of

173

MR. LEWIS ENTERS A WASHINGTON COURT TO HEAR SENTENCE PASSED FOR CONTEMPT

Right—Earl Houck, head of UMWA's legal department.

WAITING TO TESTIFY TO THE SENATE LABOR COMMITTEE AGAINST OPPRESSIVE LABOR LAWS

Mr. Lewis and Harrison Combs, UMWA associate counsel.

America and as vice president of the American Federation of Labor, I cannot, by action or inaction, acquiesce in what must be described as the ugly recrudescense of 'government by injunction.' I cannot disavow labor's principles or policies, nor am I disposed to adopt a course which will inevitably amount to a betrayal of labor's constitutional rights.

"The mine workers are God-fearing, law-abiding American citizens. They have not ceased work in defiance of their government. On the contrary, they have asserted their rights as free men to protest the unjust and arbitrary acts to which they have been subjected by individuals employed by the government.

"Without intending any personal disrespect to this court, I must respectfully but firmly stand upon those vital rights and freedoms that are rooted in our Constitution and that have been given full expression by the Congressional mandates of 1914, in the Clayton Act, and of 1932, in the Norris-LaGuardia Act."

The UMWA immediately appealed Judge Goldsborough's decision and the miners returned to work on December 7. For weeks, newspaper reporters and photographers followed Mr. Lewis no matter where he went. They camped outside of his Alexandria, Va., home. He went to work in the morning and left the UMWA building with flash bulbs exploding in his face. When he arrived at the courthouse, he had to fight his way through crowds of newsmen and onlookers. He was lampooned by cartoonists, vilified by editorial writers, and denounced by radio commentators. But Mr. Lewis held his temper, said nothing and carried the case to the Supreme Court. The government continued in technical control of the mines and the operators conducted business as usual. No move was made by either the government or the operators to break the deadlock. The miners were forced to work under the restraint of Judge Goldsborough's edict, so restrictive that the union legally dared not state its position in the newspapers or on the radio. On March 7, 1947, the United States Supreme Court announced its decision on the UMWA's appeal. The Journal reported the salient points of the decision:

"The majority of the court held:

"1. That the Norris-LaGuardia Act was not intended to apply to the United States as an employer. The court divided five to four on this question, with Justices Rutledge, Murphy, Jackson and Frankfurter dissenting.

"2. That the United States District Court had the right to issue a restraining order to preserve existing conditions while it considered its own authority. The vote on this question was seven to two, with Justices Murphy and Rutledge dissenting. (In simple language, the decision of the court, in effect, means that President Lewis and the UMWA should have obeyed the injunction until the issues involved were determined by the court on their merits.)

"3. That miners working in government-seized mines are U. S. employees. This decision was by a six-to-two vote, with Justices Murphy and Frankfurter dissenting. Justice Rutledge expressed no opinion on this question.

"4. The court OK'd the merging of civil and criminal contempt in a single proceeding. The vote was seven to two, with Justices Murphy and Rutledge dissenting.

"5. The fine of $10 thousand against President Lewis was affirmed. The fine of $3,500,000 against the UMWA was reduced to $700 thousand for criminal contempt, conditional upon the UMWA's withdrawing its contract termination notice, and thereby purging itself of contempt, within five days after issuance by the Supreme Court of a mandate. Otherwise, the $3,500,000 stood."

The UMWA immediately complied with the Supreme Court's order, but the mines still were being operated by the government under the restraint of the Goldsborough injunction.

On March 17, 1947, Rear Admiral Joel T. Boone, pursuant to a clause in the Krug-Lewis agreement, released his report, "A Medical Survey of the Bituminous Coal Industry." This massive document deplored in dispassionate detail the lack of adequate medical and sanitary facilities in a large majority of America's mining communities. This study, the only one ever made of an entire American industry, sustained Mr. Lewis' arguments for the Welfare Fund in every detail. It said:

"The present practices of medicine in the coal fields on a contract basis cannot be supported. They are synonymous with many abuses and they are undesirable and in many instances deplorable.

"The evidence is convincing that three-quarters of the hospitals are inadequate. The distances involved in transporting an injured miner from the mine to the hospital is recorded for 188 mines. The average distance is seventeen miles.

THE MINERS RETURN TO THE AFL AND MR. GREEN GETS A PAID-UP UMWA MEMBERSHIP

"The distances range from one to 160 miles.

"If it is custom and tradition that mine families shall exist in squalor, it is time for that custom and tradition to be abolished.

"Theoretically, the miners' wages allow for the extra hazardous nature of their occupations. Yet evidence clearly indicates that their earnings do not permit sufficient reserves in savings, bonds or personal insurance to compensate them in case of permanent disability resulting from accidents and serious illnesses."

On March 25, 1947, a tragedy occurred which Mr. Lewis later described for the House Labor Committee in these words:

"On Tuesday, March 25, disaster occurred at the Centralia No. 5 mine, at Centralia, Ill., operated by the Centralia Coal Company, which was in turn operated by the Bell & Zoller Coal Company of Illinois.

"One hundred and eleven coal miners were killed in that explosion. They left ninety-eight widows; they left seventy-eight orphans; and six of these men left dependent mothers or fathers.

"The reason for the small number of orphans

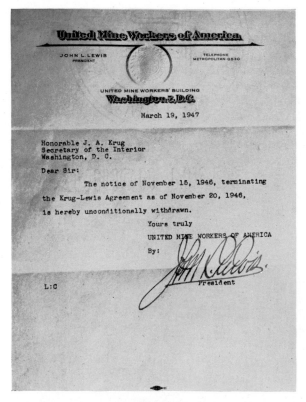

THE SUPREME COURT DIRECTED MR. LEWIS TO WITHDRAW 1946 CONTRACT TERMINATION

to the total number of men killed, as miners' families go, is due to the age of the men employed. The average age of the employees of this mine was fifty-five."

Mr. Lewis blamed Secretary Krug. He told the House committee:

"I previously have made the statement that places the responsibility for the disaster on government officials. I said that these men at Centralia died through the criminal negligence of J. A. Krug and I reiterate that statement now and I shall prove it beyond peradventure at this hearing.

"I have not said that J. A. Krug by an affirmative act killed these men. I say that J. A. Krug, by his inaction, has permitted them to

---

DURING A BRIEF RECONCILIATION BETWEEN THE MINE WORKERS AND THE AFL IN 1947

Left to Right—Mr. Lewis, 13th vice president of AFL; Daniel Tobin, Teamsters; William Green, AFL president; George Meany, AFL secretary-treasurer; William L. Hutcheson, Carpenters.

THE HORROR OF ANOTHER MINE DISASTER IS REVIEWED BY UMW LEADERS, MARCH 26, 1947

Left to Right—John T. Jones, District 16 president and head of Labor's Non-Partisan League; John O'Leary, vice president; John J. Mates, District 9 International Board member and assistant to President Lewis, Mr. Lewis.

---

die while he withheld from them succor which it was within his power to give.

"In no instance, regardless of his obligations under the contract he signed, regardless of his own code, declared and promulgated by him as being fair and reasonable, and which he has sole authority to enforce, has he, in the interest of safety, removed any supervisor or mine manager or closed down a single mine because danger was imminent.

"Now, as a matter of fact, when the inspector's report was filed with him in the month of November, 1946, it showed that the mine was not rock-dusted. It showed that coal dust existed there in excessive quantities. The report also showed that there was insufficient air in the mine and that it was not properly ventilated.

"Whenever the inspector's report shows those conditions, danger is imminent. It may come at

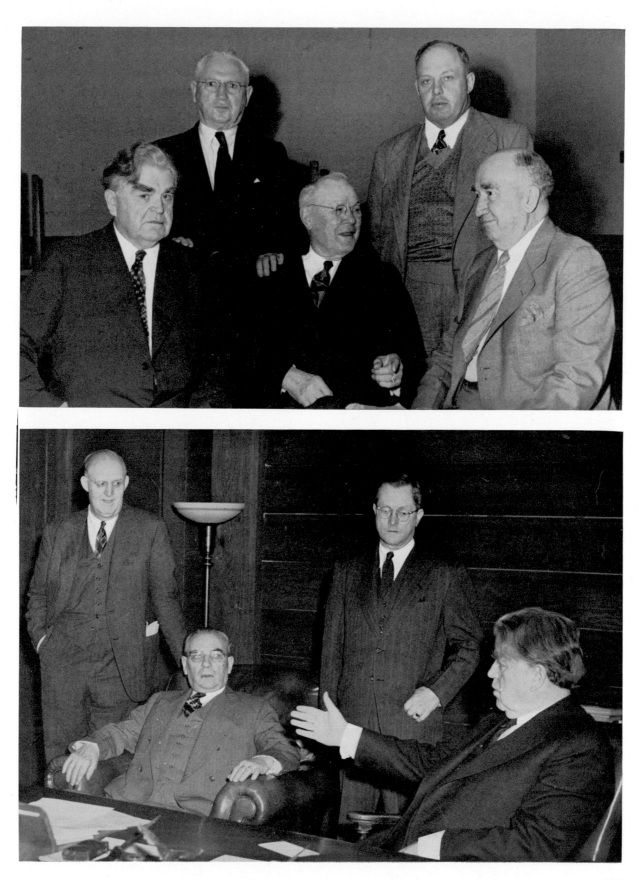

"THESE 111 MEN AT CENTRALIA WOULD HAVE MINED A LOT MORE COAL HAD THEY LIVED"

---

any moment, or it may be deferred, according to the mysteries of nature and the providence of God.

"But Mr. Krug did nothing.

"You may think that he is worthy of the trust imposed in him, but I think he is dishonorable and without a moral conscience on his side, a friend to the coal operators, a scheming, a designing politician, unfaithful to his trust."

Mr. Lewis then said:

"As constructive suggestions, I offer:

"1. That the Congress enact a joint resolution asking the President to remove J. A. Krug from his office for cause.

"2. That the Congress enact, at once, legislation or an amendment to the existing legislation making it mandatory for a federal inspector of mines to close down mines found in violation of the law or the federal code of safety standards, and give him the authority to do so.

"3. A third suggestion to the Congress—and primarily to the House of Representatives because this type of legislation has to originate in the House—that a joint enactment authorize the Treasury of the United States to remit to the United Mine Workers of America the three-quarters of a million, more or less, for fines for contempt, on the basis of reasonable doubt of a five-four decision of the Court and with this stipulation, that this money remitted be placed in a trust fund with the trustees appointed by the Congress to care for the widows and the children of the Centralia and the Straight Creek disasters, including the recovery of those bodies and the future education of the more than 200 children who are victims."

Finally spurred into action, Mr. Krug ordered 518 unsafe mines closed on April 3, an action described by Mr. Lewis as "Krug's deathbed confession." The shutdown order came only after Mr. Lewis disclosed startling figures provided by the director of the Bureau of Mines, Dr. R. R. Sayers. At the House hearing, Mr. Lewis revealed:

"On March 28, I received the following letter from Dr. Sayers:

" 'In compliance with your request of March 28, 1947, I am submitting the following information:

" '1. Total number of mine inspections made during calendar year 1946 by qualified inspectors of the Bureau of Mines is 3,345.

" '2. Number of mines found to be complying entirely with the Federal Mine Safety Code, clear of all violations, is two.

" '3. Approximate average number of violations of the code per mine in government possession is twenty-seven.' "

Mr. Krug tried to alibi himself by shifting blame to Mr. Lewis. He said the UMWA president should have told the men not to work in the mine. Mr. Lewis gave the House committee his answer:

"Now, in fact, Mr. Krug called Drew Pearson to his office and they spent the afternoon there preparing a defense against this situation and the point of it is that John Lewis caused the explosion that occurred in Centralia because he had copies of the inspector's report and did not do anything about it. Of course, I knew about the Centralia mine and, of course, I knew about every other mine that is unsafe in this country.

"The director of the Bureau of Mines said there were only two mines that did not violate the code.

"In ordinary circumstances, the members of

the mine safety committee can remove the men from an unsafe mine, but immediately following the November report of the inspection of that mine the contract was terminated by the organization. The Coal Mines Administrator, Mr. Krug, went into court and secured a 'yellow dog' injunction to restrain those men from stopping work and terminating that contract.

"We were driven back to the mines by the power of the government and the support of Congress and a decree of the federal court, sustained by the Supreme Court. Driven back to the mines!"

On March 29, the International officers called for one week of mourning. Their letter to the membership said:

"We recommend that the designated memorial period, in accordance with our agreement, shall begin March 31 and end Sunday, April 6. During this period, coal production will cease and memorial ceremonies, church services and other exercises should be conducted to honor our dead and to pray to God in His infinite mercy to provide consolation for the bereaved families. The cooperation of the clergy and churches should be invited and accepted.

"We, who are privileged to speak for our dead and for those pathetic widows and orphans and for the future safety of our people, say that this killing must stop. It must be stopped now. The American people must be aroused to the stark realities of the situation and the casualties of the coal industry. Coal is already saturated with the blood of too many brave men and drenched with the tears of too many surviving widows and orphans.

"As an effective protest against these horrors, we believe that the industry should suspend work, meditate, pray and resolve for a safer and more secure future for those working in the coal mining industry."

Mr. Lewis lamented that it took a tragedy such as the Centralia disaster to goad the federal government into action on behalf of the mine

MR. LEWIS TO SEN. O'MAHONEY: CENTRALIA MINE DISASTER VICTIMS WERE "MURDERED"

workers. He told the House Labor Committee on April 3:

"These disasters occur with impunity, and each time there is a disaster in the industry, the newspaper columns are filled with stories of probes, investigations, experts being rushed to the scene of the disaster, rescuers at work. Rescuers for the dead? And endless repetition! The public is sorry for the victims—and people on the street say, 'Oh, isn't that too bad!' And it ends there—and nothing is done—and the widows wait—and the orphans grow up in poverty and in ignorance and in deprivation of opportunity—because some one found it cheaper to kill their fathers than to protect them—and the public was too busy with its own affairs to care very long—or to do anything about it."

He later told the committee what the aftermath of the Centralia tragedy provoked the government to do:

"It is surprising what the memorial period has produced.

"In all these months, we have been unable to get Mr. Krug and Captain Collisson to agree to an appointee for a trustee for the Welfare Fund, but since the memorial period they have agreed to a trustee. From the list of eleven eminent

MR. LEWIS, APRIL 3, 1947: GOVERNMENT FAILED TO ENFORCE OWN MINE SAFETY CODE

Americans that we submitted many weeks ago, they have agreed on one trustee, Mr. Thomas Murray of New York, former receiver for the Interborough, director of Chrysler Corporation, director of banks, head of a big engineering company. He is now a trustee and next Tuesday Mr. Murray, Captain Collisson and I will sit down to make the first effort to administer the Welfare Fund.

"So we are getting a trustee. We have gotten Admiral Boone's report. It looks as though we are going to have some law enforcement; 518 mines will be shut down until they are made safe. Really, it is surprising!

"In addition to that, we are getting examination of these conditions by Congress. It is surprising what the memorial has produced, but it is sad that this had to happen before we could get that consideration."

Mr. Lewis went on to lay the miners' case for a federal safety law and the Welfare Fund before Congress and the people:

"I called the roll of the victims of this indus-

180

try for a five-year period for you gentlemen a while ago: 300 thousand-odd mine-made victims. Some died—more than 6 thousand. Some lived; some lived blind, some with twisted backs, lost limbs, paralyzed bodies, broken bones, the flesh burned from their faces until they are grinning spectres of men.

"We want a welfare fund for them, at the cost of this industry, a charge on the cost of production.

"Many men in Congress have assailed us for wanting to do something for these victims of our basic industry, an industry essential to the United States and its future, because society would not do it for our people.

"If we must grind up human flesh and bones in an industrial machine—in the industrial machine that we call modern America—then, before God, I assert that those who consume coal, and you and I who benefit from that service—because we live in comfort—owe protection to those men first, and we owe security to their families after, if they die. I say it! I voice it! I proclaim it! And I care not who in heaven or hell opposes it! That is what I believe! And that is what the mine workers believe!"

Mr. Lewis answered the states' righters' opposition to a federal mine safety law by showing that the same men opposed safety legislation in their own states. He added:

"A uniform national safety code is highly desirable from a competitive and economic standpoint because the operators of one state that has poor administration of mining laws have a distinct economic advantage over those operators in states where the law is enforced and they are required to spend money for guarding the lives of the men."

He used his home state of Illinois to illustrate how little value some state administrations place on the lives of the miners:

"I would like to point out that appropriations for mine safety in part of the central mining states are on the average much less for the protection of miners, the mining industry, the property values represented there, than they are for the so-called wild life of game and fish. That goes in states that are not game and fish states, too.

"For instance, in 1940, Illinois, with 45 thousand men employed in its mines, had sixteen state inspectors. The state mining department appropriation was $329 thousand. But it had 147 state game wardens, who required an appropriation of $1,888,000.

"Now, Illinois has no game of any kind or wild life except catfish and rabbits.

"A few ducks light on the Illinois River every

ANOTHER ROUND OF CONTRACT TALKS STARTS WITH BITUMINOUS OPERATORS, APRIL, 1947

Left to Right (left side of table)—Mr. Lewis, John O'Leary, UMWA vice president; Thomas Kennedy, UMWA secretary-treasurer; John Owens, District 6 president; John T. Jones, District 16 president.

spring and fall but don't stay long. Illinois appropriates $329 thousand for the protection of the lives and property of a great, basic industry employing 45 thousand men; but it appropriates $1,888,000 for these rabbit shepherds."

When some of the smoke from the Congressional hearings on the Centralia disaster had blown away, it could be seen that not all of the results were good. Dr. Sayers, director of the Bureau of Mines, was rewarded for his objective report on mine safety conditions by being fired. Secretary Krug recommended to President Truman that Dr. James Boyd be appointed to replace Dr. Sayers. At a Senate hearing on Dr. Boyd's nomination, Mr. Lewis said:

"On the basis of Mr. Boyd's own testimony, he possesses no qualifications for the position. By his own admission, he knows nothing of the problems of the coal mining industry.

"He says he has book learning, but, of course, it takes more than book learning to save the lives of the coal miners in this industry and to give them that protection to which, as citizens and human beings, they are entitled under the laws of their country.

"This man says that all the director of the Bureau of Mines needs to be is a good administrator, so that he can hire specialized talent. How will such a man know whether he is hiring qualified or unqualified talent if he possesses no knowledge of the industry himself?"

Dr. Boyd was not confirmed at this time.

The trustees of the UMWA Welfare and Retirement Fund—Mr. Lewis, Captain Collisson and Thomas E. Murray—held their first meeting in New York City on April 8, 1947, and announced that the fund contained $18 million. The trustees approved a resolution for payment of a $1 thousand death benefit to each UMWA member who had died since June 1, 1946, the date when the fund had begun to accumulate. They also ordered a survey of individual cases of miners or their families who were destitute as a result of sickness, disability or retirement.

The first death benefit checks were sent on

May 16, 1947, to the next of kin of victims of the Centralia disaster.

The Anthracite Health and Welfare Fund also began functioning at the same time. In May, 1947, the trustees announced a grant of $575 thousand to the Barton Memorial Hospital of Jefferson Medical College, Philadelphia, for research into miners' diseases, particularly anthracosilicosis or "miner's asthma"; research to prevent miners' diseases; care of miners suffering from anthracosilicosis and tuberculosis; and rehabilitation programs for sick miners.

The Anthracite Fund also inaugurated a $1 thousand death benefit program, retroactive to June 1, 1946. Priority in both funds was given to benefit payments for deaths suffered in coal mining accidents.

Captain Collisson reminded the soft coal operators that the Smith-Connally Act would expire on June 30, 1947, and that the government, at that time, would have to relinquish control of the mines. The operators now were ready to sit down with the union and negotiate. The talks started at the Shoreham Hotel in Washington on May 15. The Southern operators attended but refused to participate, still contending that freight rate differentials made it impossible for them to sign a contract which would commit them to industry-wide wage standards.

Meetings with the Northern operators went on the next day. Mr. Lewis, John O'Leary, Thomas Kennedy, John Owens, Hugh White, president of District 12; Henry Allai, president and board member for District 14, and W. A. (Tony) Boyle, president of District 27, participated for the UMWA. Charles O'Neill, George Campbell, Harvey Cartwright, Hubert Howard, Harry M. Moses and P. L. Shields represented the operators. This conference adjourned without agreement on May 31.

Negotiations with the Southerners had begun on May 28, but it was soon apparent that they would negotiate only on the basis of depriving the UMWA of hard-won gains—the mine safety code, portal-to-portal pay, the Welfare Fund. The conference broke up on June 4.

Informal talks with the Northern operators continued through June. On June 30, the mines were returned to the operators. With the government no longer dealing with the UMWA, coal industry management quickly moved to sign a new agreement. An agreement in prin-

---

FIRST CHECKS FROM UMWA WELFARE FUND GO TO WIDOWS OF THE CENTRALIA DISASTER

Capt. N. H. Collisson *(left)* and Mr. Lewis sign $1,000 death benefit checks.

ciple was reached on July 3 and a subcommittee composed of John Owens and Percy Tetlow for the UMWA, and Harry Moses and Charles O'Neill for the operators, was selected to draft the contract. It was signed in Washington on July 8 and was made effective from July 1, 1947, until June 30, 1948.

It was a good contract. It raised the basic daily wage from $11.85 to $13.05. For the first time, the operators agreed to the Welfare Fund and increased royalty payments from 5 to 10 cents a ton. The mine safety code was written into the new agreement. The working day was reduced for inside workers from nine to eight hours a day, portal-to-portal, and the working day for outside men was cut to seven and one-quarter hours from the previous eight.

Because of the enactment of the restrictive Taft-Hartley Law two weeks before, the UMWA insisted on elimination of no-strike and penalty clauses. Mr. Lewis demanded and won insertion of the famous "able and willing" clause which provided for "employment of persons employed in the bituminous coal mines covered by this agreement during such time as such persons are able and willing to do work."

By June 11, 1947, virtually all operators in the United States, including those in the South, had signed the soft coal contract.

It had taken sixteen months! Now the UMWA had a contract with the operators, themselves, providing a Welfare and Retirement Fund financed as part of the cost of coal pro-

duction. A long, costly battle had been won, and a living monument to John L. Lewis and the United Mine Workers of America was being built.

The 1947 anthracite negotiations set a new record for brevity. They lasted one day. The hard coal miners won a $1.20-a-day wage raise and an increase in their Welfare Fund royalty from five to ten cents a ton. The relationship between the anthracite miners and operators had been stabilized to the point where neither side gave notice of termination of contract.

As the Journal commented: "Bituminous operators should take a lesson from their anthracite brethren."

The legislative pendulum was swinging, at this time, to the extreme of anti-labor legislation. The UMWA and President Lewis, John T. Jones and the staff of Labor's Non-Partisan League fought grim defensive battles against bill after bill introduced in the Seventy-ninth and Eightieth Congresses.

MR. LEWIS MAKES ANOTHER UNITY PROPOSAL, THIS TIME AS AN AFL SPOKESMAN IN 1947

Left to Right—Emil Rieve, CIO Textile Workers; Walter Reuther, CIO Auto Workers; Jacob Potofsky, CIO Clothing Workers; Albert Fitzgerald, CIO Electrical Workers; William Green, AFL president; Philip Murray, CIO president; Dan Tobin, AFL Teamsters; Mr. Lewis, William Hutcheson, AFL Carpenters; George Meany, AFL secretary-treasurer.

UMWA WINS $1.20-A-DAY WAGE BOOST AND 10-CENTS-A-TON WELFARE FUND ROYALTY IN '47

Seated, Left to Right—John O'Leary, UMWA vice president; Mr. Lewis, Thomas Kennedy, UMWA secretary-treasurer. *Standing, Left to Right*—Ezra Van Horn, operator chairman of the joint wage conference; Charles O'Neill, chief operator spokesman; Harry M. Moses, captive mines spokesman.

It was the Eightieth Congress that threw the book at organized labor. The Senate Labor Committee was evenly divided between Republican and Dixiecrat reactionaries and a disunited group of liberals. The labor-haters, headed by Senators Robert A. Taft and Joseph Ball, introduced bills, all of which were restrictive in nature. Other Senators introduced milder legislation. On March 7, 1947, Mr. Lewis appeared before the committee to oppose all of the proposed legislation. He said:

"I appear in opposition to the enactment into law by the Congress of regulatory, punitive and restrictive laws dealing with labor unions and their memberships. We are the one great country in which economic freedom still exists. The first duty of the Congress and of all of the citizens of our country is the conservation of this priceless heritage.

"The United States entered the world war with certain laws guaranteeing and implementing the rights and privileges of labor unions to organize and to bargain collectively for the welfare of their members. Now, after the winning of this, the greatest war the world has ever known, it is proposed that the liberties and rights of the workers shall be limited, restricted and annihilated.

"The Eightieth Congress can strengthen our free enterprise system by acting to maintain the economic freedom and liberties of the workers. The Eightieth Congress also can strike what might well be a fatal blow to this system by attempting to shackle the workers with restrictive and punitive laws."

Mr. Lewis detailed his objections to some of the provisions of these restrictive laws, many of which were later incorporated in the Eightieth Congress' Taft-Hartley Act:

"The proposal to set up a Federal Mediation Board with a high-priced personnel subject to political appointment is unnecessary and constitutes more government control by a bureau-

185

cratic agency. A conciliation service in the Department of Labor, properly strengthened, is sufficient for the needs of conciliation and mediation in labor disputes. Any independent board would simply be carrying over into peacetime the regulations and red tape that characterized the wartime agencies and which the people are so emphatically insisting shall cease. Labor has had enough of these boards and bureaucratic meddling in its affairs.

"The proposed so-called cooling-off period of sixty days constitutes the placing of labor in irons during this period of time. The right to strike is a fundamental right of the worker.

untary contract was restored. They could bargain for their goods and services. They could withhold their goods, if the price was not valid in their judgment, and they could withhold their services, if the price was not sufficient in their judgment. Take away or limit the right to strike in America and you turn the clock back to the Middle Ages, you strike down freedom and substitute the absolute form of government!

"Labor organizations are non-profit voluntary associations. They are treated under the law the same as other non-profit and voluntary associations such as churches, fraternal organizations, citizens' groups, and the many and varied

ANOTHER MINE DISASTER TOOK LIVES OF 27 MINERS AT OLD BEN NO. 8 IN JULY, 1947

Hugh White, District 12 president *(left)*, and Mr. Lewis talk with miners at the scene.

When the right to strike is limited or taken away from the workers in this country, the form of government in America is changed. The only difference between serfdom and freedom is the right of voluntary contract. When men were serfs in the Middle Ages, they had no power to contract. They could not barter for their goods or their services. Someone else had that power. When workers were made free, the right of vol-

non-profit associations that we have in this country. To single out our labor organizations and to say that they will be liable to suit in federal courts, notwithstanding the laws governing the procedure in suits against voluntary labor organizations, is discrimination and lack of equal protection of the law under our Constitution."

But the reactionary coalition steamrollered through its punitive Taft-Hartley law. Its outright repeal still is one of the UMWA's primary objectives. The officers' report to the 1948 Convention tells the story of its passage:

"On April 12, the Hartley Bill was voted out of House committee after hearings devoted to the testimony of spiteful anti-union employers.

These men were received graciously and given great leeway in their testimony while union representatives were given short shrift and were harassed and badgered throughout their testimonies.

"On April 17, 1947, the House by a thumping majority of 308-107, passed the infamous measure.

"The Taft Bill was passed by the Senate when Senator Taft succeeded in ramming it down the throats of the few protesting Senators.

"The conference report on the Taft-Hartley Bill abandoned all pretense that the House and Senate Committees wanted a fair bill. Congressman Fred Hartley's statement that 'there

votes could be mustered against the measure. Fifty-four Senators voted for the bill.

"On June 20, President Truman vetoed the legislation and returned the bill to the Congress with a sizzling message. However, he did not follow up his stinging rebuke with any concrete attempt to change the vote of Democrats who had supported the bill.

"Stampeding House members barely controlled their impatience to hear the message read and within one hour had voted to override the veto, 331 to 83. Senator Taft attempted to steamroller a final vote in the Senate, but a handful of liberal Senators were able to block

was more in the bill than meets the eye' and Senator Taft's remark that 'three-fourths of the measure was advocated by the employers of the nation' were amply confirmed.

"The intent and purpose of the law is to destroy every type of closed shop or union shop agreement. It destroys labor's traditional non-partisan policy. A union officer or paper cannot issue information on a candidate for public office. Secondary boycotts, regardless of purpose, are forbidden. Lawyers are assured controlling voices in labor-management affairs.

"On June 4, the report of the conferees was presented to the House and accepted by a vote of 320 to 79. In the Senate, only seventeen

BEFORE AFL DID THE GREAT FLIP-FLOP OF 1947 IN ITS STAND ON TAFT-HARTLEY LAW

Left to Right (the AFL Executive Council)—Felix Knight, Carmen; William Birthwright, Barbers; W. C. Doherty, Letter Carriers; David Dubinsky, Ladies' Garment Workers; Dan Tobin, Teamsters; George Meany, secretary-treasurer; William Green, president; William L. Hutcheson, Carpenters; Matthew Woll, Photo Engravers; Joseph Weber, Musicians; George Harrison, Railway Clerks; Harry C. Bates, Bricklayers; Mr. Lewis.

his high-handed action. Senators Murray of Montana, Pepper of Florida, Johnston of South Carolina, Taylor of Idaho, and Morse of Oregon led a fight to change seven votes needed to sustain the veto. For eighteen and a half

MR. CHING APPARENTLY ISN'T CONVINCING MR. LEWIS OF HIS POINT, MARCH 18, 1948

hours, Senators Taylor and Morse held the floor until an agreement was made to vote two days later. This move was made to enable the workers of the nation to protest to their Senators against the bill. Thousands upon thousands of telegrams, letters and cards poured into senatorial offices but it was useless. Senator Taft, joined by twenty renegade Democrats, led the Republican-National Association of Manufacturers forces to a sixty-eight to twenty-five victory, six more votes than needed."

After passage of the bill, Mr. Lewis charged that Senator Taft, by the act, sought to "reduce the workers of America to the status of second-class citizens." He said: "Free-born Americans will forever resent that classification by Taft and his ilk in Congress. It is obvious that the Republican Party sold out to financial interests for cash contributions in the last elections. There is one thing that can be said about the Republican Party—they stay bought."

But Mr. Lewis had an answer for organized labor. Boycott the law! It was a simple proposal. All unions would pledge to have nothing to do with the newly constituted National Labor Relations Board. The board would have no cases and the law would become inoperative.

This proposal was made to the AFL Executive Council in Chicago in September, 1947. Mr. Lewis convinced the Council members that his way was the only way to nullify the act. Robert Denham, Taft-sponsored general counsel for the NLRB, had made it plain that union officers who refused to sign non-communist affidavits could not present any cases before the board. Council members decided that the only effective way to oppose the act was to refuse to sign the affidavits. William Green said:

"The Executive Council decided that the Taft-Hartley law is reprehensible, vicious and destructive of the civil and legal right of workers. It could not conform to the Denham ruling."

Mr. Lewis said:

"I do not suggest that Denham's ruling is wrong. As a matter of fact, it may be expressly and concisely in accordance with the iniquitous Taft-Hartley Statute. Denham's ruling and the statute grant an option to labor organizations to file affidavits or withhold such filing. I choose to exercise my option negatively.

"What does Mr. Denham propose to do about it?"

But the AFL Executive Council presented that united front only until the AFL convention opened in San Francisco in October, 1947. In the interim, all of the Council members except William Hutcheson of the Carpenter's Union capitulated and decided to file affidavits.

In what is perhaps the greatest statement of his career, Mr. Lewis warned the AFL Convention delegates that they were making a terrible mistake. The AFL obviously was ready to bow down to the Taft-Hartley Law by adopting an amendment to its constitution stating that the AFL vice presidents were not Federation officers and, therefore, need not sign the Taft-Hartley non-communist affidavit. The hierarchy of the AFL knew that their thirteenth vice president, John L. Lewis, never would sign. Mr. Lewis told the delegates:

" 'Thou shalt not muzzle the ox that treadeth out the corn.' So runs the Scripture. But the

"GREEN: WE DISAFFILIATE, LEWIS" IS THE NOTE SENT TO THE AFL, DECEMBER 12, 1947

"TAFT-HARTLEY LAW IS THE FIRST UGLY, SAVAGE THRUST OF FASCISM IN AMERICA"

Mr. Lewis makes an historic address to the 1947 AFL convention in San Francisco.

Congress of the United States designated 15 million workers in this country, organized into one form or another of unions, as being cattle that treadeth out the economic corn of our country, and the Congress placed an economic muzzle on each of you. What are you going to do about it? Oh, I see. You are going to change our constitution. God help us!

"The Taft-Hartley Statute is the first ugly, savage, thrust of fascism in America. It came into being through an alliance between industrialists and the Republican majority in Congress, aided and abetted by those Democratic legislators who still believe in the institution of human slavery. It was bought and paid for by campaign contributions from the industrial and business interests of this country, and the Republican Party and the Democratic minority made good by forging these legislative shackles for you and the men and the women who pay you to represent them intelligently.

"It creates an inferior class of citizens, an inferior category and a debased position politically for the men and women who toil by hand or brain for their daily subsistence and to safeguard the future for their loved ones.

189

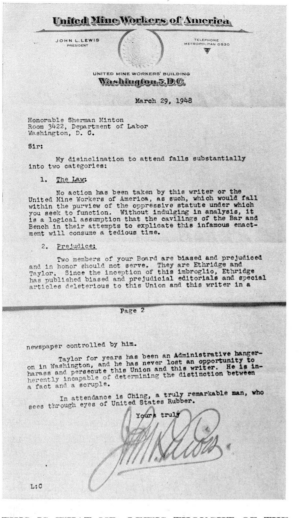

THIS IS WHAT MR. LEWIS THOUGHT OF THE TAFT-HARTLEY FACT-FINDING BOARD OF '48

"It symbolizes and parallels historically what happened in Italy before the coming of fascism, and it symbolizes and it parallels historically what happened in Germany before the coming of nazism. In each country, labor was regimented by oppressive and punitive laws. Its leaders were persecuted and, when the labor unions were made to be devoid of influence and power, the liberties of all the people were taken away.

"Now comes the Taft-Hartley Act, which tries to do that thing here in America, where we always believed heretofore that we had a free labor movement. We even presumed at times to lecture the representatives of labor in other countries and chide them because they didn't have a free labor movement. And yet when this statute is enacted—some seventy-three pages in length in the printed copy—it contains only two lines that say labor has the right to organize and thirty-three pages of restrictions which dare labor to try to organize. When that comes to pass, the welkin is filled with the outcries and the lamentations of our great leaders of labor in this country, calling upon high heaven to witness that all indeed is lost unless they can grovel on their bellies and come under this infamous act.

"I am one of those who does not think that all is lost. I represent an organization whose members believe they pay their officers to fight for them, not to deliver them into slavery. And four weeks before this convention assembled, we found our great leaders beating the drums in their own private little conclaves, trying to devise ways and means to have this convention call the Taft-Hartley Act a good a act, with a minimum degree of criticism from their membership.

"The question of signing the anti-communist affidavit, which is only one small feature of the abrogations of this act, has occupied the minds of our leaders and the columns of the public press now for more than six weeks, and at last we come to the fatal and unhappy day when men who purport to lead the mighty hosts within the American Federation of Labor cry aloud and say, 'There is nothing else for us to do— nothing else for us to do!'

"I will tell you what you should do, at least once in your lives: You should do your duty by your membership!

"I suppose it is hardly necessary for me to say that I am not a communist. I suppose it is hardly necessary for me to say that I was fighting communism in America, with the other members of my organization, before many people in this country knew what communism stood for in America and throughout the world. In the early 1920's, our organization paid for the research and study of the most serious analysis and compilation of communist activities in industrial America that ever has been gotten out, before or since, and that story was published in all the metropolitan newspapers of this country in seven serial issues. That story was made a Congressional document and is on file for anyone who cares to read it. It exemplifies what I say, that the United Mine Workers of America has been in the vanguard of our citizenship in opposing the cast iron Oriental philosophy of communism or any other damned kind of 'ism' in this country. And we expect to remain in that position. We don't expect to change our principles too often. And we do expect some support from the American labor movement, because we think that our attitude reflects the attitude of the rank and file in these great organizations of labor who work for a living and who want a country tomorrow in which their children and their grandchildren can live.

"The signing of the affidavit isn't the only thing that an organization has to do to conform to this act. This act is a trap, a pitfall for the organizations of labor, and I am surprised that those who have been attempting to analyze it haven't looked down the road just a few months or a year to find out some of the things that are inherent in this act.

"This act was passed to oppress labor, to make difficult its current enterprises for collective bargaining, to make more difficult the securing of new members for this labor movement, without which our movement will become so possessed of inertia that there is no action

and no growth. In a labor movement where there is no growth, there is no security for its existence because deterioration sets in and unions, like men, retrograde."

Mr. Lewis warned that, after the affidavit has been filed, the act still lists conditions which must be met in order for a petition to be received and acted on affirmatively. He enumerated the exhaustive and complex data that unions must file with the Secretary of Labor, including the compensation of its principal officers, its dues and initiation fees, its method of electing officials, its procedures for ratifying contracts and for authorizing strikes, and its financial status in minute detail. Mr. Lewis went on:

"And I assert, without qualification, that there isn't an organization in the American Federation of Labor that can make that report in a manner it can feel assured will be satisfying to the labor-hating, labor-baiting general counsel of the National Labor Relations Board—who has been hired to persecute and prosecute your unions and

"JUST ONE MORE," URGE PHOTOGRAPHERS AT THE 1948 TAFT-HARTLEY BOARD HEARING

make the life of your unions and their members more difficult.

"Oh, someone may say, 'I have talked to Mr. Denham.' Yes, I know a number of gentlemen have talked to Mr. Denham, and he has said that (A), (B), and (C) won't be necessary. That is all right for you gentlemen who have talked with Mr. Denham and convinced him of the purity of your motives and the fact that you will vote right on occasion. But how about some of the rest of us who haven't talked to Mr. Denham and who don't propose to talk to Mr. Denham privately? Do you think Mr. Denham will give us that consideration? Or will Mr. Denham, with the great powers vested in him by this act, continuously say to a few gentlemen in the American Federation of Labor, 'The reports filed by your union are not satisfactory'?

"Suppose he deems them satisfactory only while we are 'good' in his estimation. And if an organization follows a policy not to his liking, will he put his research workers and young

---

MR. LEWIS GIVES THE 1948 TAFT-HARTLEY FACT-FINDING BOARD A PIECE OF HIS MIND

lawyers to work on these filed accounts and dig up the discrepancies?

"There are things in here to which I cannot conscientiously swear of my own knowledge. What happens if I so swear and there are errors in it?

"Well, on the form prepared by Mr. Denham —to which you gentlemen may attach your John Hancocks—appears the following warning. I am quoting:

" 'Any fraudulent statement or misrepresentation in this affidavit is subject to punishment of $10 thousand fine or ten years imprisonment, or both, as provided for by Section 35-A of the Criminal Code.'

"I wonder on whom do you think Mr. Denham would use that clause? Oh, he wouldn't use it on the good boys. He wouldn't use it on those unions that are willing to grovel before him and before the Taft-Hartley Act, but he probably would use it on the type of union that believes this act to be a despicable adventure, inimical to the interests of all Americans, debasing to conform to, and not in concert with the guarantees accorded every citizen by the Constitution of the United States. That is the kind of people on whom Mr. Denham will invoke his ten years or his $10 thousand fine arrangement. If we had had this act and had our Mr. Denham in the last coal controversy, I ask you, do you think he would have given Judge Goldsborough a lift? Do you think he would have sent his young lawyers into court to make averments as to the inadequacy of the returns and the misrepresentations contained in those returns? And we could have taken the next ten years in appealing from the decision and have hired more lawyers, because the damage would have been done and the unions would have been convicted in the newspapers and the so-called court of public opinion in America!

"I wonder whither are we drifting. Members of the Executive Council—in their several meetings—have said each to the other, 'We must stand for the repeal of this un-American statute and we must resist and withhold support from all modifying amendments that seek to make it virtuous. It is so completely bad that it can't be made virtuous, and enough amendments cannot be attached to it to make it virtuous; so we will stand against its modification by amendment and we will ask the American people to

THE 1948 DISPUTE ENDS AS SEN. BRIDGES IS NAMED WELFARE FUND NEUTRAL TRUSTEE

Left to Right—Sen. Styles Bridges of New Hampshire, Mr. Lewis, Ezra Van Horn, operator trustee.

---

join us in asking for its complete repeal.' Then your president and other officers of your organization made known that position in public.

"And now we meet this afternoon and the distinguished committee on laws comes in here with a report that says, in effect: 'No, we won't permit Congress to amend it; we will debase ourselves and amend our own constitution to make it unnecessary.' What a paradox! What a paradox! How much heart do you think that will give the members of our organizations out in the industrial centers of this country when they see their great leaders, with all the pomp and ceremonials of a great convention, kneeling in obeisance before this detestable and tyrannical statute? Do you think that will encourage them?

"What effect will it have upon the ordinary citizen not related or concerned intimately with labor organizations? When you organize and implement your plans to go out and ask a Con-

gressman or Senator who fashioned this iron collar—that has been placed about your neck and sets you apart from your fellow man—to free you from this collar, what are you going to say to him when he answers: 'Why, Mr. Blank, I understand your organization has amended its constitution to permit you to accept the great virtues of this act, and that you overrode the opposition in your convention, in your wild clamor to be the first to sign up. How can you be opposed to the act when you fight to receive its emoluments? Surely Mr. Taft must be right when he says the rank and file of labor have been liberated under this act from the tyranny of their own leaders.'

"And is it true that the leaders of our movement are to be the first of our mighty host of 8 million members to put their tails between their legs and run like cravens before the threat of the Taft-Hartley Statute?

"I am reminded of the Biblical parable, 'Lions led by asses.' Is this true of this mighty host of 8 million workers in the American Federation of Labor, each filled with enthusiasm and ambition, each having responsibilities and dreams for himself and his family, each looking for-

193

ward to the realization of a substance that will carry him through the evil days that must come to every man? I think of that mighty host trying to advance across the plains of America, led and flanked and having their thinking done for them by intellectually fat and stately asses!

"I think you should think about these things. God knows, you are paid enough for thinking! I am, too, but I do try to shut my mouth occasionally and think once in a while, and that is what the American Federation of Labor should do.

"The great brains in Congress who enacted this measure under the tutelage of the lawyers employed by the National Association of Manufacturers, in a moment of mental aberration, put an optional clause in this statute. They made it optional whether or not you would conform to the obligations of the act. It is not mandatory and it is not illegal, and it does not put anyone in defiance of the act if he fails to file that

---

THE ANTHRACITE WELFARE FUND PROVIDES A SILICOSIS TREATMENT FOR JOHN FLANNERY

affidavit, because it is an option. And they unwittingly gave to labor the greatest chance to destroy this statute that will ever come to us.

"All we needed to do when we met in Chicago was to do nothing, and the act would have been discredited; there would have been no cases filed before the board, and its only functions would have been functions solely in the interests of the employer. The sense of fair play of the American people would not have permitted this government to spend money to utilize the savage devices of this statute solely in the interests of the great industrialists and employers of this country who now are making larger profits than ever before in the history of our country or any other country.

"We lost that chance. We lost it by bickering among ourselves. We lost it by failing to take counsel with each other in good faith. We lost it because we could not overlook our small animosities or our little ambitions or our private dreams.

"Time went on, and from the Council meeting in Chicago to the advance meetings of the departments in this city before the convention, the

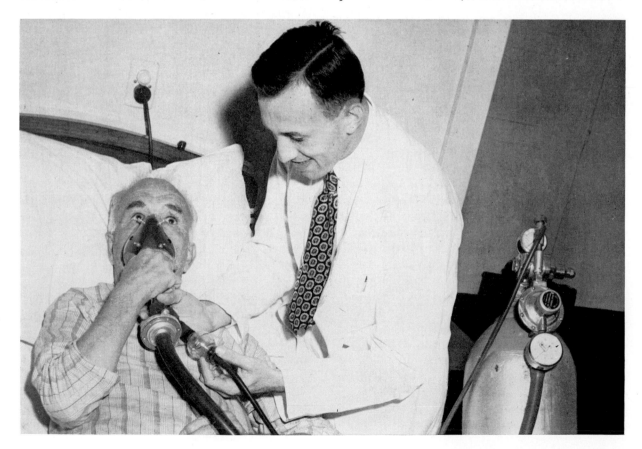

waiting world had a right to believe that labor could no longer exist in free America unless it was permitted by some stubborn man to sign an affidavit—to run the risk of being prosecuted under that affidavit in the months to come.

"I wonder what built up the labor movement in this country? Laws and statutes that protected the organizers of our movement when they went out to the meetings? Oh, no! The founders of our Federation had no such protection. They had to fight for the right to be heard. They had to fight for the right to hold a meeting. Men had to sacrifice and sometimes die for the right to join a union. Those were the conditions under which this movement of ours was created. It is a monument to the unselfish sacrifice of millions of men through decades of time and to the unswerving devotion to principles of the great leaders of our movement who have preceded us.

"Well, what are we going to do? Are we going to abandon that policy and that course of action

BACK TO COURT AS MR. TRUMAN USES TAFT'S "SLAVE STATUTE" AGAINST THE UMWA, 1948

Left to Right—Harrison Combs, UMWA associate counsel; Welly K. Hopkins, senior counsel; Mr. Lewis, Earl Houck, head of UMWA legal department.

that created us, that made strong and courageous men out of our members and great leaders out of their representatives? And are we now going to cry aloud, like a voice in the wilderness, that we must have a law that will prevent men and women from leaving our unions?

"That is what this clause in the constitution amounts to. Some people are afraid that a federal labor union will leave the American Federation of Labor because some raiding organization will pass by long enough to stop and get on a ballot. I make the averment to you that unless a majority of the members of a local union want to change their affiliation or leave that union, the contracting organization does not have to be on the ballot.

THIS WAS THE MINE WORKERS' CONSIDERED OPINION OF THE 1948 TAFT-HARTLEY FINES

"Oh, you might say, it makes it easier for the officers if we do this. What do I care about that? I think sometimes, as we grow successful in mature years and we get a little heavier, we are a little more indolent. And I think that is one thing about the American Federation of Labor. Some of us need to revise our perspective and wonder how we would have done this job ten years ago or twenty years ago; how we would have approached it and how we would have executed it.

"I am fairly familiar with the history of the American Federation of Labor. You can look at these charts on your tables there and you can see that in 1934, after two years of the New Deal, the membership of the American Federation of Labor was 2,600,000. You can look at the membership today and will see it is 7,600,-000—a great increase, but not too much to be proud of because after all, how did the Amer-

ican Federation of Labor get those members, substantially speaking? Why, those unions followed along after the armored divisions of the United Mine Workers of America and mopped them up. That is how you got them. Some of your unions adopted the technique of the industrial organizations. You refused to do that twelve years ago when the representatives of the United Mine Workers came before you pleading to take in the millions of the great mass production industries, and you said no, perhaps just as you will say no today when the representatives of the United Mine Workers rise in this convention to ask you to look whither you goest.

"The CIO, which we would like to have in membership in our great Federation now, never

196

would have been the CIO if the American Federation of Labor had listened to the words of the United Mine Workers of America, which offered them the services of their men and the millions of their treasury. That is what we offer you now. Had we been able to agree in 1934 and 1935 and 1936 in our councils of this Federation—yes, even in this very city and in this same hall in 1934—we wouldn't have 7,600,000 members today. The American Federation of Labor would have had, in my considered judgment, an enrollment today of 25 million workers in its ranks in American industry.

THE '48 CONTRACT TALKS; OPERATORS FILE MORE SUITS TO PREVENT PENSION PAYMENTS

Left to Right (clockwise around table)—Mr. Lewis, John Owens, UMWA secretary-treasurer; John T. Jones, District 16 president and conference secretary; Clarence Donaldson, District 2 vice president *(standing)*; William Blizzard, District 17 president; George Titler, District 29 president; Harvey Cartwright, Indiana Coal Operators and conference chairman; H. K. Cook, Tennessee operator; Joseph E. Moody, Southern Coal Producers Association president; George H. Love, Pittsburgh Consolidation Coal Co. president; Charles O'Neill, chief operator spokesman; Harry M. Moses, representing steel industry captive mines; George F. Campbell, Illinois Coal Operators; J. Roy Browning, Illinois Coal Operators.

"Oh, you may say, that is the word of a prophet without too much honor in his own country. Yes, but it is the word of a worker in the ranks, and it is the word of one who has worked in the industrial workshops of this country, and who has carried the flag of organization throughout our great modern industries. And it is the word of one who knows something about the dreams of the men and women who work for a living, and who knows something about their responsibilities and their burdens. And I say to you, as my calm and considered judgment, I say to you now that if you take this action today recommended by your committee, in my judgment, you will live to regret it. You will live to regret it!

"That is only the opinion of one and may not be well received on the part of some of you. If there ever was a time in the history of the organized labor movement, in the history of our country, when unity of purpose, unity of the structural form of our movement, unity of policy and objectives were needed in the interest of every man, woman and child under our flag, then that time is now. Yet we quibble over details. We swallow a camel—the Taft-Hartley Act—and we strain at gnats.

"Your committee comes in here with a constitutional amendment, which, of course, I am trying to oppose—just for the record—that puts in the printed word of the constitution the claim that the American Federation of Labor will only have two officers. Well, that is not true. The Federation will continue to have fifteen officers—thirteen members of some kind of an Executive Council and a president and secretary, which makes fifteen—although your constitution will say that you have only two officers. Of course, the Council is going to have some duty, and if its members are not officers of the Federation, what will they be?

"You know, to me that smacks of the communist technique: to lie to escape responsibility. That is what that is; that's a lie!

"Is that what you want to do, or do you want to be men, and stand foursquare, and look the Congress in the face, and look Taft and Hartley in the face, and look Denham in the face and say: 'We want our rights as free men, and we are going to have them.'

"You know, if you grovel enough in this convention you will probably have more to grovel for next January and March, because when the Congress and the enemies of labor find out how easy you are they will give you more to grovel for. Did you ever think of that? Hadn't you better fight a little now than fight more down the road? Or would you rather run?

"Well, gentlemen of the convention, I represent an organization—the United Mine Workers of America. They pay me; and they are not going to run with you. They don't like to run. I will say this, that the mine workers don't hesitate to tell me that they don't pay me to run, either, in the wrong direction.

"We are not going to run with you. I don't know what the Congress will do next session. That depends a great deal on what this convention does. If they see we are on the run, they will take courage and they will fashion some more sharp spears to accelerate our speed even greater. Conceivably, they might pass a bill next session that takes away the optional features of the act; makes it twenty years in the pen for not signing this affidavit or sends out a provost-marshal guard to corral some of us; charges us with treason or high crimes and misdemeanors. That is the next logical step. That is what happened in Italy and in Germany,

1948 DEADLOCK IS BROKEN AS COURT OK'S PENSIONS; MR. LEWIS BEFORE FACT BOARD

isn't it? God knows, it had been happening in Russia for a long time before that—even before we made them our allies. Sometimes I think we must have known what we were doing when we made them our allies. That's questionable, though.

"Isn't that the next step? If you resist the power of the state, the central government will be used against you; and if you don't resist, it will be used against you that much more quickly, because they won't lose any sleep at night worrying about what to do with a labor movement that is fleeing before the storm. And that is what you will be doing if you pass this damnable amendment that you have before you.

"So, friends of mine, take your choice. Some of you are boasting you have the votes to do it. Perhaps you have, but that isn't all you need after you do it, because you will have additional troubles. You will have some trouble in your own membership in this country. And how many of you think that you are going to have an easy time in the future after you qualify under this act and after you amend your constitution? How many suits do you think will be filed against you?

"You know that under this act any place where the employer alleges an unfair labor practice, he can ask the board for an injunction, and the board has no power but to petition for the injunction from the court on a prima facie presentation of facts by the employer, not subject to review in advance. That injunction will cut you off from your membership, whatever the circumstances. And what are you doing today by this proposed amendment to this constitution? You are repealing the 1919 injunction policy articulated by that convention, the words of which were written by men in this convention at the instigation of President Gompers. You are repealing that, and you are humbling yourselves in abasement before the return of government by injunction.

"Have you thought of these things? Hastily, perhaps, some of you—some of you looking at the immediate considerations. I am trying to look at the future of our labor movement. I am here to say that if we have the courage to stand together, then we are strong enough and powerful enough to protect our membership, our unions and our country from the detrimental effects of this most despicable act. If we don't stand together—well, divided we fall.

"Now, I won't keep you much longer. I fear greatly you are bored. I have tried to be as brief

---

A HANDSHAKE FOR FACT-FINDER DAVID COLE AS PROGRESS IS MADE IN THE 1948 TALKS

Left to Right—Mr. Lewis, Waldo E. Fisher, Mr. Cole and E. Wight Bakke of the government fact-finding board.

as possible. It is a most serious question with me. If I have seemed exceedingly earnest, it is because I feel the weight of the great responsibility.

"I ask you to believe that, as far as I can translate it and interpret it, I am representing the undivided thought and spirit of the men who compose the organization that I have the honor to represent.

"One thing more. It is always well to have a little zest in an undertaking. I wish to say this to you: I care nothing about the title of vice president. I care nothing about the numbers that are attached to the names of the members of the Executive Council. I have often wondered why we had those titles and those numbers. I would just as lief sit on an Executive Council that was called an Executive Board. That is what the United Mine Workers have, an Executive Board, with no numbers, no titles. It isn't a question of being demoted in honorable position. There is nothing personal about it. It is a matter of principle as to whether or not I should accept a position on a denatured governing body of this organization which will live a continuous lie as long as in service, because that board, whatever you call it, will be the officers of the American Federation of Labor. And it simply is not true that the American Federation of Labor will have only two officers.

"But if you do elect to take this astounding action, I can only say to you that you will be voting this speaker off of the Council of the

THE STRAIN OF NEGOTIATIONS SHOWS AS THE UMWA OFFICERS SIGN 1948 SOFT COAL PACT

Left to Right—Thomas Kennedy, vice president; Mr. Lewis, John Owens, secretary-treasurer.

American Federation of Labor. I will not be a candidate for election to this debased board.

"Perhaps that makes no difference. Perhaps you will say, 'John Lewis is trying to hold a gun to the head of the convention.'

"That is not true. I don't think anyone can hold a gun to the head of this convention. I am simply telling you what I think on principle, so that you can make your decision with full knowledge of what it means. As far as that is concerned, on this particular issue, I don't think that the Federation has a head. I think its neck has just grown up and haired over.

"So, gentlemen of the convention, I know you must be appreciative, as I, of the portents of this possible action. I know you are just as anxious to serve your membership in this Federation. It is a question of policy how to do it—to arrive at your decision.

"Call the long roll when you will, and the decision—whatever it may be—will be yours."

The AFL disregarded Mr. Lewis' warning. The convention amended the constitution. To cap its anti-UMWA position, it also voted to distribute the UMWA's District 50 membership among AFL unions which claimed jurisdiction over the district's members. These actions, coupled with the failure of the AFL to act effectively on the mine workers' unity program, convinced the UMWA it was not getting value received for its per capita payments to the AFL. So, in November, Mr. Lewis scribbled a memorandum in pencil which he sent to the president of the Federation. It said:

"GREEN, AFL

WE DISAFFILIATE

LEWIS"

The veteran UMWA leader, Vice President John J. O'Leary, died suddenly of a heart attack in St. Luke's Hospital, San Francisco, on October 27, 1947. At the 1948 UMWA convention, Mr. Lewis said:

"John O'Leary was one of the most stalwart

of our warriors through the years. He died in battle for the principles of his organization. Just a year ago this month, in the city of San Francisco, at a convention of the American Federation of Labor, where your representatives were urging the rest of the labor movement to follow the UMWA through the walls we had breached, John O'Leary was doing his part, day by day, on the floor of that convention, in committees and in conferences. He extended his strength to the point of producing the nervous strain that resulted in the attack that caused his death far from home."

Thomas Kennedy, after twenty-two years as UMWA International secretary-treasurer, succeeded Mr. O'Leary as the vice president of the International Union. John Owens, president of District 6 and special assistant to Mr. Lewis, became secretary-treasurer. Adolph Pacifico became District 6 president and Alvin Douglass and R. C. Owens were named vice president and secretary-treasurer, respectively.

Mart F. Brennan, District 7 president, took Mr. O'Leary's place as trustee of the Anthracite Health and Welfare Fund. W. A. Boyle, District 27 president, filled the vacancy as special assistant to Mr. Lewis.

Another change occurred in October, 1947, when John Kmetz, for ten years International Executive Board member from District 1, was sworn in as Assistant Secretary of Labor, succeeding Philip Hannah of Ohio. Both had started as breaker boys in the mining industry.

The coal operators' line-up also changed when Joseph E. Moody was hired to represent the Southern Coal Producers Association. He, like his predecessor, former Senator Burke, had no experience in the coal industry.

$1 WAGE BOOST, 20 CENTS FOR WELFARE WON IN ANTHRACITE, AS IN SOFT COAL, IN 1948

Left to Right—Thomas Kennedy, vice president; John Owens, secretary-treasurer; Mr. Lewis.

In July, 1947, Dr. R. R. Sayers, former head of the Bureau of Mines, was appointed chief of the newly-created Medical Advisory Board for the Bituminous Welfare Fund. The trustees established the board and asked it to study types and standards of medical and hospital service to be furnished to miners in their communities; to suggest policies for physical rehabilitation, industrial hygiene and sanitation; to conduct research on industrial ailments; and to assist local health authorities and operators in carrying out recommendations in Admiral Boone's medical survey of the industry.

The initial phase of the fund's work—payment of death benefit claims—was in good order and the fund appeared ready to expand its work in accordance with the contract. Then, on January 17, 1948, Thomas E. Murray resigned as the neutral trustee in a dispute over pension payments. Having broken up the board by their stubborn opposition to any program, the operators and Ezra Van Horn, their trustee, began haling Mr. Lewis, the mine workers' trustee, into courtrooms, before government boards and fact-finding agencies. The ensuing two-year wrangle provoked by the operators inspired still another anti-UMWA campaign by editorial writers and radio commentators.

On January 20, Mr. Lewis informed George M. Humphrey of the M. A. Hanna coal interests, and Benjamin Fairless of "Big Steel," that Mr. Murray had resigned. Mr. Humphrey and Mr. Fairless were the key men through whom Mr. Lewis had won industry consent to the fund in the 1947 contract. He asked them to call the operators' negotiating committee to a meeting with the UMWA to work out a settlement within the next five days. Mr. Lewis wrote:

"Van Horn consistently has refused to agree to any proposals which seek to activate the pension fund. The dispute has impaired and prevented activation of the Welfare Fund in whole or in part and thus defeats one of the major provisions of the 1947 agreement."

Four days later, Mr. Fairless replied that the problem was one that could be solved only by the fund's trustees. He said that he represented only about 5 per cent of the national tonnage and that Mr. Lewis should address any request to reopen the contract to the signatories of the bitu-

---

UMWA WINS ANOTHER FIGHT FOR THE UNION SHOP IN THE CAPTIVE MINE INDUSTRY, 1948

Mr. Lewis waits as Harry M. Moses (*right*) signs the bituminous wage agreement.

AWARDING THE FIRST ANTHRACITE PENSIONS AT HAZLETON, PA., ON SEPTEMBER 17, 1948

Left to Right—Mr. Lewis, John Close, 72; Albert Fox, 67; Wash Fedora, 73; Thomas Kennedy, UMWA vice president.

---

minous agreement. Mr. Humphrey, also, declined and suggested that Mr. Lewis refer the matter to the president of the Pittsburgh Consolidation Coal Co.

Mr. Lewis took them at their word. He notified the signatories of the 1947 agreement, on February 2, that the deadlock between the trustees "constitutes an outstanding, unresolved dispute, national in scope."

It remained so and on March 12, 1948, Mr. Lewis wrote the UMWA membership:

"For eight months, the bituminous coal operators, through their trustee, Ezra Van Horn, of Cleveland, O., have dishonored the 1947 wage agreement and defaulted under its provisions affecting the Welfare Fund.

"This fund on March 6, 1948, had assets amounting to $29,494,032.87, all lying unused in banks. Such welfare payments as have been made during the past eight months have been made from the funds accrued under the 1946 agreement, and are limited to the payment of death benefits and inadequate relief in individual distress cases.

"During the past year, and throughout the hard winter which has afflicted the nation, our membership has continued loyally, and with a sense of public duty, to break all records in the production of coal. This service increased the profits of the coal companies and should have won some consideration for human values; but instead has made them contemptuous of their contractual and moral obligations.

"The winter is now gone. This office proposes to go forward in requiring the coal operators to honor their agreement. Your ears will soon be assailed by their outcries and wails of anguish. To relieve themselves, they need only to comply with the provisions of the agreement which they solemnly executed on July 8, 1947.

"Please discuss this matter in your local unions so that our membership may be fully advised. You will later hear more from this office on this subject."

The matter was discussed in the local unions and on March 15 the coal miners began to leave the pits. When the miners stopped work, the "wails of anguish" began. The bituminous operators wrote Mr. Lewis on March 19 that they were not responsible for the tie-up in the fund. They said they had made their payments into the fund and that a dispute among the trustees was not a contract violation.

Mr. Van Horn proceeded to file the first of his suits to prevent operation of the fund. On the same day, March 20, Cyrus Ching, director of the Federal Mediation and Conciliation Serv-

NATIONAL SECURITY PROBLEMS REVIEWED BY CIVIL, MILITARY LEADERS, NOVEMBER, 1948

Left to Right—Malcolm Muir, Newsweek Magazine; Winthrop Aldrich, board chairman, Chase National Bank; Gen. Omar Bradley, Army chief of staff; Robert R. Young, board chairman, Chesapeake & Ohio Ry. Co.; Arthur H. Sulzberger, publisher, The New York Times; Mr. Lewis.

ice, wired Mr. Lewis an invitation to attend a meeting with the operators at his office. Mr. Lewis replied:

"Obviously, you think time is expendable. The group of individuals you have asked to your Monday meeting is the kept outfit that hangs around the Shoreham Hotel to constitute a false front for the coal industry. They are the same outfit who, for eight months, have dishonored the existing agreement in the coal industry. It is preposterous to assume that any progress will be made at your meeting, as these men merely carry out instructions of their principals.

"There are a half dozen men who can speak with finality on matters of policy affecting the coal industry. They are Messrs. Fairless of Steel, Humphrey of M. A. Hanna, Harriman of Union Pacific, Buchanan of Old Ben, Francis of Island Creek, and Alexander of Pocahontas Fuel.

"In view, however, that you have made a public announcement of such a meeting, and with every desire to avoid any discourtesy to you

personally, the UMWA, out of deference to your request, and purely as a matter of routine procedure, will have a representative committee present at your meeting."

After his meeting, Mr. Ching suggested that the miners return to work and that a three-man fact-finding board be selected to report on the dispute. The mine workers' committee—John Owens, W. A. Boyle and John T. Jones—declined.

Mr. Ching turned the dispute over to the White House and President Truman promptly invoked the Taft-Hartley Law. He appointed a Taft-Hartley fact-finding board before which the UMWA would be legally compelled to appear. Federal Judge Sherman Minton was appointed chairman and the other members were Mark Ethridge, publisher of the Lousiville Courier-Journal, and George W. Taylor, former chairman of the War Labor Board.

The board summoned Mr. Lewis to testify before it, but he wrote Judge Minton that he was "disinclined" to attend because he felt the board was biased. Mr. Lewis cited anti-UMWA editorials published in Mr. Ethridge's newspaper and said that Mr. Taylor "has never lost an opportunity to harass and persecute this union." The letter ended:

"In attendance is Ching, a truly remarkable man, who sees through eyes of United States Rubber."

In a circular letter to the UMWA membership, Mr. Lewis relates events of the next few days:

"On March 29, the chairman of the President's board of inquiry issued and had served upon me by U. S. marshals a subpoena commanding me to appear before his board at 2:00 P.M. on that same date, the subpoena saying, among other things, 'Fail not at your peril.'

"On the afternoon of Monday, March 29, the U. S. District Court for the District of Columbia issued an order to show cause why I had not responded to the board's subpoena, and a marshal served the same upon me at 9:00 P.M. at my home in Alexandria, Va.

"On Tuesday, March 30, our attorneys appeared before U. S. Judge Curran to oppose issuance of the order requested by the board. Judge Curran, in a twenty-minute hearing, overruled our attorneys and ordered the U. S. marshal to serve upon me another order to compel me to attend the hearing of the board at 2:00 P.M. the same day.

"At 2:00 P.M. on March 30, under compulsion of the court order, I appeared before the board of inquiry and made answer to all questions asked of me by the board.

I AM A CANDIDATE FOR RE-ELECTION TO THE ONLY OFFICE I WANT: MR. LEWIS IN 1948

MARCH 11, 1949, BROUGHT A WORK STOPPAGE TO EMPHASIZE THE FIGHT FOR MINE SAFETY

John Owens *(left)*, UMWA secretary-treasurer, and Mr. Lewis at UMWA headquarters.

"On Wednesday, March 31, the board of inquiry made a report of its findings to the President of the United States.

"I asked you on March 12, 'to discuss the matter in your local union.' Such discussions as may have been held, or which you may hereafter desire, have been and will continue to be on your own initiative. As far as I know, it is

205

UNITED CONSTRUCTION WORKERS' A. D. LEWIS IN NEW YORK DURING THE 1949 TAXI STRIKE

still the inherent right and privilege of American citizens to continue to exercise the right of free speech and freedom of assembly.

"I, therefore, now repeat that you are not now under any orders, directions, or suggestions, expressed or implied, from me or any of the union officers to cease work or to continue to cease work in protest to the present dishonoring (as we see it) of the 1947 contract."

The board's report charged that the circular letter to the membership of March 12 had "induced" the miners to stop work.

On April 3, President Truman ordered Attorney General Clark to seek a Taft-Hartley injunction against Mr. Lewis and the UMWA to force the miners back into the pits. Judge Goldsborough again entered the picture and the same day issued another restraining order without a hearing.

Mr. Van Horn's second suit to prevent activation of the fund was filed on April 6. It warned all banks, under legal peril, that they would be held responsible for any disbursements of Welfare Fund money. On the same day, the UMWA

offered to meet with the operators, in obedience to Judge Goldsborough's order.

Judge Goldsborough next scheduled a hearing for April 12, directing Mr. Lewis and the UMWA to show cause why they should not be held in contempt of court because of the miners' refusal to return to work.

The four-month stalemate over the naming of a third trustee for the fund ended on April 10, when Mr. Lewis and Mr. Van Horn agreed on Senator Styles Bridges of New Hampshire, whose name had been proposed by Speaker of the House Joseph Martin.

On the day of the contempt hearing, April 12, the trustees—Mr. Van Horn dissenting—voted to start pension payments. Mr. Lewis immediately telegraphed all local unions:

"Pensions granted. The agreement is now honored."

The men returned to work, but Judge Goldsborough held that the return to work at this time did not constitute satisfactory compliance with his order.

He proceeded with the contempt case and on April 20 found the International Union and Mr. Lewis guilty of civil and criminal contempt of court. Judge Goldsborough levied fines of $1,-400,000 on the UMWA and $20 thousand on Mr. Lewis for criminal contempt. No fine was imposed for civil contempt. The case wound its way to the U. S. Supreme Court, which, on November 7, 1949, sustained Judge Goldsborough. The check which Secretary-Treasurer Owens wrote to pay the UMWA's fine was the largest ever written for a fine imposed by a United States court.

In a statement explaining the Bridges-Lewis pension plan, the new neutral trustee said pension payments should start immediately on the basis of $100 a month to men who were at least sixty-two years old, who had twenty years' service in the industry, and who retired after May 29, 1946, date of the Krug-Lewis agreement. This was a compromise. Mr. Lewis had proposed retirement at sixty. Mr. Van Horn wanted the age to be sixty-five.

Payments, however, could not be made because Mr. Van Horn still had the funds tied up with his complicated legal actions. By now, suits No. 1 and No. 2 had been dropped and he had instituted No. 3.

206

Miss Josephine Roche, former Colorado coal operator and friend of the miners, became director of the Welfare Fund in April, 1948. She had been technical assistant and consultant to Mr. Lewis on fund affairs since December, 1947.

With the Welfare program still stymied by litigation and dispute, the UMWA moved into 1948 contract negotiations in Washington. Talks began on May 18 with Mr. Lewis challenging the authority of the Southern Coal Producers Association to bargain for Southern companies. The association, as such, was not a party to the existing agreement. It complained to the general counsel of the NLRB, Robert Denham, who obtained another Taft-Hartley injunction from Judge Goldsborough. He ordered the UMWA to bargain with the SCPA. The UMWA complied and as talks resumed, June 7, Mr. Lewis said:

"As representatives of labor, we sit here under attainder; in reverse, your limbs are unshackled. You have no fear of the thought police, and when annoyed by our conduct, you can, at will, invoke additional processes of government to dragoon us. Free collective bargaining? You have reduced the words to mockery.

"We have at present no wage proposals. Assuredly, the mine workers expect improvements. You and your industry are magnificently opulent. Your 1946 profits were without parallel. In 1947, you increased them twice and even thrice. In recent months, you have levied additional heavy increases upon each ton of coal sold. You are digging deep and without restraint into the national purse. From time to time you raise outcries against the men who mine your coal; and, while the gullible public is bewildered by your outcries, you pluck more doubloons from the consumers of coal. In this fashion, and with hardened conscience, you have become the most corpulent of our native fat cats.

"We assume that you would deplore any impairment of your abnormal income after July 1. Such an assumption would seem to be a logical predicate for the making of a new wage agreement before that date. Under such circumstances, the mine workers will be glad to consider any offer affecting the terms of a possible new contract which you may persuade yourselves to utter. Just in passing, may we suggest that as a condition precedent to a new contract, the mine workers will expect guarantees incident to the honoring of the current agreement in the matter of its welfare provisions."

THE MINERS' INTERNATIONAL FEDERATION MEETS AT UMWA HEADQUARTERS, MAY, 1949

Left to Right—Achille Delattre of Belgium, MIF president; Mr. Lewis, Sir Will Lawther of Great Britain, MIF secretary.

Trustees Bridges and Lewis voted a few days later—Mr. Van Horn dissenting—to begin paying benefits from the funds thus far blocked by the operator trustee. The miners and operators, meanwhile, continued negotiations until the operators walked out on June 15. The next day, Ezra Van Horn filed his suit No. 4 to tie up the Welfare Fund, and on June 19 President Truman again invoked the Taft-Hartley Law and appointed a board to report on the contract dispute.

Then, dramatically, on June 22, the very day that Mr. Lewis was to testify, the miners' big break came. The same Judge Goldsborough who twice had shackled the union with injunctions and severe fines, now ruled for the miners. He upheld the Bridges-Lewis pension plan, called it a "business-like" proposal, and threw out Mr. Van Horn's No. 3 suit, which had challenged the plan. Judge Goldsborough's decision said:

"There seems to be nothing that shocks the mind at the idea that the members of the United Mine Workers who have worked for twenty years under the ground and are sixty-two years old should get $100 a month pensions . . . It is just enough to give them a little dignity. The court does not think that there is any justification in law or sound reason for this complaint."

When Mr. Lewis appeared before the inquiry board later that day, he told it that in the light of Judge Goldsborough's decision he was confident that the operators and the union could reach an accord on their own. The three members—David L. Cole, a Patterson, N. J., lawyer; E. Wight Bakke of Yale University, and Waldo E. Fisher of the University of Pennsylvania—agreed to let the parties try to settle their own differences.

The operators quickly got down to genuine collective bargaining and in three days, on June 25, a joint statement was issued by the negotiators announcing that a wage agreement had been signed. At the same time, the operators removed the last legal roadblock to the Welfare Fund by instructing Mr. Van Horn to drop his suit No. 4.

Two major changes were made in the new contract. The statement said:

"The wage agreement between the bituminous coal operators and United Mine Workers of America, to become effective on July 1, 1948,

provides: (1) An increase in wages for each union employee of a flat $1 per day; (2) An increase in the Welfare and Retirement Fund of 10 cents per ton, making the total payment into this fund 20 cents per ton.

"All other terms and conditions of the previous wage agreement remain as they were."

Basic wages were now $14.05 a day.

The anthracite agreement, which followed quickly, again was arrived at through free collective bargaining without benefit of courts or presidential boards. A series of conferences was held beginning on May 27 and the agreement was reached on July 3. It amended the 1947 agreement, provided for a wage increase of $1 a day and doubled the Welfare Fund royalty to 20 cents a ton.

In the bituminous industry, the captive mine operators refused to sign the new contract, once again bringing up the issue of the union shop. On July 2, Harry Moses, representing steel industry captive mines, filed a Taft-Hartley charge of unfair labor practices against the

TAKING A WALK IN 1949 TO GIVE SOUTHERN OPERATORS TIME TO COUNT THEIR TONNAGE

Left to Right—Samuel Caddy, District 30 president; Mr. Lewis, Ray Thomason, District 29 International Board member.

MAY 31, 1949: ANOTHER HEARING, ANOTHER PLEA TO CONGRESS FOR SAFETY LEGISLATION

UMWA with General Counsel Robert Denham of the NLRB. The charge was that the UMWA's union shop agreement with the industry, in existence since 1939, and since 1941 in the captive mines, was illegal because the miners had not voted in an NLRB election on the issue.

The captive mine employees gave their answer on July 6, end of their vacation. They did not return to work. Mr. Denham rushed to court, seeking still another Taft-Hartley injunction. But Judge Goldsborough, instead of issuing one, mediated the issue and got the steel industry operators to sign the same agreement as the rest of the industry with the understanding they could carry their NLRB charge on through hearings and into the courts, if necessary.

The NLRB later ruled that the union shop clause violated the Taft-Hartley Act, but the case later became academic with the signing of the 1950 contract. That agreement contained a new union shop clause, written to satisfy operators' objections and the legalistic language of the Taft-Hartley law.

The UMWA Welfare and Retirement Fund continued to expand its functions. Dr. Warren F. Draper became executive officer of the medical and hospitalization program in August, 1948. An outstanding medical administrator, he had served as public health officer under General Eisenhower in Europe.

The historic moment finally had arrived when the dreams of Mr. Lewis and the UMWA came true. Pension check No. 1 of the United Mine Workers of America Welfare and Retirement Fund was handed to the first pensioner, Horace Ainscough, a retired coal miner from Rock Springs, Wyo. Trustee Lewis presented the check in a ceremony on September 9, 1948, in the International Executive Board room at UMWA headquarters in Washington.

Next step in the fund's expansion was the establishment, starting in October, of ten regional medical offices in the bituminous coal fields.

The year 1948 was a presidential election year, and Mr. Lewis, like many American workers, found himself "between Scylla and Charybdis," without a candidate to support. The Republican presidential candidate was Governor Thomas E. Dewey of New York. Mr. Lewis

209

ignored Governor Dewey. Of the Democratic candidate, President Truman, Mr. Lewis had this to say in his opening speech to the 1948 UMWA convention at Cincinnati:

"It is unfortunate that a President of the United States should use all the vast powers which the people have conferred upon him and use all the money which is in the treasury, paid there by taxes, to prosecute a group of citizens against whom he has a malignant personal hatred. It is a sad commentary that a President of the United States would stoop that low. And yet that's the record, and it devolves upon you to determine what you are going to do about it when you have a chance to decide whether or not Harry Truman is going to be the future President of the United States.

"He is a man totally unfitted for the position. His principles are elastic and he is careless with the truth. He has no special knowledge on any subject and he is a malignant, scheming sort of individual who is dangerous not only to the United Mine Workers, but also dangerous to the United States."

As the 1948 UMWA convention opened, the International Union was in its best financial condition in its long history. It had weathered the concentrated opposition of the federal government and the coal operators for two years and had emerged from the struggle stronger than ever. The organization had paid two huge fines for contempt of court, but the membership considered them small premiums to pay for the tremendous insurance policy that was the Welfare Fund.

In appreciation and approval of the victorious policies of their International officers, the delegates unanimously voted to increase Mr. Lewis' salary to $50 thousand a year and to raise the salaries of Vice President Kennedy and Secretary-Treasurer Owens to $40 thousand annually. Salaries of other union officials, also, were raised.

Remembering their bitter experiences with the "Little Steel" formula and the failure of the OPA to hold prices during World War II, the delegates adopted a resolution condemning all forms of wage and price controls. They, also, called for guaranteed regular employment in the bituminous coal fields. On this important question, Mr. Lewis said:

"When market conditions in the bituminous industry become so poor that they threaten stability of our contract and the working conditions of our people, when the disparity of employment gets to a point where it constitutes a rank injustice and lack of opportunity for our members to work, the UMWA, itself, may find it neces-

---

A DISCUSSION OF MINE SAFETY LEGISLATION DURING THE 1949 CONGRESSIONAL SESSION

Left to Right—Mr. Lewis, Sen. Matthew M. Neely of West Virginia, Sen. Elbert D. Thomas of Utah.

PUTTING THE QUERY TO THE SOUTHERN COAL
ASSOCIATION: WHOM DO YOU REPRESENT?

At the microphone is Joseph E. Moody, president, Southern Coal Producers Association, facing Mr. Lewis *(in background)*.

sary to advise our members how many days a week they need to work. We have that contractual right. It is a matter of self-preservation for the investors in the industry. If the operators can't give any leadership on the commercial side of this industry, the United Mine Workers of America can and will."

The convention stood in silent prayer in memory of Vice President O'Leary and former President Frank J. Hayes. Mr. Hayes died in Denver, Colo., on June 10, 1948.

The convention raised dues to $4 a month for working miners and initiation fees to $50, primarily to help defray union costs in connection with welfare activities. They also decided to hold conventions every four years instead of every two.

In his closing address, Mr. Lewis said, without mentioning the name of Governor Dewey:

"Some politician said recently that the Taft-Hartley Act at least gave labor the right to organize and protected them in that enterprise. That man has not even read the act. The act does just the reverse. If he will take the copy of the statute as printed by the Government Printing Office, and read it, he will find one line in the preamble which says that 'labor has the right to organize,' but following that he will find seventy-four pages of restrictions that dare labor to try to organize."

Mr. Lewis went on:

"If war comes—and war may come—it will be your sons who will march forth with the other sons of our Republic to protect America. It will be you, with others similarly situated, who will create the productive wealth, the lethal weapons and the goods of commerce to maintain our country—if war comes. And I assert that this must be done as free men, and not as serfs to those who would protect and entrench their own privileges by denying equal privileges and equal rights to those who earn their living by the sweat of their brow.

"There are some strange undercurrents abroad in our land. There are those—who profess to fight communism—who are secretly hoping that the alternative of communism as they see it, in some form of fascist type of government, will eventually triumph in America. There are rich men in America who are so fearful for the preservation of their wealth and privileges, who profess to be so alarmed at the rising strength of the common man as exemplified in our modern labor organizations, that they would willingly

211

trade to accept the regulations and the proscriptions of a possible man on horseback.

"I am one of those who believe that the function of the government is to serve the people, not to oppress the people."

Mr. Lewis, as chairman of the Board of Trustees, reported on January 14, 1949, that in its first twenty months of operation the Welfare Fund had paid approximately $68 million to 260,123 beneficiaries. He noted that death benefit applications were being processed within twenty-four hours of receipt by the fund and that "disability and pension cases require only a few days, although each case is carefully investigated." By May 1, less than four months later, the figures had climbed to almost $107 million disbursed to 344,168 beneficiaries.

The trustees announced on April 8 that they had voted to make pensions available at sixty years instead of sixty-two. The resolution was offered by Senator Bridges on the basis of an actuarial investigation made at his request. Mr. Lewis had been contending for the sixty-year retirement age ever since the fund's inception. Mr. Van Horn still dissented.

One of the most dramatic humanitarian projects of the fund began early in 1949. This was the program to rehabilitate paraplegic miners, those unfortunate victims of the mines whose spinal cords have been severed by cave-ins, paralyzing them from the waist down. Before the

days of the Welfare Fund, these tragic men lay in bed, helpless and poverty stricken, waiting to die. The fund began to send these men to hospitals, where they learned again to walk, learned a trade and, most of all, regained hope.

Dr. Draper announced another project on October 26, a public health program "to correct the serious deficiencies and improve the deplorable living conditions in coal mining communities."

Dr. Draper said that the program would have four phases: 1. Hospital care for disabled miners; 2. Home and office care for the disabled; 3. Hospital and medical care for working miners; and 4. A program of public health and preventive medicine. The first three phases already were in effect and the fourth was just beginning, he said.

While the Welfare Fund was rounding out its programs, Mr. Lewis began anew the fight for mine safety legislation. Senator Matthew M. Neely of West Virginia introduced a UMWA-sponsored bill at the opening session of the Eighty-first Congress which would give federal mine inspectors authority to close down unsafe

OFFICERS ANNOUNCE TRUCE IN 1949 DISPUTE AT NOVEMBER POLICY MEETING IN CHICAGO

Left to Right—Vice President Thomas Kennedy, Mr. Lewis, Secretary-Treasurer John Owens.

THINGS AREN'T AS BAD AS THEY MIGHT BE, MR. LEWIS TELLS OPERATOR HUBERT HOWARD

mines. The bill was supported by five other Senators: Francis Myers of Pennsylvania, Homer Capehart of Indiana, Robert S. Kerr of Oklahoma, Paul Douglas of Illinois, and Lister Hill of Alabama. A similar bill was introduced in the House by Representative Melvin Price of Illinois. On May 28, 1949, Mr. Lewis told the Senate Committee on Education and Labor:

"Since 1930, the depths of the depression, confusion and turmoil have reigned on the public scene. Those nineteen years must be vivid in the memory of each of us, and while we were otherwise occupied keeping up day-by-day with the daily sensations of the press, and attempts of Congress to legislate wisely for the interests of all Americans, more than a million and a quarter Americans employed in coal mines—an essential industry—were maimed, mangled, and butchered with impunity by those charged with the responsibility for their protection, with no redress for the men so affected. A million and a quarter!

"A million and a quarter men! If I had the powers of a Merlin, I would march that million and a quarter men past the Congress of the United States—the quick and the dead. I would have the ambulatory injured drag the dead after them, so that the Congress might see; and I would have the men whose eyes were shot out and who were disemboweled in the mines crawl in that procession along the cobblestones so that

the Congress might see them trailing their bowels after them.

"Thou shalt not kill—should that not run in the underground passages of our great mining industry in this country?

"Yet, does anyone recall when anyone was criminally punished for killing a coal miner underground? During this nineteen-year period, when these million and a quarter men were maimed and mangled, how many coal operators were killed, the men who supervised the operation of the mines, the men who operated these mines for profit, the men who took the profits?

"I wonder how much the mine workers of this country will take sometime from people of that ilk, who fatten on the industry.

"The days run on and men continue to die. These lobbyists for the operators and National Coal Association have been petitioning this committee to delay.

"You know, this industry breaks more backs than any other known industry. And what happens to a man whose back is broken in a mining community? Why he lies in some remote cabin up a canyon or creek until he dies. The UMWA Welfare Fund, which some of these sutlers and camp followers do not like, is finding hundreds of these broken-back cases. A man lay in a ten-foot square log cabin up a creek for twenty-three years without control over his kidneys and bowels. And these human leeches come down here and say to Congress, 'Don't legislate!' "

The Congress, as usual, never even put it to a vote. It was not until July, 1952, that any bill giving mine inspectors authority to close unsafe mines was written into the law.

The coal industry lost a veteran leader at this time in the death of Charles O'Neill, who had been chief spokesman for the bituminous operators for many years and had dealt with Mr. Lewis since both were young men. Mr. O'Neill started his career as a miner and rose in the industry to become president of the Central Pennsylvania Coal Operators Association. At one time he had been secretary-treasurer of District 2, UMWA. Mr. Lewis attended his funeral and visited Mr. O'Neill's family to offer his condolences.

Associate Supreme Court Justice Frank Murphy, who had won the respect of Mr. Lewis as governor of Michigan during the CIO organ-

213

izing days, died July 19, 1949. Mr. Lewis telegraphed Justice Murphy's brother:

"The untimely death of your distinguished brother will be mourned by the millions of Americans whose cause and whose rights he has championed. He never faltered in his earnest work of establishing equality of privilege for all Americans, however situated."

During the strike of the United Steelworkers, CIO, in the fall of 1949, and while the miners, themselves, were on strike, Mr. Lewis once again tried to promote labor solidarity. He proposed to AFL President William Green that the nine largest international unions in the AFL and the UMWA contribute $250 thousand a week for an indefinite period to aid the steel workers in their struggle.

Philip Murray, president of the steel workers and of the CIO, approved the idea but said the fund should be for the benefit of any labor organization in conflict with management, not for the steel union alone.

MR. LEWIS ANNOUNCES THE 1949 THREE-DAY WEEK AS OPERATORS BALK AT NEGOTIATING

Mr. Green replied in a lengthy letter some time later. In vague terms, he wrote about the desirability of labor unity. He wondered whether the steel workers had asked for help. He did not indicate his position on the UMWA's proposal.

Mr. Lewis replied to Mr. Green on October 16:

"You have justified my judgment. I did not think you would do anything. You didn't. You rarely do. Unfortunately, you follow invariably your well-known policy of anxious inertia. You cry aloud for labor peace and labor security, but seldom do anything to achieve it.

"I note that you are going to Europe with nine of your associate executives. While there, doubtless, you will adjust the European situation. When you adjust it satisfactorily and return to your own country, I may write you again.

"At the moment, I am too busy to continue a fruitless discussion."

With the Democrats, who were pledged to repeal of the Taft-Hartley Law, in control of the Eighty-first Congress, labor hoped the statute could be wiped from the books. The fight for repeal began early in 1949. UMWA Vice President Thomas Kennedy, in a statement to the Senate Labor Committee, reiterated the mine workers' demand for outright repeal and, in a reference to Senator Taft's legislative maneuvering, declared:

"We will no longer stand idly by and allow this Lucifer of labor relations to make a Roman holiday of what should be the most serious of legislative deliberations. He deliberately seeks to dupe, deceive, distort and distract the public. His is the hairy hand of Esau but the voice of Jacob. We condemn him for his hypocrisy and his consistent hymn of hate."

Taft-Hartley supporters dragged out hearings on the repeal measure in committee until June, when it was reported that William Green and Philip Murray had agreed to four amendments to the law, one of which would have retained the injunction provision. Mr. Lewis, on June 6, telegraphed each member of the Senate:

"Reports are current that Green and Murray, acting for their respective interests, have secretly agreed with certain Senators to accept at least four oppressive amendments to proposed legis-

THE SOFT COAL DISPUTE DRAGS ON INTO 1950 STILL WITH NO OFFER FROM THE OPERATORS

Left to Right (clockwise around table)—J. William Wetter, T. G. Gerow, Hugh Lee, George H. Love, Frank Amos, all operators; John T. Jones, District 16 president, conference secretary; Harvey Cartwright, operator and conference chairman; Truman Johnson, operator; Adolph Pacifico, District 6 president; John Owens, International secretary-treasurer; Mr. Lewis, Thomas Kennedy, International vice president.

---

lation seeking to repeal the infamous Taft forced-labor statute. These amendments would perpetuate government by the injunctive process in America and would continue to degrade American citizens—members of labor unions—by imposing upon them a continued status as second class citizens.

"If such reports are true, they constitute a foul betrayal of American labor by Green and Murray, as well as a pusillanimous compromise of the American principles of equality and freedom upon which our Republic is based. The Democratic members of the Senate are pledged by their party platform to repeal the Taft forced-labor statute and remove its shame from American life. They should each honor their pledge. The Republican Senators who are not beholden to special interests antagonistic to labor should permit their intelligence and their conscience to function in a manner that will not dishonor the millions of American workers who pray for equality of privilege and treatment with all other citizens under the law."

By the middle of June, it became apparent that the battle to repeal the act had been lost. Mr. Lewis wired Senators Matthew M. Neely of West Virginia, Claude Pepper of Florida and James E. Murray of Montana, congratulating them on their fight for repeal. He told them they had been abandoned by other Democrats and added:

"Taft, of course, is the son of a rich man, obsessed with the fixation that it is his heritage and his mission to regulate the lives and retard the laudable ambitions of the sons and daughters of the poor."

Thus, the UMWA again faced negotiations with the Taft-Hartley noose still around its neck and the operators eagerly ready to spring the trap. Their grand strategy was the big stall: Meet with the union, say "No" and wait for the government to use the Taft-Hartley Law once more.

In an unprecedented move, the Southern operators, on April 21, 1949, notified the UMWA they were terminating their contract and demanded negotiations separate from the rest of the coal industry. Mr. Lewis accepted for the UMWA and suggested that the conference be held in Bluefield, W. Va.

The next step was taken by the union on May 13. Mr. Lewis notified Benjamin F. Fairless, president of U. S. Steel, and Harry Moses, head of the corporation's captive mines, of termination of the contract. They agreed to meetings with the UMWA in Philadelphia, beginning a month later.

Talks with the Southern Coal Producers Association started in Bluefield on May 25. Mr. Lewis immediately challenged Joseph E. Moody, SCPA president, to prove that he represented all the companies he claimed. Two groups of producers had seceded from the Southern association the previous day. The UMWA allowed the Southerners a week to straighten out their credentials. The talks were resumed on June 3 and lasted one week, but without result.

The International officers, on June 8, sent a letter to the UMWA membership. It said:

"Exercising its contractual option under the agreement in all anthracite and bituminous districts, the UMWA is hereby authorizing a brief stabilizing period of inaction, during which a cessation of all mining will occur. It will be effective Monday, June 13, and work will be resumed on Monday, June 20.

"This period of inaction will emphasize a lack of general stability in the industry and the dangers which will accrue therefrom if current harmful practices are not remedied. It will contribute constructively to the abatement of current economic demoralization; it will not adversely affect the public interests; it will help preserve property values in the industry; and it will help preserve the living standards of the mine workers."

One day after the start of the "brief stabilizing period of inaction," Mr. Lewis wrote the rest of the soft coal operators in the North and West terminating their 1948 agreement. Operators and union negotiators met for two days at White Sulphur Springs, W. Va., designated the sessions "the National Conference," and recessed on June 24, while the operators considered the UMWA proposal for a three-day work week after expiration of the contract.

The operators rejected the proposal at the next session and, on June 30, a letter from the International officers to the UMWA membership said:

"The wage contract in all bituminous districts expires on June 30. Three wage conferences of magnitude are in session. Additional time is required to realize expectations for a new agreement. It is desirable that this time be utilized under conditions of the least possible strain upon our membership, the industry and the public. You are, therefore, advised and instructed as follows:

"All members in all mines heretofore under contract will return to work Tuesday, July 5, and produce coal three days; namely, Tuesday,

PLANNING STRATEGY ON FEBRUARY 8, 1950, AS GOVERNMENT FACT-FINDERS INTERVENE

Left to Right—Mr. Lewis, Secretary-Treasurer John Owens, Welly K. Hopkins, senior counsel.

**MR. LEWIS STUDIES THE COAL OPERATORS AS
1950 CONTRACT TALKS RESUME IN CAPITAL**

Mr. Lewis *(left)* and Vice President Kennedy.

Wednesday and Thursday. Each following week thereafter, until you are further advised, the work days will be Monday, Tuesday and Wednesday, on which days coal will be produced. All other work, except the production of coal, may be performed without restrictions, in accordance with the usual practice.

"In all mines west of the Mississippi River, the production of coal is not restrained by the three-day limitation. Coal production in that area must begin on Monday and continue consecutively during the week for the number of days worked by the mine; however, under no circumstances is coal to be produced on Saturday, which is, under this policy, an idle day as such.

"Operators of all mines will be expected, under this policy, to maintain the same terms, wages, hours and conditions of employment heretofore existing under the agreement expiring June 30. Local unions will immediately report to their proper district the identity of any coal company refusing to cooperate with this policy.

"The arrangements herein set forth are subject to change without notice upon receipt of authorized instructions by the local union from the UMWA."

The three-day work week remained in effect during the entire summer of 1949. Led by the Southerners, many of the operators, using the union-directed three-day week as a pretext for another blow at the Welfare Fund, stopped their royalty payments.

Mr. Lewis appealed to James D. Francis, president of the Island Creek Coal Co., to abandon "your mad and vengeful attack on the existence of the fund" and pay what was owing. He appealed also to I. F. Freiberger, chairman of the board of the Cleveland Trust Co., as a man of influence, to direct Mr. Francis to "abandon his mad policy of making war on ailing men and dependent women."

Nothing came of either appeal. The operators continued to default on their payments so, on September 16, the Welfare Fund trustees announced they had adopted the following resolution:

"Resolved that following the date of September 17, 1949, the trustees authorize a temporary suspension of payments by the fund to beneficiaries for pensions, disability benefits, death benefits, widows' and orphans' assistance, and

217

for medical and hospital service incurred subsequent to September 17, 1949; except that in emergency hospital and medical cases, as determined by medical administrative officers of the fund, payments may be made for hospital care and attendant medical care in such cases. Suspension of payments by the trustees is a temporary expedient, to continue until funds are available for resumption of benefit payments, at the discretion of the trustees."

The soft coal miners immediately began to stay away from work in protest against non-payment of Welfare Fund royalties and the anthracite miners staged a sympathy work stoppage. Mr. Lewis told reporters at White Sulphur Springs on September 22 that George Love, president of the largest commercial company in the industry, Pittsburgh Consolidation Coal Co., and George Humphrey of the M. A. Hanna interests, had the power to end the dispute but chose to stall negotiations in hopes of destroying the Welfare Fund. Mr. Lewis added:

"They have deliberately estopped the making of an agreement while they campaigned vigor-

---

FEBRUARY, 1950, BROUGHT GUARDED OFFERS FOR NEW CONTRACT FROM COAL OPERATORS

Left to Right—George Titler, District 29 president; Ed. J. Morgan, District 23 president; Mr. Lewis.

ously against the three-day work week. They got much public support in their opposition to the three-day work week and apparently have convinced the individual mine worker throughout the entire industry that the continuance of the three-day week was not constructive and meant that the mine workers indefinitely would have to continue the hardship of part-time employment with no hope that the operators would voluntarily agree to a change in the status quo.

"So we suggested to Mr. Love that he was like Samson. He was so successful in putting his shoulders to the columns and supports of the temple that he pulled it down about his ears, and instead of having a three-day week, the mine workers individually have decided that, until he changes his attitude, he will have a no-day work week."

The protest work stoppage in the three anthracite districts and in soft coal fields west of the Mississippi River ended October 3. The International officers wired district presidents in these areas:

"The suspension of mining in the western and anthracite areas is not now vital to the pending wage negotiations. To minimize loss to all parties, all mine workers in the before mentioned areas are requested to return to work and resume coal production Monday, October 3, until further notice. This policy affects anthracite Dis-

A "BREAK" IN THE 1950 CONTRACT TALKS AS COURT FINDS UMW NOT GUILTY OF CONTEMPT

Left to Right—Mr. Lewis, Pete Graeff, UMWA staff *(in background)*; Paul K. Reed, special international representative.

Mr. Sewell Avery, representing the great gypsum company and Montgomery Ward and other interests as he sits there; and the representatives of the great major insurance companies which have large investments in industrial enterprises and have representation on these boards.

"So we have a combination of powerful financial leaders, not necessarily great in number but tremendously influential in the magnitude of their financial representation. That includes practically all the major automobile companies, with the exception of Ford. It includes practically all of the steel industry. It includes those coal commercial interests closely identified with the steel industry. It includes the insurance companies. It includes the DuPont family and their great investments; their holdings, of course, being 23 per cent of the stock of General Motors, which means control, for all practical purposes. It includes the Mellon empire and their banks. And all taken together make a tremendous group of immense power who apparently have decided to make this struggle in steel final and significant in American economic history.

"Therefore, there has been no progress in the

tricts 1, 7, and 9 and bituminous coal Districts 10, 13, 14, 15, 21, 22, and 27. District presidents will please execute this policy." Mr. Lewis explained that with the approach of winter, coal from these districts was needed for home use.

The government interrupted the negotiations by summoning both sides to a meeting in Washington on October 7 called by Cyrus Ching, director of the U. S. Mediation and Conciliation Service. Mr. Ching lectured the parties, the meeting adjourned, and the negotiators trooped back to West Virginia.

Weary of the operators' stalling, Mr. Lewis named to reporters at the White Sulphur Springs conference with northern operators, on October 13, the men and corporate interests dictating the policies of the coal companies and fighting a war of attrition against the mine workers and their Welfare Fund:

"Those interests include all the companies interested in steel. They include the representation on their board of directors from various industries, such as Mr. Walter Gifford, representing the empire and all the employees of the American Telephone and Telegraph Co. as he sits on the board of the United States Steel;

THE LONG BATTLE IS WON, MARCH 5, 1950, AND THE WORD GOES OUT TO THE MINERS

coal negotiations. They have elected to fight this out, and create this crisis, and there is nothing that labor can do either in the coal industry or the steel industry but to await their pleasure."

In a new move to prod the government to take Taft-Hartley action, the Northern and Western operators walked out of the White Sulphur Springs conference on October 21. Their deliberate stalling had failed to goad the UMWA into taking a walk. Mr. Lewis acted to resume meetings with an important segment of the industry soon after. Early in November, he wired Governors Henry Schricker of Indiana and Adlai Stevenson of Illinois in response to letters stating concern over the coal reserves in their states. He told them the steel companies had huge stockpiles cached in Indiana and Illinois and suggested they appeal for release of some of this coal. He asked both governors to arrange conferences between the mine workers and the Illinois and Indiana operators.

At a news conference during a National Policy Committee meeting in Chicago on November 7, Mr. Lewis said he had advised Governor Stevenson to confer with George B. Harrington of the Chicago, Wilmington & Franklin Coal Co., who was blocking agreement in Illinois. These moves were fruitless.

The Policy Committee, as a matter of public interest, then voted a three-week truce and all miners returned to work from November 9 to 30. They had been out fifty-one days.

With the truce about to expire, the Policy Committee met again, this time in New York City, and on December 1 Mr. Lewis announced that the three-day work week would be resumed in all mines on the following Monday, December 5. The committee also authorized executive officers and scale representatives "to make wage contracts with any or all individual coal companies."

In the next three months, the UMWA reached agreements with companies producing 64 million tons of soft coal annually—approximately 15 per cent of total production.

The operators meanwhile began to move the controversy into the courts. First was the suit by Charles I. Dawson of Louisville for a federal court order to force his seating as the operators' new Welfare Fund trustee and seeking to tie up the fund's money pending the court's ruling. Mr. Dawson had been elected by the operators, but the incumbent, Ezra Van Horn, had not submitted his resignation to the other trustees.

Next, the Southern Coal Producers Association, on December 28, complained to General Counsel Robert Denham of the NLRB that Mr. Lewis and the UMWA were guilty of Taft-Hartley "unfair labor practices." They asked

---

THE OPERATORS THROW IN THE SPONGE AND UMWA'S 1949-50 "MARENGO CAMPAIGN" ENDS

Left to Right—John Owens, International secretary-treasurer; Thomas Kennedy, International vice president; Mr. Lewis, John T. Jones *(standing)*, District 16 president and joint conference secretary; George H. Love, representing Northern operators; Joseph E. Moody, president, Southern Coal Producers Association; Harry M. Moses, representing H. C. Frick Coal & Coke Co.

MARCH 8, 1950, AND THE UMWA TURNS ITS ATTENTION TO A NEW ANTHRACITE CONTRACT

Left to Right (clockwise)—Mr. Lewis, Michael J. Kosik, District 1 president; Thomas Kennedy, International vice president; Mart F. Brennan, District 7 president; John Boylan, secretary, Anthracite Board of Conciliation; Ralph E. Taggart, Edward Griffith, Robert L. Birtley, H. J. Connolly, anthracite operators; Joseph Kershetsky *(foreground)*, District 9 president.

Mr. Denham to seek an injunction to end the three-day work week. This was Mr. Lewis' comment:

"Taft, flamboyant oppressor of the poor, asked the President to herd the coal miners into the lethal gas chamber of the infamous Slave Statute.

"Denham, hatchet man for the Hi-Profit Tong, is urged by the coal operators to lay about him and create an orgy of legal bloodletting at the expense of the taxpayers.

"The only issue current in the coal industry is whether mine workers shall be paid a base underground rate of $14.05 per day as the operators insist, or $15 per day as the mine workers insist. Should the machinery of the State and the money of its citizens be now utilized to oppress the mine workers and cripple their union, merely to save the prosperous coal operators 95 cents per day?"

In Illinois, the miners stayed home on the first work day of the new year, 1950. Restlessness at lack of a contract was spreading through the coal fields. By January 30, 100 thousand men were idle despite a previous wire from Mr. Lewis

to district presidents:

"Will you please transmit to our members who are idle this week my suggestion that they resume production next Monday."

Mr. Denham petitioned the United States District Court, on January 18, for an injunction against alleged unfair labor practices by the UMWA as charged by the Southern producers. Without waiting for an NLRB ruling as to whether the practices were unfair, Judge Richmond B. Keech, on February 9, issued a Taft-Hartley injunction denying the union the right even to discuss them with the operators.

Despite strings attached to an operators' offer to resume soft coal negotiations, Mr. Lewis had agreed to meet them on February 1. On the day before the conference was scheduled to open, however, President Truman intervened with a proposal that both sides appear before a special presidential board of inquiry and that the miners return to work pending a finding by the board. Mr. Lewis declined on grounds that the miners "do not wish three strangers, however well-intentioned but necessarily ill-informed, to fix their wages and working conditions."

The operators and the UMWA met on February 1, as scheduled. On February 2, the operators walked out of the negotiations for a second time. On February 6, President Truman invoked the national emergency provisions of the Taft-Hartley Law and named a fact-finding board composed of David L. Cole, who had been chairman of the 1948 Taft-Hartley board; W. William Wirts, Northwestern Univer-

221

sity law professor; and John T. Dunlop, Harvard economics professor.

By now, virtually all soft coal miners were out of the pits. They were angry—at the nine months of operator stalling on a new contract and at having the Taft-Hartley Law used on them once again. The only bituminous miners working were those covered by individual contracts with small companies.

The Taft-Hartley fact-finding board's attitude toward the dispute was, surprisingly, a patient one. Chairman Cole apparently had no intention of taking any hasty action that might jeopardize the reaching of an agreement. On February 11, after two meetings, the board made a preliminary report to Mr. Truman. It criticized the refusal of the operators to bargain on wages but stated there was a shortage of coal amounting to an emergency and requiring resumption of production. President Truman acted at once and had the Justice Department request a Taft-Hartley ten-day restraining order. Judge Keech issued the order immediately.

It directed the miners to resume work under the terms of the 1948 contract and ordered both the operators and the union to resume negotiations. Mr. Lewis, forthwith, complied. He sent one telegram explaining the injunction and instructing the district presidents to comply, and a second telegram to the operators requesting a resumption of negotiations. The miners, however, remained away from work.

Mr. Truman, meanwhile, had reconvened the fact-finding board and instructed it to observe the court-directed negotiations between the UMWA and all the soft coal operators. In a few days, enough progress had been made in the talks so that sub-committees were named by the union and operators for specific discussion of wages and hours. Mr. Lewis proposed a shorter work day and employment guaranteed for 200 days annually. These were rejected by the industry.

On February 17, the three International officers sent another communication, this time a direct appeal to the membership. It said:

"We now call upon you to join us in complying forthwith with all of the court's directives. Accordingly, you are hereby officially instructed to terminate the work stoppages in which you are now individually engaged and to return, forthwith, to work."

BEFORE THE WAGE STABILIZATION BOARD ON JANUARY 10, 1951, TO OPPOSE WAGE FIXING

UMWA Vice President Thomas Kennedy *(left)* and Mr. Lewis.

Judge Keech, at the request of the Justice Department, on February 20, cited the UMWA for civil and criminal contempt. He renewed the Taft-Hartley restraining order for another ten days. Once again, UMWA officers were haled into court to show cause why they should not be held in contempt because of the miners' continuing work stoppage. Secretary-Treasurer John Owens, as the chief UMWA witness, related the several efforts to get the men back to work. After three days of trial, Judge Keech took the case under advisement on March 1. The next day the Judge gave his ruling. The government had failed, he said, to prove any case. The officers of the UMWA had made every effort to bring a halt to the work stoppage. The union was not guilty of contempt of court. President Truman quickly sent a message to Congress asking authority to seize the mines. But it took less than twenty-four hours after the not guilty ruling for the UMWA and the soft coal industry to reach agreement on a new contract. Once more, the complete futility of trying to settle collective bargaining disputes by injunction had been proved. The coal industry, for ten months, had stalled and stalled and stalled. It had used every weighted legal device provided to employers by the Taft-Hartley Act. The strategy and tactics had failed. The coal miners, despite the shackles placed on their union, had refused to be bludgeoned back into the pits.

Late on the afternoon of Friday, March 3, 1950, Mr. Cole of the fact-finding board announced that the industry and union had reached agreement in principle. A drafting committee was named by both sides to write the new contract. Mr. Lewis summoned the National Policy Committee to meet in Washington on Sunday, March 5. The drafting committee reported agreement on all details the same day. The draft of the contract was immediately ratified by the Policy Committee and negotiators affixed their signatures to the National Bituminous Wage Agreement of 1950 that afternoon. Essential provisions were: across-the-board wage increases of 70 cents a day, bringing basic wages to $14.75 a day; an increase of 10 cents a ton in operator payments to the Welfare Fund, bringing royalties to 30 cents a ton; a new Welfare Fund Board of Trustees with Mr. Lewis, chairman, Welfare Fund Director Josephine Roche, neutral trustee, and Charles Owens of

COALDALE, PA., LABOR DAY, 1950: THOUGHTS ABOUT FREE MEN AND A LOOK TO THE FUTURE

New York, operator trustee. The operators dismissed approximately $15 million in damage suits against the UMWA and agreed to pay defaulted Welfare Fund royalties by March 15, 1950. The contract was to terminate on July 1, 1952, but could be reopened by either party after April 1, 1952. Mr. Lewis wired all UMWA district presidents:

"New contract has been approved by the International Policy Committee and executed by the bituminous coal operators. All mines will resume work."

Mr. Lewis told reporters:

"The mine workers emerged from this struggle with additional bread-and-butter money for their families, with additional life and death money for their stricken and ailing in the form of additional revenue for their Welfare Fund, with their union intact, with their membership unimpaired, and with all labor benefited by the discrediting of the Taft-Hartley abomination."

The anthracite agreement was signed on March 9 and won the same benefits for the hard coal miners as were included in the soft coal agreement. These negotiations had been overshadowed by the tremendous struggle in the bituminous industry, but hard coal miners suffered the same long months of stalling by the

223

operators. The anthracite operators, to their credit, however, did not walk out of negotiations, nor run to the courts seeking Taft-Hartley injunctions.

With the mine workers' struggle out of the way, Mr. Lewis once more tried to initiate action on labor unity. On March 6, he wrote to Walter P. Reuther, president of the UAW:

"The Executive Board and the Policy Committee of the United Mine Workers of America, assembled in Washington today, gave consideration to the fact that your union for some weeks past has been engaged in a struggle against the Chrysler Corporation and that you are facing oncoming negotiations with other important segments of your industry. We are conscious of the fact that your union, in order to protect its interests, may be forced to make expenditures of a substantial nature and that it conceivably could be an advantage to your union and its members to be assured of additional financial support from other segments of organized labor.

"I, therefore, advise that the Executive Board of the United Mine Workers of America, with the National Policy Committee concurring,

BASIC WAGES RISE TO $16.35 A DAY AS UMW WINS $1.60 INCREASE ON JANUARY 18, 1951

Left to Right—Harry M. Moses, Bituminous Coal Operators Association; Mr. Lewis, John T. Jones *(standing)*, District 16 president; Joseph E. Moody, Southern Coal Producers Association. *In background*—Justin McCarthy, director, UMWA News Bureau.

has authorized me to inform you that the United Mine Workers of America will advance the United Automobile Workers, immediately if you wish, a cash loan of $1 million, to be used for such purposes as your organization may require in its present emergency.

"Our Policy Committee likewise hopes that this action on the part of the United Mine Workers of America will be emulated by other great unions in the Congress of Industrial Organizations and the American Federation of Labor, to the end that your union may be assured of success in its present struggle."

Mr. Reuther turned down the offer of the loan. He said the UAW would appreciate "outright contributions."

Nothing had come of Mr. Lewis' proposal to the AFL to establish a fund to aid striking steel workers in 1949. But during the height of the soft coal dispute, the United Steelworkers, CIO, had made $500 thousand available to the UMWA. Taking this as a sign that the CIO was interested in discussing labor unity, Mr. Lewis wrote to Philip Murray, Steelworkers and CIO president, on March 7, 1950:

"The Executive Board and Policy Committee of the United Mine Workers of America have authorized me to extend the thanks of the United Mine Workers of America and its membership to the United Steelworkers of America and its membership for their appreciated gift of one-half million dollars, made on February 8.

"Conditions did not permit the usage of this money. We, therefore, return the original check in the same amount, uncashed, and properly marked 'Void.'

"During recent months, each of our great unions has been engaged in major conflict with

---

A $1.60-A-DAY PAY BOOST IS WON FOR THE ANTHRACITE MINERS ON JANUARY 26, 1951

Seated—Ralph E. Taggart *(left)*, Philadelphia & Reading Coal & Iron Co.; Mr. Lewis. *Standing*—Edward Griffith *(left)*, Glen Alden Coal Co.; UMWA Vice President Thomas Kennedy.

the most powerful associated group of financial interests in America. The idea seems increasingly prevalent in industrial and financial circles that our great industrial unions should be attacked and crippled, one by one. This idea should be knocked in the head.

"United Mine Workers of America offers to negotiate with the United Steelworkers of America a mutual aid pact for common defense, wherein the assets of both organizations, or a stipulated part thereof, would be made available, each to the other, under emergency conditions. The potential advantages to our respective memberships of such an arrangement are self-evident."

Mr. Murray rejected the UMWA's proposal, stating that such a fund would serve "no useful purpose," and on April 5 came up with a labor unity proposal of his own. He wrote to all American labor organizations suggesting formation of a top level committee to work out policy on economic, legislative, and political issues. Mr. Lewis replied the next day:

"I refer to your letter of April 5.

"It will be referred for consideration to the International Executive Board of the United Mine Workers of America, which will assemble

April 18. The executive officers will recommend to the board that it authorize participation in your suggested joint committee."

The board approved the Murray proposal unanimously and enthusiastically. But the AFL, after due pondering, hedged on Mr. Murray's offer. The AFL would meet, William Green stated, only with the CIO. Specifically rejected was the idea of allowing unaffiliated unions to join the talks. This meant the UMWA.

Mr. Murray acceded to the AFL's restricted proposal and, on May 25, the AFL and CIO met. Two days of talks resulted in appointment of a sub-committee to study organic unity—as demanded by the AFL—and the hope of labor unity did not die but faded away.

With the end of the 1949-1950 coal dispute, the Welfare Fund reorganized its activities and, on June 1, pension payments were resumed. Hospitalization and medical services became available on July 1. A new program of services for disabled miners and dependents, maintenance aid for aged widows and dependent children, and the extension of medical and hospitalization services to widows and dependent children was announced October 12.

The communists invaded South Korea in June, 1950, and United Nations forces struck back. America stepped up mobilization and emergency legislation was rushed through the Congress. Labor's advice on mobilization policy was sought by W. Stuart Symington, chairman of the National Security Resources Board. A program initiated by John Owens, the miners' representative at the Symington conferences, was adopted in part when the government agreed to name a top-level twelve-man advisory board to include three labor representatives. The other labor officials rejected Mr. Owens' motion to include Mr. Lewis, however, and named Philip Murray, CIO president; William Green, AFL president, and A. J. Hayes, president of the Machinists' Union. The board was soon lost in a maze of bureaucratic agencies and accomplished virtually nothing.

Soon after start of the "police action" in Korea, William Green, without anyone having brought up the suggestion, proposed a "no-strike" pledge for the duration. Mr. Lewis sent him the following memorandum:

"You know, Bill, that I am ever distressed when I have to disturb the calm placidity of your ordered existence. Yet I suggest that the rights of American workers in industry should not be bartered to appease your innate craving for orthodox respectability. Consideration of the following items is, therefore, indicated:

"1. Although the mine workers have espoused labor unity, you have stipulated them out of the unity conferences. It follows that any mess that you cook up with the CIO, if you can cook up any mess with the CIO, will of course have to be eaten by you, and you alone. We do our own cooking.

"2. You have stipulated the mine workers out of representation on the select, star chamber labor committee which you designated to please Symington. We gently advise that we will not be bound by your deliberations or commitments conducted or made in our absence. We do our own committing.

"3. The press chronicles you as plodding about the country seeking someone to whom you can give a 'no-strike pledge.' I am sure that you will pardon me when I suggest that the mine workers are not yet ready for you to sell them down the river. Restrict your pledges to your own outfit. We do our own no-striking."

The off-year Congressional elections of 1950 brought some unity on political matters among labor groups but the lack of a top-level policy helped to return some of labor's worst enemies to the Eighty-second Congress. The UMWA's Labor's Non-Partisan League confined its activities to coal mining states and helped send the union's friends to Washington. On September 19, 1950, Mr. Lewis wrote to R. Livingston Ireland, president of the Ohio Coal Operators Association, concerning a candidate:

"Taft's secret political handlers propose to have him enter coal mines to cozen the men underground. This will be bad from the standpoint of coal production.

"Taft was born encased in velvet pants and has lived to rivet an iron collar around the necks of millions of Americans. He is the relentless, albeit witless, tool of the oppressors of labor.

"You should refuse him entry to mines where Americans toil. The underground workings are necessarily confined, and the air therein is easily contaminated. The effluvia of the oppressor is ever disagreeable and could enrage the men to a point of evacuation of the mines. This we would both deplore!"

An amusing incident occurred in the fall of 1950 as the result of a suggestion to President Truman that Mr. Lewis be named U. S. ambassador to Moscow. This brought a reply from the Chief Executive that he "wouldn't appoint John L. Lewis dog catcher."

Mr. Lewis wrote to State Senator Neal Bishop of Denver, Colo., who had made the suggestion to Mr. Truman:

"Conceivably it is true that the President's choice of words was again unfortunate. One could, however, persuade one's self that he was thinking only in terms of problems of State and

had no intent to belittle or sneer gratuitously at a private citizen. Assuredly, the President of the United States would not permit his personal feelings to sway his judgment on appointments to public office.

"Presidential appointment to the office of Dogcatcher would postulate creation of a new federal bureau with its accompanying personnel of thousands of employees and, in consequence, an increase to the tax burden.

"Naturally, the first duty of the Bureau of the Dog, if staffed by the undersigned, would be to collect and impound the sad dogs, the intellectual poodle dogs and the pusillanimous pups which now infest our State Department. This would be gravely disturbing and would, perhaps, cause profound unrest throughout our national canine fraternity.

"The President could ill afford to have more brains in the Dog Department than in the Department of State and, from this standpoint, his remarks to you are eminently justified."

SOUTH AFRICAN TRADE UNION LEADER VISITS MR. LEWIS IN WASHINGTON HEADQUARTERS

A. A. Addio-Moses and Mr. Lewis.

227

**DISCUSSING AMERICA'S DEFENSE PROBLEMS
WITH ODM CHIEF WILSON, FEBRUARY 1, 1952**

**50,000 AUTO WORKERS AT FORD RALLY HAIL
"MR. ORGANIZED LABOR" ON JUNE 23, 1951**

It was in the fall of 1950 that major Northern operators in the bituminous coal industry established a new agency to do business with the UMWA. For many years, the operators had joined forces only at contract time and then had gone their separate ways when the agreement was signed. One of Mr. Lewis' complaints against the industry had been lack of a responsible, permanent collective bargaining agency with which the union could discuss mutual problems at any time. The new agency was the Bituminous Coal Operators' Association. Harry M. Moses, for thirteen years president of the H. C. Frick Coke Co., was chosen president. The association represented operators producing about one-third of total soft coal production and was openly dominated by the steel industry.

Mr. Lewis was soon to test the workability of the new association. Late in 1950, the UMWA president began informal, secret discussions with Mr. Moses looking toward a wage adjustment in the soft coal contract. The meetings were in sharp contrast to the knock-down and drag-out battle of 1949-50 and on January 18, 1951, Mr. Lewis announced that the UMWA and the bituminous operators had agreed to an amendment which raised wages for all miners $1.60 a day as of February 1, 1951, bringing the basic daily rate to $16.35. The contract termination date also was amended so that on or after March 31, 1952, either party, by sixty days prior notice, could end the agreement.

Of the amended contract, Mr. Lewis said:

"It's a bread-and-butter agreement. The matter has been handled in a statesmanlike manner by the industry, to the mutual advantage of operating interests and the mine workers and to the country as a whole. There has been no tumult or shouting. No public apprehension has been created. The country is now freed from any thought of a so-called coal crisis for an indefinite period of time."

The anthracite operators signed a similar agreement on January 26. Before the announcement of the new agreements had been made, Mr. Lewis appeared before the newly-created Wage Stabilization Board on January 10, 1951, to say:

"The wage structure of our country cannot be stabilized by the arbitrary fiat or decree of an agency of government, in substitution for the great structure of collective bargaining between industry and labor which is the result of at least a hundred years of experimentation between the interests involved.

"We see no necessity for wages to be stabilized in the sense that the wage structure must be frozen. The word stabilization, as it is used, sometimes has a misleading application. Stabilization of our economic structure is effected when reasonable tranquility prevails and when the ordinary machinery of relationships is working in the normal manner. The ability thus to stabilize has brought its own reward in our country and has produced an economy which is the marvel of the present age and something unequaled in any other civilized country.

"There is no reason now to think that that same productive capacity—enhanced and expanded to whatever degree may be necessary by the requirements of the nation in its domestic and foreign policies—cannot continue without the necessity of undertaking from a government center to dictate every act, prescribe every rule, apply the slide rule to every rate, and try to take over the enormous task which constantly requires the attention—and the complete attention—of the leaders of industry and labor."

Concerned over increasing big-business domination of the government mobilization program by $1-a-year executives still on the payrolls of their corporations, the AFL and CIO in December, 1950, formed the so-called United Labor Policy Committee. But, as usual, the organizations saw fit to "euchre out" the UMWA —as Vice President Thomas Kennedy put it. The ULPC, also, effectively prevented any UMWA participation in the government's defense establishment. ULPC policy was to work with the Wage Stabilization Board—which the UMWA opposed—in the fixing of wages. It selected the labor members of the WSB. But they soon resigned in protest against an arbitrary 10 per cent ceiling on wage increases voted by the industry and public members of the board. Mr. Lewis complimented them in the vain hope that that would be the end of the WSB. But, after some conferences at the White House, the AFL and CIO officials announced that they were returning their representatives to the WSB in return for some changes in the mobilization set-up promised by Mr. Truman.

Ten years had passed since the final big organizing triumph by the CIO in the automobile industry—the signing of the UAW contract with the Ford Motor Co. in June, 1941, a victory won primarily because of the able UMWA representatives assigned to the task by Mr. Lewis. The occasion called for a celebration by Ford workers at the River Rouge plant, Dearborn, Mich. Invitations to attend went to CIO President Murray, UAW President Walter Reuther, and to Mr. Lewis. Upon learning the miners' leader had accepted, Mr. Reuther directed the UAW executive board to declare an official "boycott" of the meeting. Mr. Murray was conveniently busy with other matters. Despite the obvious snub by their officials to the man who has devoted his life to the labor movement, more than 50 thousand auto workers turned out to hear "Mr. Organized Labor," as he was introduced, issue a new call for labor unity:

"The form of division in American labor is not the fault of the rank and file. It is the fault of those leaders with responsibility of leadership and who, after all, are paid for representing the best interests of the membership that pays them. And who is there who can successfully say that it will not be to the benefit of every member of organized labor, and his children beyond him, and to Americans as a whole, to unify the strength of these 16 million men behind a recognized and accepted policy, with unified leadership before our adversaries at the conference table?

"While we are working for structural and policy unity in the labor movement in this country, I have a little suggestion to make that might hold us up until our leaders can get in the happy

---

MANAGEMENT NEGLECT BROUGHT DEATH TO 119, SAID MR. LEWIS AT WEST FRANKFORT, ILL.

To Mr. Lewis' right is John J. Forbes, director, U. S. Bureau of Mines. To the rear in street clothes is Louis Austin, District 11 International Board member.

THE CAMERA RECORDS MR. LEWIS' EXPRESSION OF GRIEF AND ANGER AT THE HORROR OF THE WEST FRANKFORT, ILL., MINE DISASTER OF DECEMBER 21, 1951. ONE HUNDRED AND NINETEEN MINERS WERE KILLED. THEY LEFT 301 DEPENDENTS—109 WIDOWS, 175 CHILDREN AND OTHERS

A GRINNING SEN. TAFT DEFENDS THE TAFT-HARTLEY STATUTE AT MINE SAFETY HEARINGS

Left to Right—John T. Jones, District 16 president and head of Labor's Non-Partisan League; Sen. James E. Murray, Montana; Mr. Lewis; Sen. Robert Alphonso Taft, Ohio; Harold J. Sloman, U. S. Bureau of Mines.

frame of mind where they can agree with each other. This is a simple little suggestion. I suggest that the great organizations of labor in this country that are able to, and can afford to, can immediately create a huge fund for the common defense of the great unions and organizations of labor in this country. I know of at least forty unions in the CIO and in the AFL which are able financially tomorrow, if they wish, to contribute a million dollars each into that revolving trust fund.

"If they would do so, we would have that $40 million trust fund to be put behind any union in distress or danger from Ford or General Motors or United States Steel or anyone else. I would be happy to recommend to the UMWA that they put in $10 million, so we could have a $50 million fund. We might set up that little device right away, while we argue with each other on Sunday what we should do on the week days as to unity."

As usual, no other leader picked up the idea.

The anthracite industry lost four of its top people in 1951. Ralph E. Taggart, chairman of the Anthracite Operators' Wage Negotiating Committee and head of the Philadelphia & Reading Coal & Iron Co., died April 30. On May 2, John Boylan, former president of District 1 and secretary of the Anthracite Board of Conciliation, died. Four days later, John Gallagher, UMWA international representative and administrative auditor, died. Mr. Taggart's successor as chief spokesman for the hard coal operators, Edward Griffith, president of the Glen Alden Coal Co., died on October 25.

Two of the UMWA's leaders in the soft coal fields also died. Abe Vales, District 19 president, died August 16, 1951, and his successor, Charles Hicks died January 16, 1952.

The Bituminous Welfare Fund's fourth fiscal year ended June 30, 1951. A report showed that the fund had a balance of nearly $100 million; that its revenues for the four years were more than $360 million; and that more than $254 million in benefits had been paid to 721 thousand men, women and children in the soft coal areas of the nation. All costs of administration and office equipment during the four years had been only a little more than $7 million, or less than 2 per cent of revenues. Next step in the fund's fight against misery, disease, destitution, and death was the plan announced, on October 10, 1951, to form a non-profit corporation, financed with Welfare Fund money, to build ten hospitals in coal mining areas where such facilities were non-existent or inadequate. The fund early in 1952 established a disaster service to provide quick financial relief for families of mine disaster victims. Welfare Fund crews now are sent into disaster areas immediately to expedite payment of death benefits and to determine whether miner's families need extra help.

ONCE AGAIN THE UMWA BEGINS THE FIGHT FOR FEDERAL MINE SAFETY LEGISLATION

Left to Right—Mr. Lewis, Rep. C. W. (Runt) Bishop of Illinois, who lost a relative in the West Frankfort disaster; Sen. James E. Murray, Senate labor committee chairman.

A never-ending job for Mr. Lewis and the UMWA is that of seeking ways to improve the economic condition of the coal industry.

An example of the type of contribution the union seeks to make to the industry is the action Mr. Lewis took in December of 1951 when he announced details of a coal export plan designed to expand foreign markets for coal. At a news conference after a meeting of the Policy Committee, Mr. Lewis said:

"The Policy Committee was informed of the efforts of the officers of the union to secure a broadening of the coal export trade, not only to Europe but also to certain areas in the Pacific where coal is costly and in insufficient quantity.

"The present ocean rate is about $14.50 a ton to lay coal alongside the docks in Europe, and with coal costing about $10.50 at Hampton Roads, that makes a total of $25 a ton, too high a cost to be absorbed by the economy of the nations that are fighting back in Europe. The high price of coal results in European governments buying vast tonnages of coal mined behind the Iron Curtain—Poland, Silesia, East Germany and Czechoslovakia. And, unfortunately, American taxpayers have to provide many of the dollars that are used by these European governments to buy this coal mined be-

233

MR. LEWIS LISTENS AS COAL OPERATORS TESTIFY AGAINST A FEDERAL SAFETY LAW

hind the Iron Curtain.

"There are no reasons why this coal should not be delivered practically at cost and why transport should not be in government-owned ships allocated to some agency that will operate them at an approximate cost of operation. American coal laid down in Japan now costs, in Japanese ports, $30.50 a ton. Indian production, upon which Japan has been relying to augment her own limited production of coal, is insufficient to supply Japan's expanding economy. Recently, Japan has made a deal with the Russians to obtain Manchurian coal at $20 a ton. There is no reason why American coal can't be laid down in Japan for a price that will enable them to use American coal.

"The justification of the American merchant marine, and the using of taxpayers' money to subsidize it, is merely to create a device to carry American goods to market. Some 375 Liberty ships are now leased out to private operators and many of them are engaged in transporting coal, but transporting coal at high charter rates that are, in a large way, dictated by Lloyd's in-

surance company. We think these Liberty ships should be allocated in sufficient numbers to a private enterprise, which might be created, to transport this coal from our ports at approximately the cost of transport, and that the government should carry the insurance upon the bare bottoms and that the pool to be organized should carry the charges-off for losses of cargo in the event of loss.

"That coal export plan will result in more employment, more sales, more railroad tonnage and more taxes for the government. It's sensible; and it will enable the United States to continue in the coal-exporting business even in normal times."

Government officials sat on the plan for several months until, in the spring of 1952, it was reported the officials who had been "studying the matter" had decided that with summer coming on Europe probably wouldn't need much American coal.

The UMWA carried its demand for adequate mine safety legislation back to Capitol Hill again early in 1952. Mr. Lewis told Congress:

"On the night of December 21, 1951, 119 miners were killed in the Orient No. 2 disaster at West Frankfort, Ill. They left 301 dependents, 109 of them being widows, 175 children, and 17 other dependents.

"The destruction of the 119 lives underground in the brief moments of one night aroused temporary nation-wide horror and indignation. Day by day, year after year, however, the same human tragedy, the same immeasurable loss of economic values, has been recurring throughout the coal mining industry in mine fatalities and mine injuries, in women widowed and children orphaned, in husbands and fathers crippled and incapacitated, and their chief earning power destroyed.

"How many shocks do we wish? How many shocks does it take to move us? Do we live only on shocks and thrills and sensations and the debasement of human values and the wastage of human life? Yet these coal operators come before this distinguished committee and they say, in effect, 'Leave us alone, leave us alone.' In the face of this appalling record, all they want is to be left alone to emulate this horrible record of their operation of this industry on safety."

Mr. Lewis then recited the "appalling record": One hundred and nineteen men, the same number who were killed at West Frankfort, dying every seventeen days from 1900 through 1950 in mine accidents; since mine deaths first were recorded in 1839, 114,025 miners killed; 571 major disasters, killing 13,131; twenty-five of these disasters each bringing death to more than 100 men.

He added:

"It is something to go down the rows of 100 burned and dismembered and blackened corpses lying on the cement floor of a gymnasium in a public building and look at them and know that a few hours before they were walking about in the form of men, even as you or I, and that there they lay, disfigured, changed from the form of human beings to something beyond imagination, and then be expected to emerge from that scene of horror with patience and with tolerance for the men who come before this committee and say: 'Don't pass any legislation. Let me continue to do as I will. I hope some day to be able to operate my mine without killing so many men. But don't rush me! Don't rush me!' That is what they say.

"It might be noted in passing that the establishment of the Welfare Fund in the coal industry was fought just as bitterly, just as violently, just as persistently, as the same operators now fight any attempt to create more safe conditions in the mines. The same men now come before the Congress, before the members of this distinguished committee, and plead for the right of the states to continue this abominable record of slaughter unequalled in the civilized world. I sometimes wonder why the great God above doesn't punish them while they are speaking their brutal language before the Congress of the United States."

The Congress finally passed a compromise federal mine safety law in July, 1952, giving the U. S. Bureau of Mines' inspectors authority for the first time to shut down unsafe mines.

There still are many other goals to be fought for and won. Even as this book is written, a new "Bloody Harlan" occurs in Clay and Leslie Counties, Ky., where anti-union coal operators

---

MINE SAFETY HEARINGS MOVE ACROSS THE CAPITOL TO THE HOUSE OF REPRESENTATIVES

Left to Right—Charles Ferguson, acting UMWA safety director; Rep. Augustine B. Kelley, Pennsylvania; Mr. Lewis.

have instituted a reign of terror, which is either overlooked or participated in by local law enforcement authorities. There, gun thugs have tried to assassinate Tom Raney, District 30 International Executive Board member. Other valiant men, seeking only to bring a better way of life to the mine workers in this last pocket of resistance to UMWA organizers in Eastern Kentucky, have been ambushed and critically wounded.

Mr. Lewis' battle for a single, strong, unified American labor movement goes on. As a concrete example of this, the United Mine Workers of America, in June, 1952, set aside $10 million to aid their embattled brothers in the steel industry, during their fifty-three-day-long suspension of work in June and July, 1952.

The chronological story must end. It is well that it end with the words of a rank and file mine worker. They are the words of Horace Michael Ainscough of Rock Springs, Wyo., who, when he was handed pension check No. 1 from the UMWA Welfare and Retirement Fund by Mr. Lewis, said:

"I accept this check, Brother John L. Lewis, and I am deeply grateful for receiving check No. 1 from the pension fund. I am not thinking of myself so much as I am of others. I am thinking of the widows, the orphans, the older men and their families, the sick and the aged, the dependents of the Welfare Fund and the joy it will bring into their hearts. These people cannot be here today to thank our president, John L. Lewis. With the deepest humility, I offer this fervent prayer—God bless the day John L. Lewis was born."

UMW WELFARE FUND PENSIONER NO. 1: "GOD BLESS THE DAY JOHN L. LEWIS WAS BORN"

Mr. Lewis hands the first pension check to Horace Michael Ainscough, 62, of Rock Springs, Wyo., September 9, 1948.

THE THUNDERING VOICE

DOWN THROUGH THE YEARS, John L. Lewis has dedicated his life—his thoughts, his words, his actions—to the struggle for the dignity of the coal miners of America and their families.

Why? What processes of mind and heart, what philosophies and visions have guided him through the vicissitudes and obstacles which have beset his path? Why have the sturdy, God-fearing, fiercely independent American coal miners followed the same rocky path? What faith has enabled them to endure hardship, poverty, social ostracism, and vilification? Whence has come the strength to fight—as men must fight—to be free? What are the basic beliefs that have bolstered them down through the dark, bitter years of their struggle?

From time to time, as the years have gone by, President Lewis has reflected on these profound matters. He has paused to express his deep feelings about the men of the mines—their problems and their beliefs.

The following lines are his words. They were spoken in many places at many different times. They present a condensation of his ideas on the matters that most deeply concern him—the men in the pits and the great American industry in which they toil. And they show, as nothing else could, the mutual faith and the mutual understanding which exist between the UMWA and John L. Lewis.

* * *

I am proud of the record of the United Mine Workers of America. I am proud of the record of every leader of our organization and, most of all, I am proud of that fealty and that support and that strength and that backing that has always come to our leadership from the men back in the local unions who mine and load the coal, who pay the freight for our organization.

I am proud of the leadership that the UMWA has given to American labor. Its officers and representatives have lent their services to other organizations, to teach them the ways of organization and collective bargaining out of the fullness of our strength and out of the wealth of our experience.

I am proud of the contributions that the UMWA has made to the coal industry of America. For long years before the United Mine Workers of America completed the organization of the industry, the coal companies paid no taxes, comparatively speaking, to the United States Treasury. They had no profits. They had no earnings. They were living on their reserves and eating up their capitalization paying salaries.

The American coal operators never would have mechanized their mines unless they had been compelled to do so by the organization of the mine workers. The UMWA holds that labor is entitled to a participation in the in-

International Presidents: 1890-1952

JOHN B. RAE
1890-1891

JOHN McBRIDE
1892-1894

P. R. PENNA
1895-1896

M. D. RATCHFORD
1897-1898

JOHN MITCHELL
1898-1907

T. L. LEWIS
1908-1910

JOHN P. WHITE
1911-1917

FRANK J. HAYES
1917-1919

JOHN L. LEWIS
1920—

creased productivity due to mechanization. We decided the question of displacement of workers by mechanization years ago. We decided it is better to have a half a million men working in the industry at good wages and high standards of living, than it is to have a million working in the industry in poverty and degradation.

There can be no increase in the standard of living in America except as we create new values by increased productivity. For example, in England now, the per capita coal production is a little over a ton per man per day. The United Kingdom has only one great natural resource in volume and that is coal. Forty to 45 million people are literally standing on billions of tons of coal that is as good as any coal in the world. They lack the aptitude to pick up enough of it to keep themselves warm.

The British mine worker has to live and accept his pay on the basis of the amount received by the employer from one ton of coal per day.

Many years ago, the British miners' union, a large organization of miners, officially opposed the introduction of machinery and the use of power and automatic machines in the mines.

The British mine owners were perfectly content to accept that point of view and to take from the industry all of the increased revenue, against what they should have plowed back to put the industry on a modern basis.

The result has been that the British mines have become obsolete in every economic sense. England is staggering economically because of that fact; while, on the contrary, here in America we have increased the productivity per man per day until it is now 7.7 tons, or seven times that of Great Britain, and it is delivered to our consumers at prices less than one-third of the cost in Britain. And yet our industry pays a wage structure, on a weekly basis, that is three and one-half times that of Great Britain.

Had it not been for the position of the United Mine Workers of America, not only to accept and encourage, but also to demand modernization—constant modernization of our mining industry—and to demand cooperation of our membership with that policy; had it not been for that, economic and political America would have been in just the same position as the British Empire today, because coal is the element upon which our superstructure of economics rests. True, we have some substitutes. They

merely have gone to make up part of the increased consumer requirements of heat units in this country. Our country still requires more coal than it did at any time in history. That is a normal process, notwithstanding that perhaps 300 million tons, more or less, are displaced by the competition of natural gas, fuel oil, hydroelectric power, and other substitutes. But that is all right. As long as those things are economically preferable, they should be encouraged.

Some genius may solve the question of harnessing solar energy. I think it will be a happy day when that comes. I'd like to dream of a civilization where men don't have to go underground into the mines, just as long as those men have a chance to be absorbed into the economy.

You know, in our form of economy, there are three parties to benefit as a result of these improved techniques—a new chemical formula, a new invention, a new process. I am among those who do not believe that God ever put an idea in the mind of an inventor for the sole advantage of an employer. The parties to benefit from that improved technique and that increased productivity are: the investor and the employer who has his investment made more secure and more profitable; the worker who is able to have a higher wage, shorter hours, improved conditions and greater protection against evil days; and, the public which draws its reward from having a unit of manufacture at lesser cost.

The United Mine Workers of America desire that the distribution of the advantages and benefits of the machine shall not be restricted to the few, but that all of the personnel in the coal industry shall participate and be on a more or less equal level. The narrow wage differential between skilled and more highly skilled miners comes about as a matter of deliberate policy.

A man gets $19 a day now for running a modern continuous cutting machine. We see no reason why he should be raised to $23 a day merely because the machine has raised productivity, because that would mean that we would have $4 less to distribute elsewhere around the mine. You can't keep some men in the classification of pot boys or janitors, while you make another man in the same mine a preferred citizen by allowing him a higher rate. As a matter of fact, and in the realm of human relations, you merely make him an agent of the company, who will conspire with management to get wage increases for himself, to the great detriment of the mass of men employed.

The mine workers rely upon the UMWA to secure for them a fair participation in the economy of the country. And the UMWA does not believe in wage controls. It does not believe in price controls. It does believe that the mine workers can secure their fair participation in the nation's economy without strict government control over that economy.

The collective bargaining structure of our country represents the sum total of the efforts through the years of countless numbers of men, representing industry, labor and the government, who have participated in the gradual crystallization of these formulas. Collective bargaining efforts have justified themselves. Those efforts, in a large sense, have contributed to America's productive capacity. They have stood the tests of two world wars, as well as the tests that accrue daily in peace time.

Equality in bargaining strength is the first requisite of real labor-management cooperation. In this enlightened day and generation, there can be no industrial effectiveness or no economic rehabilitation based upon industrial autocracy, or the coercion of industrial workers by industrial management or the government. The maximum degree of productive efficiency and of financial performance can only be attained through the assurance of freedom in action to industrial workers.

Without the union and without collective bargaining, the individual worker is continually subject to individual exploitation and the whims and caprices of management, who prefer to post their wage schedules on the bulletin boards of their plants without having to take the trouble to negotiate them with the men who are going to work.

The establishment of a peaceful, working basis of industrial relations permits not only management but also the labor union to turn its attention to constructive objects. This is a fact that is all too frequently overlooked. Far too many people think of labor unions simply as militant organizations. The militant character of the labor movement is the result of the fact that labor has been placed constantly on the defensive and its legal and natural rights to organize and to bargain collectively have been denied or, at least, constantly opposed. It, therefore, unhappily follows that an entirely disproportionate part of the energy and ability of union members and labor leaders is necessarily directed to a struggle for existence and growth. In this state of almost constant struggle and strife, it is impossible for the union to make that contribution to industrial efficiency and social planning which it wishes to make and believes it is qualified to make.

It is impossible to crush the spirit of labor which desires organization. Outward manifestations may be crushed from time to time, but it always will reassert itself. To postpone acceptance of this fact is merely to help continue a system of constant friction and hostility.

The Taft-Hartley slave law is an act of oppression because it is designed not to destroy labor, as such, in a forthright manner but to prevent the logical growth of unions. And it is delaying them. If you will tell me how many members the AFL and the CIO have organized since the passage of the Taft-Hartley Act, I will be much obliged. I can tell you now. It is none.

And, furthermore, the Taft-Hartley Act, in its civil provisions, has legalized the methods of disemboweling our modern labor organizations through civil damage suits which will be filed whenever the evil days of depression come and it is possible for industry to strike down our unions one by one.

I think that the coal miners have the right to strike. Unless you change our form of government, you cannot stop a coal miner from stopping work, either individually or collectively. Not in America! Not under our concept of the privileges of citizens and their relationship in a democracy! When you enact legislation that takes away that right, you are starting a new era for America. You are throwing away our Republic and you are beginning to set up a totalitarian state.

And I might add that never in all American history has the deprivation of coal during a strike gone to a point where it hurt the country.

However, I read editorials that say my methods have advanced the use of competitive fuels and doomed coal to become a drug on the market. When the miners read that, they laugh.

240

International Officers

AT THE UMWA'S MONUMENT TO THEIR BELOVED FIFTH PRESIDENT, JOHN MITCHELL, COURTHOUSE SQUARE, SCRANTON, PA., DURING ANNUAL OBSERVANCE OF MITCHELL DAY, OCTOBER 29, 1949

Left to Right—Thomas Kennedy of Hazleton, Pa.; John L. Lewis of Springfield, Ill.; John Owens, of Cambridge, O.

International Executive Board

JOHN OWENS
Secretary-Treasurer

JOHN L. LEWIS
President

THOMAS KENNEDY
Vice President

JOHN KMETZ
District 1

JOHN GHIZZONI
District 2

FRANK HUGHES
District 3

WILLIAM HYNES
District 4

JOSEPH YABLONSKI
District 5

PETER PHILLIPPI
District 6

DAVID J. STEVENS
District 7

O. E. GASAWAY
District 8

JOHN J. MATES
District 9

SAM NICHOLLS
District 10

LOUIS AUSTIN
District 11

JOSEPH SHANNON
District 12

FRANK D. WILSON
District 13

HENRY ALLAI
District 14

JOHN T. JONES
District 16

ROBERT LIVETT
District 18

JAMES W. RIDINGS
District 19

JAMES H. TERRY
District 20

DAVID FOWLER
District 21

JOHN H. DELANEY
District 26

RAY THOMASON
District 29

TOM RANEY
District 30

They laugh because they know that any housewife whose husband can find the money will put in gas for fuel; it is clean and requires no hand labor. They also know that industry will use coal over other fuels because its lower cost appeals to industry.

I also read editorials that say that the pay I cost miners who go out on strike represents much more in any year than any wage gains I procure for them. When the miners read that, they laugh, too. They laugh because they know these things: that about 200 working days per year is maximum in the industry and that the time spent in strikes would be idle time anyhow.

I do not believe that the fact that a man strikes for a wage increase, or wants improved working conditions, or wants a decent pension arrangement, or wants shorter hours, or wants security for his old age makes him a communist. Not in America! Not in my book!

Nor do I believe it is necessary for me to state that I am not a communist and that the United Mine Workers of America is a law-abiding institution. The UMWA, in 1923, issued a pronunciamento warning American labor of communism. The UMWA, in 1927, wrote into its constitution that a communist could not be a member of the organization. The UMWA has no communists in its ranks. It is against those who promote disobedience of law and who hope to achieve their objectives by violence. The mine workers in this country have been fighting the communist movement since its inception. It is not a new thing with us. We are Americans!

I am against regimentation of industry, or the destruction of the profit incentive system that built our Republic and our country to the proportions it now occupies.

Free competitive enterprise is free relationship in commerce and in the ordinary undertakings of human existence and relationship, with only the rules laid down by governmental authority.

I think our labor unions, our trade associations, our cooperative institutions, our grain dealers' associations, our orange growers', onion growers', potato growers', sheep growers', corn growers', and hog growers' associations are all free associations—voluntary associations—which we have in this country—and are the inherent checks and balances of our economic system.

They furnish the pressures that make for the competition which results in further experimentation and adaptation of better devices, increased productivity, lower unit costs to the consumer; and those are the pressures that make the producer always alert to go forward, improve his product, lower the cost of production so as to insure that he will stay in the market. It is part of our free enterprise system.

How much for each? That is where collective bargaining comes in. Who gets so much? That is the bargaining that has been going on in the market places through 7 thousand years of known human history.

The right of the buyer to buy or not to buy, the right of the seller to sell or not to sell, the right to bargain in conference as to how much we want before we would accept: that is the difference between freedom and serfdom! In the Middle Ages, when men were serfs to landowners, they did not have the right of contract. They did not bargain for their services, the work of their hands, their brains or their goods without the consent of the master. The thing that made men free was to have the unqualified right to contract their own goods and their own services and not to contract those goods and services if they were not satisfied. That is the difference between freedom and serfdom in America.

So I look with growing alarm at the tendency of the CIO, as an organization, and the American Federation of Labor, as an organization, constantly to agree in Washington that some government board will have the right of life and death, in every economic sense, over the 62 million workers in America gainfully employed. That is the trend toward compulsory arbitration. I do not yield to any man in America, who is not a party to my employment, to have the right to say how much my wages shall be, what my working conditions shall be, and what kind of education I give my children through his fixation of my income. That is just too damned much power to give to somebody else!

I am reminded, I might say in passing, of a story about Confucius who, with his mandarins, was making an inspection one day of part of his province and came near the foot of a green mountain, and he heard a woman sobbing in grief. He approached her. She was kneeling by the side of a new-made grave. He said:

"Woman, why weepest thou?"

She said: "My husband was killed by a tiger and he lies here. Three weeks ago my son was killed by a tiger, and he lies here. Therefore, I weep."

Confucius said: "Woman, why do you not leave a country that abounds in tigers?"

She said: "The government here is not oppressive."

He turned to his retinue and his mandarins and said: "Let this be a lesson to you: that oppressive government is more to be feared than tigers."

The United Mine Workers of America do not believe in tying the miners to wages and prices imposed by the government. Nor do we accept the theory that wages should be tied to the cost of living. To accept that theory would forever condemn workmen to remain in a fixed status during the tenure of their existence upon this earth, and would offer no hope for future improvement. Merely to regulate the workmen's compensation by the rise or fall of the cost of clothing, by the price of shelter or the value of stable foodstuffs is a theory that should not be accepted in America.

We hold that the care of the human element in industry should run inherently with the cost of production. A man is just as essential as any other item in the cost of production. For instance, mining is a particularly hazardous industry. The result is a tremendous usage of manpower which, when used up or dispensed with in the ordinary way, renders these men physically or occupationally unable to enter other industries. They then either live in poverty or become a charge against the public purse and the taxpayers of the country are assessed for state aid, hospital funds and charitable organizations.

The United Mine Workers of America Welfare and Retirement Fund is conducted on the basic principle that a commodity, used generally by the public, should completely bear its own cost of production, rather than have the production of that commodity subsidized to some degree by the government.

We think that the 30 cents a ton for the Welfare Fund is an insignificant and comparatively unimportant item in the entire cost of producing coal.

We think, too, that the fund is an asset in many ways. It is a community asset because we find now that the business men and the professional men in the mining communities recognize that it turns a family from a state of pauperization to an asset to the community. They have purchasing power furnished by the Welfare Fund.

And we think, in the end, it will affect the whole picture of tax collection and assessments. We think it is fundamentally sound from the standpoint of our American form of government and the idea of preserving free enterprise, and is the basis upon which can be built up the whole economic, social, and political structure of our nation.

Our Welfare Fund is a brand snatched from the burning. I don't know anything that runs further into the emotions of a human being than the matter of our fund, with its security for our people. It is a dream that has come true, long deferred through the centuries, now established.

It is part of the social contribution of the United Mine Workers of America, of which its founders dreamed. Who can measure the contribution of the United Mine Workers of America to the national economy and the social well-being of the population? Who can successfully decry the existence of an institution dedicated to such an enterprise? Yet, 'tis done.

We have more democracy in the United Mine Workers of America than any other labor organization I know. The UMWA is one of the few national labor unions that has the referendum system of voting. All local unions of the many thousands composing the organization carry on their elections through secret ballots, counted by a board of six tellers. In addition to that, any member can run for president of the UMWA who can secure the nomination of five of those local unions. It is mandatory for his name to go on the ticket and he has a perfect privilege of contesting the election.

There is no curtailment of freedom of expression in the UMWA. I think the public and, more particularly, the members of Congress, should attend one of our conventions. I think it would be a lesson to all of them.

Under our rules, legislation cannot be killed in committees; it can be in the Congress, but not in our convention. It has to be reported out, favorably or unfavorably, or amended. The

MULE HAULAGE AND PICK AND SHOVEL COAL MINING—ILLUSTRATED IN THESE PICTURES TAKEN DURING THE 1920'S—SYMBOLIZE AN ERA OF BACK-BREAKING TOIL, LONG HOURS AND LOW PAY

TODAY CONTINUOUS MINING MACHINES MAKE AMERICA'S COAL INDUSTRY THE WORLD'S MOST PRODUCTIVE; AN INDUSTRY OF SKILLED WORKERS, SHORTER HOURS, HIGHER PAY AND SECURITY

247

mover of a resolution cannot be gagged from talking on that resolution and, believe me, the delegates to our conventions know how to talk and support their convictions.

Our organization has evolved a set of rules for the conduct of its members—a constitution, if you please—recognized as the binding contract between the individual member and the union itself, which protects his rights, his privileges and his liberty.

I am not one who proclaims that the constitution of the United Mine Workers of America, as it is written, is a perfect document. But I am one who says that, since January 25, 1890, the men of the mines have gathered in conventions, have studied, debated and counselled with each other over the provisions of the constitution. They have labored, trying to interpret the minds of their own people, trying earnestly to follow a course of action that their own consciences would permit. And from that labor comes this constitution, merged from the agony and the travail of men in the mining industry. Page after page is written in blood by men who wrote and then died in this industry.

That is why it is a great human document and a great American document, a document which has been born and emerged from the crucibles of opinion in the councils of this union over the period of the last sixty years.

So I say to each coal miner, guard and protect this document—guard and protect it—because it is born of human agony and it is the eternal bill of rights for the members of this union. In it there is no transgression upon the rights of a neighbor, a friend, a fellow citizen, or any representative of our American Republic.

In all the history of our modern world, there has not been fabricated a voluntary form of organization so comprehensive in scope, so profound and efficient in devising its policy and so capable in the administration of its affairs as the United Mine Workers of America.

Through the years I have served our organization, I have at all times been determined to serve our union and to discharge the trust imposed in me in a manner that would preserve that confidence and entitle me to the cooperation of those hundreds and hundreds of thousands of men whose problems I understand because I am one of them.

You know, there is an understanding and a bond and fraternity among mining men all over the world. Our industry is an industry apart, with specialized problems. The average man engaged in the mining industry, whether he is on management's side or labor's side, is a rather extraordinary personality.

I think the American public does not understand the American mine worker and never will. It doesn't understand how a coal miner thinks or why he thinks that way. It doesn't understand why he stops work or why he decides to go to work. We find that the average citizen has a lot of academic sympathy for the abstract coal miner. But that is as far as it goes.

But I feel that the members of the UMWA and their officers understand each other. I think I can say that from the standpoint of efficiency of operation, loyalty of membership, and mobility of action, under difficult conditions, there has never been a union like the United Mine Workers of America. They will stop. They will start. They will stay stopped. And the public sometimes doesn't know why they stop or why they start. The public forgets that the mine workers are confronted by the hard facts of life.

Life in the mines is naked and elemental. Relations are not cushioned with sophistry. Mining is the only labor which is performed underground. It requires the ability to withstand noxious gases which exude from the earth; the absence of sunshine—the absence of the violet rays essential to health—because the miners go to work most of the year before they see the sun and they come out when the sun's power has ended.

Mining is back-breaking labor. It is a laborious industry which requires the exercise of great thews and sinews and the ability to withstand fatigue.

Mining is also a task that requires skill, knowledge and training. Men never make efficient miners if they first enter the mines as adults. They have to go in at an age when they can absorb the psychology of the industry, when their reactions, nervous and physical, are such that they can adapt themselves to the industry; and to be an efficient miner they must have that training early in life.

Mining is performed amid hazards and miners do become inured to these hazards. They continually hope, hour after hour, day after day,

A REMINDER: DEATH STILL STALKS THE MEN WHOSE LONELY WORK MAKES NATION GREAT

FOR OTHERS THERE IS HOPE AND A CHANCE, THANKS TO THE LIFE WORK OF A GREAT MAN

that nothing will happen, that they will not be killed; and they finally persuade themselves they are not going to be killed and they continue to accept the hazards and take a chance.

But every man in the industry must die or be injured every six years and, if one escapes, it means another man has been injured twice. That is the mathematical record of the industry. It is appalling. It is the worst in the civilized world. The mining industry continues to be a mortician's paradise.

These hazards not only bear on the men in the mines, who, after all, become calloused to a certain degree and become inured to the danger of death that comes every day, but they also bear heavily on his family.

There is not a woman in a mining town in this country who does not gasp every morning when her man leaves to go to the mines, because she has no assurance that she will ever see him again.

Be it known to you that, aside from the hazards, the occupational diseases of the mining industry are a terrible scourge. An investigation conducted some years ago by the Bureau of Mines, the United States Public Health Service and the UMWA revealed that in our anthracite industry one man in every four was afflicted with silicosis, a progressive, malignant ailment from which men die and for which medical men have

249

evolved no adequate counter-protection, and one man in every four dies that way, because he works in an industry essential to public requirements.

And, in addition to the hazards, in addition to the diseases, in addition to the laboriousness, in addition to the degree of skill required in this industry, comes the social indignity and humiliation and constant baiting visited upon the mine workers every time they ask for redress.

They are like a wounded bull in the Mexican bull ring. Did you ever see a bull being baited in Mexico, while the population cheers and screams with delight, just as the population screams with delight when the mine workers are being baited in this country, when the courts of the country are turned loose on them, and every agency of the government is used to coerce them and denounce them and decry them and traduce them? Do you think that has any effect on the coal miners of this country?

But I do not ever hope to be able to educate the country to an understanding of the coal miner. The public does not understand, and I think never will, that almost spiritual fealty that exists between men who go down into the dangers of the mines and work together—that fealty of understanding and brotherhood that exists in our calling to a more pronounced degree than in any other industry. The public does not know that a man who works in a coal mine is not afraid of anything except his God; that he is not afraid of injunctions, or politicians, or threats, or denunciations, or verbal castigations, or slander—that he does not fear death.

The thing that gives me strength is the fact that I am able correctly to interpret the aims of my people. I know the psychology of the coal miner. I know about his dreams and his ideals and trials and tribulations. I have lived with coal miners. I am one of them. My family has been associated with the mining industry for a century and a half and an understanding of the miners' problems is inbred in me if anything is inbred in me. If there is anything in inheritance, I have got an understanding of the coal industry.

I have laid down in a mine tunnel with my face in a half inch of water, and pulled my shirt up over my head, expecting to die the next minute in an explosion I heard coming toward me. And when God performed a miracle and stopped that explosion before I died, I think it gave me some understanding of what men think about and how they suffer when they are waiting to die in a coal mine explosion.

So, I understand some of the thoughts of the coal miners of America. I know the mining industry. I have worked in the mines of many states. And when I speak, I speak the thoughts of the membership of the United Mine Workers of America, because I understand them. I remain true to them and they remain true to me.

And I say to you, the mine workers of America, that you usually have followed and supported me because you believe your cause is just.

Tomorrow a psychological wave might pass through your minds and wash away whatever influence I have as an individual and as president of the United Mine Workers of America.

The President of the United States has power which no psychological change can take away from him while he holds his office. Industrialists have the power conferred by financial resources on which labor depends for its bread. That is real power, of which I have none.

I say to you that I have no power to order you to do anything. I hold an office in the United Mine Workers of America by the consent of you who employ and pay me. I act in conformity with the rules you set up. You have not given me the authority to regulate your lives' affairs, dispose of your income or stop you from working.

As an individual, my opinions and my voice are of no more consequence in our world of affairs, or in the coal industry of the country, than the voice or the opinions of any passerby on the street. It is only when I am able to translate your dreams and aspirations into words that others may understand, that my tongue possesses any strength or my hand has any force.

I have never faltered or failed to present the cause or plead the case of the mine workers of this country. I have pleaded your case from the pulpit and the public platform; in joint conference with the operators of this country; before the bar of state legislatures; in the councils of the President's cabinet; and in the public press of this nation—not in the quavering tones of a feeble mendicant asking alms, but in the thundering voice of the captain of a mighty host, demanding the rights to which free men are entitled.

*   *   *

"You know," President Lewis has said, "it doesn't take much of a man to be a fine leader if he is right and discreet and careful about the people he picks to associate with him and picks the right kind of association to lead. That's all there is to this leadership thing."

THESE ARE THE PEOPLE

VICE PRESIDENT: Thomas Kennedy.

SECRETARY-TREASURER: John Owens.

SPECIAL ASSISTANTS TO THE PRESIDENT: John J. Mates, Kathryn Lewis, W. A. Boyle.

LABOR'S NON-PARTISAN LEAGUE: Director, John T. Jones; Representatives, Robert Howe, James Mark, Jr.

LEGAL DEPARTMENT: Director, Earl E. Houck; Senior Counsel, Welly K. Hopkins; Associate Counsel, Harrison Combs, Willard Owens.

SAFETY DIVISION: Director, C. F. Davis; Acting Director, Charles Ferguson.

UNITED MINE WORKERS JOURNAL: Editor, K. C. Adams; Assistant Editor, Cecil Owen.

UMWA DISTRICT 50 AND UNITED CONSTRUCTION WORKERS: Director, A. D. Lewis; Assistants, Luke Brett, Elwood Moffett; Comptroller, O. B. Allen; Assistant Comptroller, John V. Johnson; Legal Director, Yelverton Cowherd; Research Director, Edward E. Kennedy; Editor, District 50 and UCW News, Warren Irvin.

AIDES TO INTERNATIONAL OFFICERS: Executive Secretary to Mr. Lewis, Mrs. Elizabeth Covington; Secretary to Mr. Lewis and Clerk of the International Executive Board, Gerald Griffiths; Aides to Vice President Kennedy, Joseph Kennedy, Emmett Thomas; Executive Assistant to Secretary-Treasurer Owens, Mrs. Esther Cossel Jones; Secretary to Mr. Owens, Wayne Channell.

SPECIAL INTERNATIONAL REPRESENTATIVE: Paul K. Reed.

THE INTERNATIONAL EXECUTIVE BOARD: John Kmetz, John Ghizzoni, Frank Hughes, William Hynes, Joseph Yablonski, Peter Phillippi, David J. Stevens, O. E. Gasaway, John J. Mates, Sam Nicholls, Louis Austin, Joseph Shannon, Frank D. Wilson, Henry Allai, John T. Jones, Robert Livett, James W. Ridings, James H. Terry, David Fowler, John H. Delaney, Ray Thomason, Tom Raney.

THE DISTRICT PRESIDENTS AND SECRETARY-TREASURERS: 1—August J. Lippi, David Cummings; 2—James Mark, Edward Sweeney; 3—Frank Hughes, president; 4—William Hynes, Michael Honus; 5—John P. Busarello, Fred Gullick; 6—Adolph Pacifico, R. C. Owens; 7—Mart F. Brennan, David J. Stevens; 8—Thomas Rea, Wilbert Killion; 9—Joseph Kershetsky, Frank J. Brennan; 10—Sam Nicholls, Richard Francis; 11—Roscoe McKinney, Ralph Day; 12—Hugh White, Walter James; 13—Frank D. Wilson; 14—Henry Allai, Joseph E. Hromek; 15—Frank Hefferly, Fred Hefferly; 16—John T. Jones, William J. Morgan; 17—William Blizzard, R. O. Lewis; 18—Robert Livett, Angus J. Morrison; 19—Ray Thomason, acting president; Albert Pass; 20—William Mitch, president; 21—David Fowler, Sam Richards; 22—J. E. Brinley, Arthur Biggs; 23—Ed. J. Morgan, Jess Lovelace; 26—Freeman Jenkins, Michael Higgins; 27—W. A. Boyle, R. J. Boyle; 28—Allen Condra, E. L. Scroggs; 29—George J. Titler, D. M. Stamper; 30—Samuel Caddy, Samuel H. Caddy; 31—Cecil J. Urbaniak, Harry Bennett; 50—A. D. Lewis, chairman, organizing committee.

And in the United Mine Workers of America Welfare and Retirement Fund, a separate entity with offices across McPherson Park from UMWA headquarters in Washington, D. C.:

TRUSTEES: John L. Lewis, Charles Owens, for the operators; Josephine Roche.

WELFARE FUND DIRECTOR: Josephine Roche.

MEDICAL ADMINISTRATIVE OFFICER: Dr. Warren F. Draper; Assistant, Dr. John T. Morrison.

ADMINISTRATOR OF HOSPITAL PROGRAM: Dr. Fred M. Mott.

GENERAL COUNSEL: Val Mitch.

AIDES TO MISS ROCHE: Harmon Kelley, Mrs. Mildred Lea.

SUPERVISOR OF PENSIONS, DEATH BENEFITS AND WIDOWS' AND ORPHANS' BENEFITS: Robert Boylan.

INDEX

Credits and Acknowledgments

PICTURES: The color frontispiece is by Harris & Ewing.   Other pictures are from the files of Ace Hoffman Studios (Wilkes-Barre, Pa.); Associated Press (Wide World) Photos; Birmingham News; Bituminous Coal Institute, National Coal Association; Chase-Statler Studios; Ferguson Studio (Pittsburg, Kans.); Harris & Ewing; International News Photos; Johnstone (Pittsburgh, Pa.); Keystone Views, Inc.; United Mine Workers Journal; United Mine Workers News Bureau; United Press Photos.   The cartoons are by Fitzpatrick of the St. Louis Post-Dispatch (Page 63) and Fred O. Seibel of the Richmond Times-Dispatch (Page 84).

PRINTING: This volume was printed at the Silver Spring, Md., plant of the Cornelius Printing Co.   S. F. Workman designed the format and supervised the printing, typography and lay-out of text and illustrations.   The engravings were made by the D. C. Engraving Co. of Washington, D. C., under the direction of Lynn Anderson.   The binding was done by George Simonds & Co. of Washington, D. C.

The type for the text is eleven-point Baskerville; for the picture captions, Bodoni Bold; for the chapter titles, Bulmer Roman.   The paper is eighty-pound enamel, made especially for this volume.

EDITORIAL: Rex Lauck, who is now editing the Lewis archives for the UMWA, selected the material and wrote the continuity with the close editorial cooperation of Justin McCarthy, Allied Syndicates' UMWA News Bureau, and Barnett Bildersee of Allied Syndicates, Inc.   Mrs. Dorsey McCarthy assisted in preparation and editing of the material used.

THE SPECIAL RESEARCH PROJECT: The collection of Mr. Lewis' speeches and writings was begun in August, 1950, by Miss Ellen Lauck at the request of the International Executive Board of the United Mine Workers of America.   Miss Lauck was loaned to the UMWA for this work by David B. Charnay, president of Allied Syndicates, Inc., whose ideas and close cooperation have contributed greatly to progress on the research and the existence of this book.